# READERS' GUIDES TO ESSENTIAL CRITICISM

## CONSULTANT EDITOR: NICOLAS TREDELL

*Published*

| | |
|---|---|
| Thomas P. Adler | Tennessee Williams: *A Streetcar Named Desire–Cat on a Hot Tin Roof* |
| Pascale Aebischer | Jacobean Drama |
| Lucie Armitt | George Eliot: *Adam Bede–The Mill on the Floss Middlemarch* |
| Simon Avery | Thomas Hardy: *The Mayor of Casterbridge–Jude the Obscure* |
| Paul Baines | Daniel Defoe*: Robinson Crusoe–Moll Flanders* |
| Annika Bautz | Jane Austen: *Sense and Sensibility–Pride and Prejudice–Emma* |
| Matthew Beedham | The Novels of Kazuo Ishiguro |
| Richard Beynon | D. H. Lawrence: *The Rainbow–Women in Love* |
| Peter Boxall | Samuel Beckett: *Waiting for Godot–Endgame* |
| Claire Brennan | The Poetry of Sylvia Plath |
| Susan Bruce | Shakespeare: *King Lear* |
| Sandie Byrne | Jane Austen: *Mansfield Park* |
| Alison Chapman | Elizabeth Gaskell: *Mary Barton–North and South* |
| Peter Childs | The Fiction of Ian McEwan |
| Christine Clegg | Vladimir Nabokov: *Lolita* |
| John Coyle | James Joyce: *Ulysses–A Portrait of the Artist as a Young Man* |
| Martin Coyle | Shakespeare: *Richard II* |
| Justin D. Edwards | Postcolonial Literature |
| Michael Faherty | The Poetry of W. B. Yeats |
| Sarah Gamble | The Fiction of Angela Carter |
| Jodi–Anne George | *Beowulf* |
| Jodi–Anne George | Chaucer: The General Prologue to *The Canterbury Tales* |
| Jane Goldman | Virginia Woolf: *To the Lighthouse–The Waves* |
| Huw Griffiths | Shakespeare: *Hamlet* |
| Vanessa Guignery | The Fiction of Julian Barnes |
| Louisa Hadley | The Fiction of A. S. Byatt |
| Geoffrey Harvey | Thomas Hardy: *Tess of the d'Urbervilles* |
| Paul Hendon | The Poetry of W. H. Auden |
| Terry Hodgson | The Plays of Tom Stoppard for Stage, Radio, TV and Film |
| William Hughes | Bram Stoker: *Dracula* |
| Stuart Hutchinson | Mark Twain: *Tom Sawyer–Huckleberry Finn* |
| Stuart Hutchinson | Edith Wharton: *The House of Mirth–The Custom of the Country* |
| Betty Jay | E. M. Forster: *A Passage to India* |
| Aaron Kelly | Twentieth-Century Irish Literature |
| Elmer Kennedy–Andrews | The Poetry of Seamus Heaney |
| Elmer Kennedy–Andrews | Nathaniel Hawthorne: *The Scarlet Letter* |
| Daniel Lea | George Orwell: *Animal Farm–Nineteen Eighty-Four* |
| Rachel Lister | Alice Walker: *The Color Purple* |

| | |
|---|---|
| Sara Lodge | Charlotte Brontë: *Jane Eyre* |
| Philippa Lyon | Twentieth-Century War Poetry |
| Merja Makinen | The Novels of Jeanette Winterson |
| Matt McGuire | Contemporary Scottish Literature |
| Timothy Milnes | Wordsworth: *The Prelude* |
| Jago Morrison | The Fiction of Chinua Achebe |
| Carl Plasa | Tony Morrison: *Beloved* |
| Carl Plasa | Jean Rhys: *Wide Sargasso Sea* |
| Nicholas Potter | Shakespeare: *Antony and Cleopatra* |
| Nicholas Potter | Shakespeare: *Othello* |
| Nicholas Potter | Shakespeare's Late Plays: *Pericles, Cymbeline, The Winter's Tale, The Tempest* |
| Steven Price | The Plays, Screenplays and Films of David Mamet |
| Nicholas Seager | The Rise of the Novel |
| Berthold Schoene-Harwood | Mary Shelley: *Frankenstein* |
| Nick Selby | T. S. Eliot: *The Waste Land* |
| Nick Selby | Herman Melville: *Moby Dick* |
| Nick Selby | The Poetry of Walt Whitman |
| David Smale | Salman Rushdie: *Midnight's Chidren–The Satanic Verses* |
| Patsy Stoneman | Emily Brontë: *Wuthering Heights* |
| Susie Thomas | Hanif Kureishi |
| Nicolas Tredell | F. Scott Fitzgerald: *The Great Gatsby* |
| Nicolas Tredell | Joseph Conrad: *Heart of Darkness* |
| Nicolas Tredell | Charles Dickens: *Great Expectations* |
| Nicolas Tredell | William Faulkner: *The Sound and the Fury–As I Lay Dying* |
| Nicolas Tredell | Shakespeare: *A Midsummer Night's Dream* |
| Nicolas Tredell | Shakespeare: *Macbeth* |
| Nicolas Tredell | The Fiction of Martin Amis |
| Matthew Woodcock | Shakespeare: *Henry V* |
| Gillian Woods | Shakespeare: *Romeo and Juliet* |
| Angela Wright | Gothic Fiction |

*Forthcoming*

| | |
|---|---|
| Brian Baker | Science Fiction |
| Alan Gibbs | Jewish-American Literature since 1945 |
| Sarah Haggarty & Jon Mee | Willam Blake: *Songs of Innocence and Experience* |
| Keith Hughes | African-American Literature |
| Britta Martens | The Poetry of Robert Browning |
| Michael Whitworth | Virginia Woolf: *Mrs Dalloway* |

**Readers' Guides to Essential Criticism**
**Series Standing Order**
**ISBN 1-4039-0108-2**
(*outside North America only*)

You can receive future titles in this series as they are published by placing a standing order. Please contact your bookseller or, in case of difficulty, write to us at the address below with your name and address, the title of the series and the ISBN quoted above.

Customer Services Department, Macmillan Distribution Ltd, Houndmills, Basingstoke, Hampshire RG21 6XS, England

# Shakespeare

## Romeo and Juliet

GILLIAN WOODS

Consultant Editor: NICOLAS TREDELL

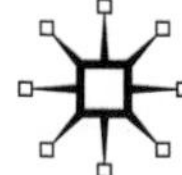



First published 2013 by
PALGRAVE MACMILLAN

Palgrave Macmillan in the UK is an imprint of Macmillan Publishers Limited, registered in England, company number 785998, of Houndmills, Basingstoke, Hampshire RG21 6XS.

Palgrave Macmillan in the US is a division of St Martin's Press LLC, 175 Fifth Avenue, New York, NY 10010.

Palgrave Macmillan is the global academic imprint of the above companies and has companies and representatives throughout the world.

Palgrave® and Macmillan® are registered trademarks in the United States, the United Kingdom, Europe and other countries.

ISBN 978–0–230–22206–9 hardback

ISBN 978–0–230–22207–6 paperback

This book is printed on paper suitable for recycling and made from fully managed and sustained forest sources. Logging, pulping and manufacturing processes are expected to conform to the environmental regulations of the country of origin.

A catalogue record for this book is available from the British Library.

A catalog record for this book is available from the Library of Congress.

10 9 8 7 6 5 4 3 2 1
22 21 20 19 18 17 16 15 14 13

Printed and bound in China

For Patricia Hesp

# Contents

# Acknowledgments

I would like to thank Nicolas Tredell and Sonya Barker for considerate and enabling editing. Thanks also to Marcus Nevitt for reading sections of this Guide and providing numerous improving suggestions. Most importantly, thank you to John Garai for unstinting love, help and support.

# Note on The Text

All act, scene and line references to *Romeo and Juliet* are keyed to the Oxford World's Classics text, edited by Jill Levenson. Other references to Shakespeare are to the Riverside Shakespeare, edited by G. Blackmore Evans and J. J. M. Tobin.

# Introduction

When Juliet invites the Romeo of her fantasy to 'doff thy name' (2.1.90), she remains blissfully unaware of that name's cultural significance. The *Oxford English Dictionary* records that 'Romeo' now describes a type (or even types) rather than an individual: 'A lover, a passionate admirer; a seducer, a habitual pursuer of women'. The very problem that Juliet discusses has become a facet of her play's existence: she ponders whether we can ever break free of our nominal, familial and social fetters, but ironically the play itself is as much bound to its (sometimes 'inaccurate') popular associations as it is to its textual context. *Romeo and Juliet* is a timeless myth (pre- and post-dating Shakespeare's conception of the play) and a timely drama (engaging with Elizabethan literary discourse, the Renaissance obsession with language, and the tensions of the early modern marriage market). Allusions to the play operate as shorthand for 'love across the divide' everywhere from pop songs to broadsheet newspaper articles, so that we might feel that there is also something inevitably clichéd about this drama. Featuring three murders and two suicides, it has the potential to be melodramatic as well as sentimental. Switches between comedy and tragedy, rarefied romance and earthy (sometimes brutal) bawdiness, work with the recurring figure of the oxymoron (a conjunction of opposing terms) to produce a formidable momentum entirely appropriate to the fast pace of the plot. It survives in two early printed editions, so that its linguistic doubling and fracturing (in puns and paradoxes) also exists at a textual level (Quarto 1 and Quarto 2).

Since its influential first performance in the 1590s to its modern-day productions on stage and screen, *Romeo and Juliet* has remained an enduring dramatic hit. However, its critical fortunes have been rather less consistent, with dissatisfied (if not dismissive) commentators sometimes casting doubt on the play's tragic status. As one of Shakespeare's first tragedies, *Romeo and Juliet* is a key text to any understanding of the dramatist's artistic development. But some critics detect immaturity in the play's writer as well as its protagonists. This Guide will trace the play's changing critical reputation from the earliest responses in the 1590s up to the twenty-first century, exploring why various features of *Romeo and Juliet* are lauded or censured at different points in time. The play's irrefutably 'canonical' status is somewhat odd, given that four centuries of criticism finds the tragedy embarrassingly raw. *Romeo and*

*Juliet* raises important critical questions about how we value tragedy and how we value Shakespeare.

In tracking the essential critical responses to *Romeo and Juliet*, this Guide interrogates the reasons for the play's grip on our cultural imagination. The first three chapters explore the chronological development of critical reactions from the sixteenth century to the end of the Victorian period. The professionalization of literary criticism in the twentieth century sees an increased diversification in critical methodologies, which this Guide reflects through thematically organized chapters thereafter. These responses reveal recurrent critical preoccupations and controversies. For example, in the eighteenth century James Howard's alternating production of the play as 'Tragical one Day, and Tragicomical another' dramatized over two performances a generic instability that subsequent critics continue to debate.[1] Likewise, the earliest satirical references to *Romeo and Juliet* fasten on to the play's elevated language: an aspect that later critics find variously distracting, artificial and thoughtfully self-conscious. Similarly, the play's romantic subject matter has been seen as insufficient material for tragedy and a radical reconstitution of tragic form; a condition of the play's timeless appeal and a culturally specific marker of its ideological constraints. This Guide surveys these different responses and explores the critical biases that shape them.

Chapter 1 addresses the play's earliest responses. It starts with a consideration of the two earliest printed editions of *Romeo and Juliet*, outlining some of their differences and assessing what those variations mean for an understanding of the 'text'. Moving on from early modern editions to early modern responses, the chapter then explores Shakespeare's own reflection on the generic meaning of the 'illicit love' story in *A Midsummer Night's Dream*, where the tale of 'Pyramus and Thisby' replays the themes of *Romeo and Juliet* in comic form. Alternatively comedic and tragic perspectives remain important in the discussion of the wider literary responses in the late sixteenth and early seventeenth centuries, as in seen in the work of John Marston, Henry Porter, John Ford and Robert Burton.

The next chapter concentrates on the later seventeenth and eighteenth centuries. It features 'criticism' in the broadest sense of the word, including scholarly editions of Shakespeare and adaptations of *Romeo and Juliet*, as well as written commentaries on the play. The adaptations of Thomas Otway and David Garrick usefully reveal the literary and ideological concerns of their cultural moment, with Otway mounting an implicit critique on the political chaos of his age, and Garrick cutting out Shakespearean wordplay to focus on the text's sentimental possibilities. This neoclassical period sees scholars such as Nicholas Rowe and Samuel

Johnson work to defend Shakespeare against accusations of imperfect technique for failing to attend to the unities of time and place. Chapter 2 also considers the work of one of the first female Shakespeare critics, Charlotte Lennox, whose writing paves the way for future feminist critics and students of Shakespeare's sources.

Shakespeare's critical popularity reaches new heights in the Romantic and Victorian periods that form the focus of Chapter 3. Like Shakespeare himself, *Romeo and Juliet* is hailed as timeless by writers such as Schlegel, Coleridge and Hazlitt. In these discussions 'love' is celebrated as a universal quality that allows the early modern dramatist to speak to all ages. The proto-feminist Anna Jameson capitalizes on Shakespeare's status as a supposed teller of moral truths to make a case for the improved treatment of real women in society: Shakespearean heroines are shown to confound nineteenth-century assumptions about gendered virtue. Part conduct book, part political tract and part literary criticism, Jameson's writing puts new emphasis on the interpretative interest of female characters, and Juliet emerges as challengingly chaste and desirous. The actress Helena Faucit continues this theme in her critical reflections on playing female parts. Their analyses stand in contrast to that of Edward Dowden, which sees the tragedy in terms of Romeo's masculine fulfilment.

Chapter 4 switches from a chronological to a thematic perspective, in response to the greater variation in methodological and ideological approaches to literature that develop in the twentieth and twenty-first centuries. This chapter considers the influence of the first professional literary critic, A. C. Bradley, and his book, *Shakespearean Tragedy*. Excluding *Romeo and Juliet* from his collection of 'four principal tragedies', Bradley established critical uneasiness with the text's generic definition.[2] Subsequent critics operate under this shadow, with H. B. Charlton defending the play as a raw experiment in genre. Franklin M. Dickey and John Lawlor likewise stress the play's supposedly immature qualities, and offer alternatively Christian and moralistic accounts of its tragedy. Nicholas Brooke distinguishes between the play's alleged early status and its youthful subject matter, developing Charlton's insight about the tragedy's experimental nature. The chapter also looks at the way Susan Snyder, Gary M. McCown and Martha Tuck Rozett have brought analysis of other generic forms (comedy, epithalamium or wedding song, sonnet sequence) to bear upon the play.

Language dominates the attention of the critics explored in Chapter 5. The early and mid-twentieth-century scholars Caroline F. E. Spurgeon and M. M. Mahood interpret the play through new close reading techniques, identifying various word patterns. Harry Levin looks at the formality of the play's language and the drama's thematic concerns with poetic and social form. James L. Calderwood retains a linguistic focus, but adopts a more theoretical perspective, examining the different attitudes shown to language by the lovers and the play's other characters. *Romeo and Juliet* functions as a 'tragedy of names' in Michael Goldman's careful close reading; Jacques Derrida's response is underpinned by the same premise, but takes a philosophical approach that investigates the very nature of language itself. The late twentieth century sees the dominance of more theoretically inflected criticism. Influenced by both Jacques Derrida and the psychoanalytical theorist Jacques Lacan, Catherine Belsey examines the relationship between the body and culture by analysing the way in which pre-existent language shapes selfhood. Insisting to the contrary on the significance of the play's historically specific moment, Kiernan Ryan sees language as evidence that cultural values are temporary, and that the play's tragedy can be averted. Writing in the twenty-first century, Laurie Maguire draws on the evidence of a bilingual adaptation of the play to demonstrate the ambivalently harmful and curative function of its language.

Chapter 6 explores criticism that looks at a particularly Renaissance form of discourse: Petrarchism. Influenced by the verse of the Italian poet Francesco Petrarca (or, in English, 'Petrarch'), Elizabethan writers developed a set of well-used literary conventions to describe love. The critics who appear in this chapter discuss Shakespeare's use of this Petrarchan mode in *Romeo and Juliet,* moving beyond accusations of poetic artificiality to historicised readings of the playwright's exploration of a dominant early modern poetic style. Rosalie Colie's generically sensitive account demonstrates how the introspection of the Petrarchan sonnet form helps translate love (traditional material for comedy) into tragedy. For Ralph Berry, the play's Petrarchan mode is self-critical, incorporating anti-Petrarchan impulses that encourage the audience to challenge the discourse's values. Writing over a decade later, Ann Pasternak Slater demonstrates that Petrarchism structures the drama's action as well as its language. This connection between lyricism and embodied theatrical action is then subject to a theorized reading by Gayle Whittier. The chapter concludes with Diana Henderson's identification of Shakespeare's innovations in recasting Petrarchan gender roles whereby the female beloved has a voice and an active role.

Psychoanalytical approaches to *Romeo and Juliet* are examined in Chapter 7. Where the critics of the previous chapter looked at the play's paradoxes of love and hatred in terms of conventional literary tropes, the writers featured in this chapter frame those emotions as psychological drives. One of the earliest of these critics, Norman Rabkin, does so through a typically mid-twentieth-century allegiance to close reading. Focusing instead on the medical aspects of his interpretation, Norman Holland suggests that the play carefully distinguishes between the young couple's love and the feuding society's hatred, as a means of negotiating difficult emotional contradictions. The feminist psychoanalytical critic, Julia Kristeva, looks at the apparently oppositional forces of love and hatred in the play, and interprets them as part of the same impulse – an aspect of a universal condition to which all adolescents of all cultures can relate. The chapter then explains the implications of Lloyd Davis's major departure from such a 'universalizing' reading when he combines psychoanalysis with a seemingly incompatible cultural materialist methodology. Hugh Grady's aesthetic account of the play tackles psychoanalytical readings in the twenty-first century.

Chapter 8 examines criticism that focuses on gender roles and sexual categories, focusing as it does on feminism, gender studies and queer theory. Coppélia Kahn shares a psychoanalytical interest with the critics of Chapter 7, but marries it with a feminist approach that finds a patriarchal structure in the tragedy. Similarly, Marianne Novy sees the constrictions of gender roles as producing the tragic dynamic of the play. Edward Snow analyses gender difference in linguistic terms, comparing the language of Romeo and Juliet and finding well-suited lovers who nevertheless experience sexuality in contrasting ways. Shifting attention from the two protagonists to Mercutio, Joseph Porter identifies a triangular relationship that enables 'queer' readings of the play. The romantic ideals of the tragedy are also put in question by Dympna Callaghan's Marxist-feminist interpretation, which sees the play as performing invidious ideological work. Challenging readings that prioritize specifically heterosexual desire, Jonathan Goldberg illuminates the queer possibilities of the text. And in the twenty-first century, Robert N. Watson and Stephen Dickey open the play out to new controversy by arguing that the threat of sexual violence is interwoven with the play's famously romantic lyricism.

The final chapter looks to two modern and extremely popular film adaptations of *Romeo and Juliet*. The chapter outlines the neo-realist features of Franco Zeffirelli's 1968 film and its representation of the young couple as innocent victims. It assesses what the film's engagement with contemporary popular culture and corresponding lack of engagement with 1960s political culture means as an interpretation of Shakespeare's tragedy. In comparison, Baz Luhrmann's 1996 adaptation has an emphatically postmodern aesthetic. The chapter explores the meaning of this mode by considering Luhrmann's fragmented use of Shakespearean language, his intertextual references to different filmic genres, and the way in which he forces viewers to become aware of their position as consumers of a tragedy.

The Guide's Conclusion summarizes the main critical findings of the 400 years of commentary on the play, discusses some of the most recent interventions into the debate, and outlines possible future directions in scholarship about the drama. Both intellectually and emotionally engaging, *Romeo and Juliet* remains a landmark piece of literature.

# CHAPTER ONE

# Patient Ears: Early Texts and Responses

## FIRST PUBLICATIONS (1597–99)

*Romeo and Juliet* opens with the description of 'Two households both alike in dignity' (Prologue 1); however, the play's lengthy publication history begins with two texts (within two years) long seen as unlike in value: the First/'Bad' Quarto of 1597 and the Second/'Good' Quarto of 1599. The word 'quarto' refers to the material form of the texts: quartos were pamphlets made by folding sheets of paper twice so that each page was a quarter of the size of the original sheet. The two *Romeo and Juliet* quartos have different titles: *An Excellent conceited Tragedie Of Romeo and Iuliet* (1597) and *The Most Excellent and lamentable Tragedie, of Romeo and Iuliet* (1599). Quarto 1 is shorter by 'more than one-fifth' – at the reckoning of Oxford editor Jill Levenson – than Quarto 2.[1] Levenson also details that Quarto 2 'contains over 800 lines which are in some ways variants of corresponding lines; and it includes passages which differ completely from their equivalents (for example, 2.5, 3.2.57–60, 5.3.12–21)'.[2] To generalize quite broadly, in the early twentieth century, the differences between the two quartos were rationalized as the difference between Good and Bad quartos (a distinction first made by the early twentieth-century bibliographer Alfred W. Pollard). Quarto 2 was considered 'Good' because it was thought that it had been printed from Shakespeare's own manuscript (or at least a closely related text); Quarto 1, on the other hand, was said to be the product of 'memorial reconstruction', where an actor illicitly sold the printer a (faulty) version of the play transcribed from memory. However, there are numerous problems with these theories (too many, in fact, to do full justice to here). There is no evidence that actors ever attempted a black-market sale of plays (there was not much money to be made from the publication of drama, so it would have been an unprofitable risk for all involved). Furthermore, some of the 'faults' ascribed to imperfect memory could equally well have other explanations (for example, a shorter text might stand for an early version of the play, or a later revision adapted for touring). Since no manuscript of a Shakespearean play survives, there is also no direct evidence that Shakespeare's holograph stands behind so-called 'Good' quartos. In any case, the desire to reach back to an 'original' text presumes that Shakespeare produced absolutely final versions of his plays. But as Levenson points out, the 'text' was constantly malleable, as it was handled and rehandled by Shakespeare, his fellow actors, adapters, revisers, bookkeepers (prompters), censors, compositors and proof-readers. Looking for a perfect copy might not only be an impossible goal, it might be a flawed one that fails to recognize the fluid nature of early modern theatre and printing.

A change in bibliographical attitudes is evident in two recent editions of the play. Jill Levenson's Oxford edition takes Quarto 2 as a copy-text, but Quarto 1 is also provided in full in an appendix. Lukas Erne has also produced a separate edition for Quarto 1 for the New Cambridge Early Quartos series. These editions manifest a desire to value *both* texts as related but separate versions of the play. In this way the editors move away from the unproven assumptions of some earlier bibliographical scholarship and open out the texts for new enquiry. Erne's Introduction to his edition is particularly helpful not only in its explanation of the history of the bibliographical fortunes of Quarto 1, but also in outlining major differences between the two texts. He usefully identifies key variations in the 'dramatic specificities' – points which make a significant difference to the theatrical performance and literary interpretation of the play(s). The shorter Quarto 1 is faster-paced than the alternatively lyrical Quarto 2. Erne explains that 'passages in which the action pauses, in which ideas and feelings are developed at some length and with considerable imaginative and verbal artistry' are easier to remove when abridging a play because they do not impact on the plot structure.[3] And the 700 lines absent from Quarto 1 but found in Quarto 2 mostly take this form, resulting in a version concentrated on breathless action and another that is more poetic. It is easy to see how the literary tastes of bibliographers might have influenced a Bad/Good hierarchy, but the fast-moving Quarto 1 has real theatrical value.

Consequent on the excision of passages of poetry is a difference in characterization between the two quartos. Most striking is the case of Juliet, whose part has 40 per cent fewer lines in Quarto 1 than in Quarto 2.[4] Thus her soliloquies tend to be much shorter. For example, in Quarto 1 when Juliet eagerly anticipates her wedding night she speaks just four lines in soliloquy:

■ Gallop apace, you fiery-footed steeds,
To Phoebus' mansion. Such a wagoner

> As Phaëton would quickly bring you thither
> And send in cloudy night immediately. ☐
>
> (11.1–4)

But Quarto 2's Juliet is considerably more talkative, with her soliloquy lasting 31 lines. Extending Quarto 1's address to the horses of the classical sun-god, the monologue in Quarto 2 is dense with imagery: vivid personification ('civil night, / Thou sober-suited matron all in black' [3.2.10–11]; 'runaways' eyes' [3.2.6]); incantatory rhythm ('Come night, come Romeo, come thou day in night' [3.2.17]); sharp-edged contrast ('Whiter than new snow upon a raven's back' [3.2.19]); paradoxes that eschew the constrictions of gender roles ('learn me how to lose a winning match / Played for a pair of stainless maidenhoods' [3.2.12–13]); starry metaphors that are both creative and destructive ('Take him and cut him out in little stars' [3.2.22]); and nature-shifting fantasy ('all the world will be in love with night, / And pay no worship to the garish sun' [3.2.24–5]). The redaction has major critical implications. Without such lines, gone is the generic novelty of a bride speaking her own epithalamium or wedding song (see McCown in Chapter 4 below), and vastly reduced is her destructive eroticism (see Kristeva in Chapter 7 below), as well as the risky extravagance of images that defy the natural order (see Snow in Chapter 8 below). Yet if Quarto 1 Juliet has less opportunity to display her linguistic talents, the attendant compression of plot intensifies the sense of her hasty activity as a heroine who arranges her own marriage and funeral.

As Erne shows, other characters are also different in their Quarto 1 and 2 incarnations. The Nurse is more closely allied with Juliet in the 1597 text and with the Capulet parents in the 1599 version.[5] She interrupts the young lovers only once in Quarto 1 (when the pair first speak to one another [4.179]) instead of three times, as in Quarto 2 (breaking up the lovers' first meeting at 1.4.224; calling to Juliet repeatedly during the window scene at 2.1.178 stage direction, 2.1.192 and 2.1.195; and foreshortening the lovers' parting after their wedding night at 3.5.37). The Quarto 1 Nurse is 'warmer' with Juliet, affectionately welcoming her charge when she returns from meeting Friar Laurence: 'Come, sweetheart, shall we go?' (16.32). This line is missing from Quarto 2 where, in contrast, the Nurse speaks to Capulet to tell him of Juliet's whereabouts (4.2.14). Furthermore, in Quarto 1 the Nurse does not join in the hyperbolic (i.e. exaggerated) Capulet lamentations at Juliet's (feigned) death, so that she is not tarred with the artificiality of the performed grief.[6]

In another characterological difference, Tybalt is less ironic in Quarto 1 than in Quarto 2. The earlier text sees Tybalt meeting Romeo with the words: 'Romeo, the hate I bear to thee can afford / No better words than these: thou art a villain' (10.35–6); but in the later text 'love' sarcastically replaces 'hate' (3.1.59–60). Tybalt also uses the word 'sir' twice when speaking to Mercutio in Quarto 2 (3.1.40, 55), but not in the earlier text.[7] Perhaps more importantly, Capulet and Montague are not as clearly bellicose in Quarto 1 as they are in Quarto 2. In the 1599 text Gregory describes the antagonism as feudal: 'The quarrel is between our masters and us their men' (1.1.18–19), a line which Erne observes is missing from Quarto 1. Furthermore, a stage direction in Quarto 1 ambiguously implies that the old patriarchs are distinct from the brawlers in the first scene: '*They draw, to them enters* TYBALT, *they fight, to them the* PRINCE, *old* MONTAGUE *and his* WIFE, *old* CAPULET *and his* WIFE, *and other citizens part them*' (1.48 SD). Far less equivocal is the dialogue of Quarto 2 (missing in Quarto 1) that characterizes the old men's belligerence:

CAPULET: What noise is this? Give me my long sword, ho!
CAPULET'S WIFE: A crutch, a crutch – why call you for a sword?
CAPULET: My sword, I say. Old Montague is come,
And flourishes his blade in spite of me.
*Enter old Montague and his Wife*
MONTAGUE: Thou villain Capulet! (*To his Wife*) Hold me not, let me go.
MONTAGUE'S WIFE: Thou shalt not stir one foot to seek a foe.

(1.1.71–6)[8]

However, not only the patriarchs' explicit attempted participation in the fight, but also their impotence is signalled here. Critics seeking to define the nature of the play's tragedy find these Quarto 2 lines telling in their bathos (see especially Snyder in Chapter 4 below).

The action itself is more clearly outlined in Quarto 1 than in Quarto 2, since in the earlier text the 'stage directions are more numerous and detailed'. So much more plentiful and illustrative are the Quarto 1 stage directions that, Erne observes, 'most editors who use Q2 as their copy text adopt many of them from Q1'. Important examples include the stage directions describing the staging of Juliet's feigned death (which are not found in Quarto 2): after drinking the potion Juliet '*falls upon her bed within the curtains*' (17.27), and once the Capulets believe her to be dead, '*They all but the Nurse go forth, casting rosemary on her* [Juliet] *and shutting the curtains*' (17.108 SD 1–2).[9] These directions make it clear that Juliet's deathlike body lies on stage as the Capulets incongruously prepare wedding festivities, providing a visual emblem of the play's tragic–comic mixture (see Chapter 4 below for further discussion of genre). Other variations between the two texts include a different time scheme (references to time in Quarto 1 are inconsistent) and independent betrothal scenes in each version (the same events are depicted but the language is different; Erne notes that Quarto 1's stage directions depict Juliet's haste and show her embracing Romeo, whereas in Quarto 2 Juliet does not touch or speak to Romeo and the language is markedly ominous: 'sorrow', 'death', 'violent ends' [2.5.2, 7, 9]).[10]

In total, the differences between the two quartos add up to significantly different texts. Erne, returning to the argument of his important book *Shakespeare as Literary Dramatist* (2007), suggests that Quarto 2 might represent a later revision of the text produced by Shakespeare for readers (hence the additional poetry and characterological complexity) and Quarto 1 an actor's text (put together from a combination of the playbook and some limited memorial reconstruction). As with most bibliographical theories, this interpretation of the distinction between the two texts is necessarily speculative. However, the fact of the multiple forms of *Romeo and Juliet* is significant for literary interpretation. Most of the literary criticism featured in this Guide is centred on the Quarto 2 version of the play. As editions of the two separate texts, such as those by Levenson and Erne, are more widely circulated, we might expect to see future literary responses that attend to the textual plurality of the play more fully (this is evident in the critical history of, for example, *King Lear*, a play which is extant in very different quarto and folio forms).

## *A MIDSUMMER NIGHT'S DREAM*

Critics and editors are divided about whether *Romeo and Juliet* was written before *A Midsummer Night's Dream* or after it; but they agree that there are striking verbal and thematic connections between the tragedy and the comedy. Shakespeare was a diligent recycler, who not only reused and remade the stories of *novelle*, chronicle histories and plays written by others, but also returned to the situations and ideas of his own work. Regardless of the direction of travel between *Romeo and Juliet* and *A Midsummer Night's Dream*, these two plays see Shakespeare experimenting with the generic possibilities of his material.

The most prominent echo (or anticipation) of *Romeo and Juliet* in *A Midsummer Night's Dream* is found in the play-within-a-play in the final scene. At this point a group of amateur dramatists ('mechanicals' or tradesmen by day) perform the story of *Pyramus and Thisby* as entertainment for the play's aristocrats. The two tales are remarkably similar in plot: two young lovers struggle to overcome the division caused by enemy parents and physical barriers (a 'wall' in *Pyramus and Thisby* and 'orchard walls' [2.1.106] in *Romeo and Juliet*).[11] In both stories a fatal misunderstanding prompts double suicide: Pyramus arrives to meet his lover at a secret assignation but finds Thisby's bloody mantle instead, and wrongly believing that a lion has killed her, he kills himself; having evaded the lion, Thisby finds her dead lover and dutifully commits suicide. Even the marketing of the two plays is similar: the title of Quarto 2 *Romeo and Juliet* describes itself as *The Most Excellent and lamentable Tragedie*, while Peter Quince reads the title of the mechanicals' play as '*The most* lamentable *comedy and most cruel death of Pyramus and Thisby*' (1.2.11–12; my emphasis).[12] The apparent oxymoron of this amateur title is repeated in a different form in the list of entertainments provided for Duke Theseus: 'very tragical mirth' (5.1.57); this is not dissimilar from the mixture promised by the title of Quarto 1 *Romeo and Juliet*: *An excellent conceited tragedie* (in Elizabethan English *conceited* could mean 'witty'). And contradictory as the mechanicals' title might sound, it is accurate: *Pyramus and Thisby* is a tragedy played for laughs. Not that its players are aware of this. Their decidedly untheatrical attempts to explain how the theatrical illusion is meant to work farcically dissolve the fiction. Thus an actor playing the part of a (moving, talking) wall explains:

■ I, one Snout by name, present a wall;
And such a wall, as I would have you think,
That had in it a crannied hole or chink,
Through which the lovers, Pyramus and Thisby,
Did whisper often, very secretly. □

(5.1.156–60)

And when Pyramus kills himself the flat-footed rhyming couplets parody the inevitability of the tragedy:

■ Now am I dead,
Now am I fled,
My soul is in the sky.
Tongue, lose thy light;
Moon, take thy flight.
Now die, die, die, die, die. □

(5.1.301–6)

Beneath the laughter is a reminder of the porous distinction between tragedy and comedy – one can all too easily dissolve into the other. Taken in the context of the fuller action of *A Midsummer Night's Dream* this generic shiftiness is all the more apparent. The larger play tells yet another story of young lovers who want to get together in spite of parental opposition; in accordance with the rules of comedy, they manage to do so. But in the midst of their happy ending, the playlet of *Pyramus and Thisby* warns the audience that the story could just as easily have gone wrong. Worse still, even a bloody end is no guarantee of tragic stature; pathos can slip into bathos. These various reworkings of the 'opposed young love' story reveal Shakespeare's fascination with the flexibility of genre. The responses of other writers of the period to *Romeo and Juliet* likewise demonstrate an interest in its generic potential; but other features, such as its language and treatment of sexual relationships, also appear to have distinguished the play.

## LITERARY REACTIONS (1599–1633)

*Romeo and Juliet* had a considerable literary and theatrical impact in the late sixteenth and early seventeenth centuries. Later critics see the play as using (and interrogating) voguish lyrical verse (see Chapter 6 below), and early responses attest to the fashionable status of the play's language. The satirist John Marston mocks the enthusiastic playgoer who stuffs his speech with theatrical dialogue; *Romeo and Juliet* is the text of choice for such fops:

> ■ *Luscus* what's playd to day? faith now I know
> I set thy lips abroach, from whence doth flow
> Naught but pure *Iuliat* and *Romio*.[13] □

Marston's satire reveals a trend for speaking in literary quotation. That *Romeo and Juliet* should typify the kind of play (later termed 'pathetique Tragedie') that would attract such poseurs indicates not only its recognizable popularity, but also the reusable and detachable nature of its elevated language.[14] Ironically, Romeo himself shares similarities with the admirers who would quote him. He is characterized not only as a lover, but as a young man in love with the fashionable language of love. Juliet teases him: 'You kiss by th' book' (1.4.223); and Mercutio mocks that he is: 'for the numbers that Petrarch flowed in' (2.3.37–8). But if the play questions (and even in places derides) the practice of recycling poetry, it was nevertheless itself quarried for poetic material. Its ready exploitation is also seen in the university drama *The First Part of the Return from Parnassus* (first performed 1601). The impoverished writer Ingenioso provides the audience with scathing footnotes in asides as his patron Gullio recounts how he wooed his new mistress:

> INGENIOSO [*aside*]: We shall have nothinge but pure Shakespeare, and shreds of poetrie that he hath gathered at the theators.
> GULLIO: 'Pardon mee moy mittressa, as't am a gentleman the moone in comparison of thy bright hue a meere slutt, Anthonie's Cleopatra a blacke browde milkmaide, Hellen a dowdie.'
> INGENIOSO [*aside*]: Marke Romeo and Juliet: o monstrous theft[.][15]

The popularity of Shakespeare and *Romeo and Juliet* with theatre fanatics is again demonstrated. Gullio's brazen plagiarism is all the more risible because of the inappropriateness of the quotation chosen. In Shakespeare's text Mercutio expands on his mockery of Romeo's love of Petrarch's 'numbers':

> ■ Laura to his lady was a kitchen-wench – marry, she had a better love to berhyme her – Dido a dowdy, Cleopatra a gypsy, Helen and Hero hildings and harlots, Thisbe a grey eye or so, but not to the purpose. □
>
> (2.3.38–42)

Here Mercutio not only pokes fun at Romeo's romantic desires, but also at the literary posture he has adopted to express them; the superlative references to a beloved more beautiful than the iconic heroines of Petrarchan and classical love are meant to sound ironic. Gullio is characterized as doubly foolish (a poetry thief lacking in basic interpretative skills); though of course not all audiences would be able to spot the precise context of the allusion (Ingenioso is required to identify the play and author, after all). Indeed Gullio's obtuseness perhaps contains something of the more general reception of *Romeo and Juliet* both in the sixteenth century and the present day: Shakespeare's play provides both a shorthand reference for romantic love and an anthology of amorous quotations – its finer nuances are not part of this kind of appreciation.

However, inexpert poetry-lovers were not the only imitators of the play. The allusions made by other dramatists indicate the creative impact *Romeo and Juliet* had on early modern theatre. Like other popular plays of the period, *Romeo and Juliet* provoked a number of parodies that attest to the play's fame and innovative nature (it is difficult to parody something that is unremarkable). These allusions illuminate features that were most striking to the play's earliest audiences. In addition to the romantic subject matter and lyrical content so enjoyed by Gullio and Marston's satirical victims, the situation of a beloved at a window, elevated above her lover, held an iconic appeal from the first, and was reworked by numerous dramatists; the following commentary highlights two representative parodies.

Probably the most popular play to make a substantial parody of *Romeo and Juliet* central to its design is Henry Porter's *The Two Angry Women of Abingdon* (printed 1599). While the play certainly functions as a successful drama in its own right, Porter produces comedy through a range of burlesque allusions to Shakespeare's tragedy. The dramatic situation playfully diminishes and localizes the tragic context of *Romeo and Juliet*: action is transplanted from Verona to the less exotic Abingdon and the 'ancient grudge' between two patriarchal households becomes a spat between two housewives. Shakespeare's 'star-crossed' lovers are replaced by a couple (Mall and Frank) matched by fathers eager to reconcile their wives to one another. If the outline seems rather loosely allusive, the window-scene works more obviously as parody:

*Enter* MALL *in the window.*
MALL: How now, whose there?
PHILLIP: Tis I.
MALL: Tis I, who I? I quoth the dogge, or what?[16]

Mall's bluntness immediately and humorously redefines the romantic imagery of the window scene. The presence of her brother Philip as the director of the wooing pointedly removes the sense of an organic passion. The lovers themselves speak in rhyming couplets that jog past any lyricism and are full of bawdy insinuation:

FRANK: ...His dutie is before you bare to stand,
Hauing a lustie whipstocke in his hand.
MALL: The place is voyde, will you prouide me one?
FRANK: And if you please I will supply the roome.[17]

Mary Bly contends that this sexual content is a significant early legacy of *Romeo and Juliet*: 'Juliet is chaste and desirous, a unique combination in the plays of the early 1590s.... Juliet's erotic fluency had a marked influence on the shaping of comic heroines in the four to five years after the play's first performances.'[18] Shakespeare's characterization of a passionate but virtuous Juliet clears the ground for sexually knowing heroines in comedy; in earlier drama such knowledge was a mark of tragic corruption. Porter's Mall is humorously emphatic about her desire to be rid of her maidenhood: 'I will not dye a maide', she swears, and then reverses Capulet's concern about Juliet's youth being 'marred' (1.2.13) by marriage:

■ Good Lord thought I, fifteene will nere be heere,
For I haue heard my mother say, that then
Prittie maides, were fit for handsome men.[19] □

Mall constantly teeters on the edge of smuttiness, demonstrating a parodic incredulity at the possibility of a woman being both sexually passionate and moral. The novelty of Shakespeare's conception is thus thrown into relief. Bly observes that Mall pointedly misquotes Juliet when she tells Frank: 'you speake without the booke'. Where Romeo decorously addressed Juliet with conventional metaphors and images, Mall and Frank take to extremes what is unconventional in the

Shakespearean relationship, as these lovers speak to each other about sex rather than love.[20] The parody articulates the transgression of the earlier play.

Other aspects of Porter's window scene likewise clarify some of the distinctive features of Shakespeare's text. Frank is delighted by the speed of his success with Mall: 'this makes me smile, / That I haue woed and woune in so small while'.[21] While it may only have taken Frank a few puns at the window to win Mall, Romeo and Juliet took scarcely more time to fall in love.

What is an intimate moment in *Romeo and Juliet*, one of the play's very few scenes of snatched privacy, here quickly becomes overcrowded. Not only does Phillip watch over the lovers, but Mall's mother interrupts the proceedings and is soon joined by her husband and his men, followed by Frank's mother and servant. This moment collapses together the comedic-romantic and tragic elements of Shakespeare's plot. In a direct allusion to Lady Capulet, Mall's mother Mistress Barnes condemns the romance: 'Ile rather haue her married to her graue' ('I would the fool were married to her grave!' [3.5.139]).[22] What is potentially melodramatic in *Romeo and Juliet* is clearly and comically so in *The Two Angry Women of Abingdon*. The light and dark imagery of Shakespeare's play generates action in Porter's comedy, as the various characters run away from and chase after one another in the dark night, with inevitably farcical consequences. *Romeo and Juliet* itself flirts with comedy (see Chapter 4 below) and critiques lyrical flights of fancy (see Chapter 5 below), but these moments are complicated by serious poetry and tragedy. *The Two Angry Women of Abingdon* provides a more straightforwardly comedic view: poetry fails to take off and the threat posed by the feuding mothers never seems truly dangerous. Not surprising, then, that the play should end happily with the eponymous angry women reconciled to one another and the couple given maternal approval. The ease with which devices found in *Romeo and Juliet* can be turned to comedy demonstrates their affinity with this genre – romance was usually a matter for comedy after all. Porter's play not only affectionately pokes fun at the Shakespearean tragedy, but it also underlines its comedic potential: two lovers can overcome objection and live happily ever after.

Allusions to *Romeo and Juliet* also work as and in comedy in John Marston's play, *Jack Drum's Entertainment* (1601). Like Porter, Marston exploits the recognizability of the window scene, which has now become the obvious venue for wooing. However, Marston comically multiplies Shakespeare's singular scene of romantic intimacy as Katherine has to contend with not one but three eager suitors: the inflated Puffe, the elderly Mamon and the true lover Pasquill, who deliberately make for the window at three in the morning with the intention of courting. Katherine shares Juliet's linguistic resourcefulness and employs it to reject two hopefuls before Pasquill enters as her real Romeo. But by the time Pasquill takes his place beneath the window the scenario has been stripped of its romance; any delicate tension between mortal danger and the confession of love is dissolved. Pasquill's role as lover is characterized (as in *Romeo and Juliet*) by densely figurative language – his description of the dawn and night resonates with imagery which marks him out as the most appropriate suitor. But while in *Romeo and Juliet* paradox is central to both the play's plot and language, it serves in Marston's play to decorate the protagonists' hyperbolic protestations of love. Conceptualizing love as fidelity in disaster, even when no danger is apparent, Katherine and Pasquill parody the love of Romeo and Juliet as the thrill of transgression (compare the view of twentieth-century critics in Chapter 7 below). Nevertheless Pasquill and Katherine successfully will potential tragedy on themselves, as the jealous Mamon, who has observed much of the love scene, decides to have Pasquill killed. Feigning death, Pasquill foils the attempted murder, but inevitably causes near-fatal confusion. Clearly Pasquill had not seen either *Romeo and Juliet* or *Pyramus and Thisby*. Fortunately he inhabits a comedy and disaster is – somewhat convolutedly – averted.

The subplot of *Jack Drum's Entertainment* also reuses Shakespeare's window scene and provides another perspective on the sexual themes highlighted by *Romeo and Juliet*. Mall's sister, Camelia, likewise uses the window for romantic dialogue. But while Mall matches up to the example of Juliet by placing one man in her heart and keeping him there, Camelia keeps changing her mind, with nearly disastrous consequences. Camelia's characterization implies that the free choice idealized in stories such as that of Romeo and Juliet, and of Pasquill and Katherine, might leave some young girls dangerously rudderless. Shakespeare's tragedy of a couple not matched together by their parents provokes an ambivalent reaction in *Jack Drum's Entertainment*: a main plot that illustrates lovers wholly (and somewhat humorously) sold on the poetry and monogamy of romantic love; and a subplot that depicts young girls as unfit to choose their own partners. Clearly the concern was not exclusive to Shakespeare's play, but in its repeated redrafting of the window scene *Jack Drum's Entertainment* associates the situation of 'unarranged' marriages very closely with a reaction to *Romeo and Juliet*.

The question of sexual freedom also dominates a tragic response to *Romeo and Juliet*, John Ford's *'Tis Pity She's a Whore* (1633). Written over three decades after the first performances of *Romeo and Juliet*, Ford's play tests the limits of the sexual transgression depicted by Shakespeare. In loving without parental consent Romeo and Juliet rebel against general social conventions, and in choosing a lover from an enemy household they break the specific laws of Verona's feud. Ford's couple Annabella and Giovanni are brother and sister, so that their sexual rebellion turns inwards but is also on a larger scale: their incestuous relationship challenges the very structure of society and the laws of God. It is: 'a tale whose every word / Threatens eternal slaughter to the soul' (2.5.1–2).[23] While Romeo and Juliet's 'disobedience' of their parents actually served a social good in its healthy exogamy, with his endogamous lovers Ford pushes the challenge of sexual freedom even further, asking if individual will should be prized over artificial social order. As we have seen, a number of responses to *Romeo and Juliet* are comedic, but Ford has a profound sense of the tragedy of *Romeo and Juliet* – not only the potential for sexual relationships to wreak havoc (*'Tis Pity* ends with Giovanni killing his sister, brandishing her heart on a dagger and being murdered by a combination of revengers and *banditti*), but also for the subject of 'love' to frame searching questions about human agency and social obedience. He does not parody or 'quote' *Romeo and Juliet* like Porter or Marston, but he seems to take pains to remind his audience of the connection with the earlier play. He gives his incestuous lovers confidants who are markedly similar in status to Friar Laurence and the Nurse: Friar Bonaventura attempts to counsel Giovanni and Putana is Annabella's 'tutoress'. The reminder of the earlier play urges the audience to accept the incestuous love as having a kind of innocence, even as Ford also explores its darkness. Ford's Parma is more corroded than Shakespeare's Verona. Friar Bonaventura and Putana are still more morally questionable than their Shakespearean predecessors: where Friar Laurence arranges a hasty marriage between two lovers, Friar Bonaventura instructs the pregnant Annabella to marry a man she does not love to cover her tracks; the Nurse advises Juliet to settle pragmatically for bigamy, but Putana 'commends' her charge for her incestuous choice. These alterations (perhaps degradations?) emphasize that there is more at stake morally in Ford's tragedy. But in explicitly taking *Romeo and Juliet* as his starting point, Ford reveals the serious dilemmas first raised by that play.

Another (very different) early response to *Romeo and Juliet* likewise treats its tragedy seriously. The play's final couplet (with a slight alteration) is quoted by Robert Burton in the second edition of his medical handbook and compendium of literary references, *Anatomy of Melancholy* (1624): 'Who ever heard a story of more woe, / Than that of Juliet and her Romeo?'[24] The reference appears in a section of the text dealing with the 'Prognostics of Love-Melancholy'. Like later psychoanalytical critics (see Chapter 7 below), Burton treats the play as evidence of real human behaviour. His writing interweaves literary references with ostensibly empirical evidence (e.g. '*Anno* 1615, a barber in Frankfort, because his wench was betrothed to another, cut his own throat').[25] Indeed he uses literary terms to diagnose love as if the fictional and the real are indistinguishable: 'Such acts and scenes hath this tragi-comedy of love.'[26]

As the 'Melancholy' subject of the text suggests, Burton focuses on the negative. 'Love-Melancholy' is essentially a form of dangerous madness and those possessed with it are 'no better than beasts, irrational, stupid, headstrong, void of fear of God or men, they frequently forswear themselves, spend, steal, commit incests, rapes, adulteries, murders, depopulate towns, cities, countries, to satisfy their lust... madness, to make away themselves and others, violent death.'[27] Situating the woeful story of Juliet and her Romeo in this context, Burton's text serves as an important caution against assuming that early modern audiences all swooned sympathetically and ecstatically at Shakespeare's play. Burton's allusion implies that the young lovers are not innocent victims of fate, parental tyranny or social disorder, but are rather pathologically unhinged disturbers of the peace. When critics idealize the couple, it is worth remembering that the celebratory stance on romantic love is culturally conditioned; attitudes to love in early modern society were far more equivocal. Indeed the changing status of love and sexual relationships is adumbrated by the evolving criticism on *Romeo and Juliet*, as the following chapters of this Guide will show.

CHAPTER TWO

# Well-Seeming Forms: Seventeenth and Eighteenth Centuries

Though Samuel Pepys unequivocally condemned the play as 'the worst that ever I heard in my life', the critical and theatrical reception of *Romeo and Juliet* in the period after the Restoration was more generally ambivalent: at once highly praised and pointedly censured (even 'corrected').[1] Responses to the play (and to Shakespeare more generally) take quite different forms: the theatre staged freely adapted versions of *Romeo and Juliet*, while in the study new scholarly editions appeared that reflected on the particulars of the 'original'. Neoclassical tastes dominated literary appreciation, insisting on adherence to prescriptions about generic form. Against this background the editors Nicholas Rowe and Samuel Johnson explained and defended Shakespeare's lack of concern for such technicalities as the unities of time and place. Johnson celebrated instead what he understood as Shakespeare's instructive natural humanity, but criticized him for moments when 'conceit' damaged this vision. David Garrick's theatrical 'alteration' of *Romeo and Juliet* removed much of such wordplay from the Elizabethan text. But the period begins with a more thoroughly adapted staging of the play.

## THOMAS OTWAY (1679)

1679 saw the first performance of Thomas Otway's tragedy, *The History and Fall of Caius Marius*, an adaptation of *Romeo and Juliet* and its substitute on the stage until the mid-eighteenth century. Although not a piece of formal criticism, Otway's play nevertheless provides an insight into the seventeenth-century conception of *Romeo and Juliet*. Otway wrote at a time of extreme political tension in England. Panicked by (false) accusations of a Catholic conspiracy to assassinate Charles II (the 'Popish Plot'), the nation was in the grip of the Exclusion Crisis – an attempt to exclude the King's brother, the Duke of York, from his role as heir presumptive to the throne, because of his Catholicism. In rewriting *Romeo and Juliet*, Otway sets the play in Republican Rome, manipulating ostensible distance from the seventeenth-century English situation to speak to it safely.

Otway's title substitutes a patriarchal ruler for the lovers and (misleadingly) promises a more traditionally tragic focus on a single, politically significant figure. The changed situation of Republican Rome also remakes the feud as central political disorder: the civil discord between two households becomes a violent battle for the Consulship of Rome, raising questions about who has the right to rule and what that right entails (pressing matters in late seventeenth-century England). Otway uses the story to provide what Sue Owen describes as 'a powerful royalist message against ingratitude (the perceived fault of factious subjects), banishment (the unjust fate of the heir to the throne), and exclusion (the avowed goal of political opposition)'.[2] However, the action focuses on the plight of the lovers Marius Junior and Lavinia, the children, respectively, of Marius and Metellus (Marius's former supporter, now with the opposition). As Michael Dobson points out, with his interest in 'the sufferings of helpless private citizens' Otway 'discovered the formula for affective tragedy'.[3]

This intensification of affect also finds Otway giving a more extended consideration to the emotional problem of loving one's enemy than Shakespeare does. Marius Junior and Lavinia are really torn by their competing loyalties for lover and family; in *Romeo and Juliet* the lovers are afflicted only by the impracticality of the situation. Otway's couple long to be obedient: they have fallen in love with one another because their parents had initially arranged their marriage; they now strive to follow parental demands to fall out of love. By contrast, Romeo and Juliet love one another not only without their parents' consent but also without their knowledge. For Marius Junior, the trial of being a good son is integral to the nature of the tragedy; this worry never occurs to Romeo. In *Romeo and Juliet* a combination of masculine temper, the logic of the feud and, crucially, simple misfortune precipitates the deaths of Mercutio and Tybalt; in *Caius Marius* the young lover makes a conscious choice to turn from his beloved and do his father's violent bidding. This is no hot flash of vengeance, like Romeo's, but a doomed attempt to reconcile his personal desire with his identity as his father's son. Otway thus depicts the young lovers as victims of the older generation's violent discord with far less ambiguity than in *Romeo and Juliet,* where Romeo murders Tybalt on account of his own temper (and Tybalt starts the fight against his uncle's express prohibition).

The conclusion of *Caius Marius* also differs in structure and tragic meaning from *Romeo and Juliet.* In a moment of pointed irony reminiscent of *The Duchess of Malfi,* Marius Junior kills the Priest without realizing he is 'the only man' who could do him 'good'.[4] Otway also accentuates the pathos of the death scene by having Lavinia wake in time to talk with Marius Junior before his poison does its work (an innovation that will be copied differently by subsequent adaptors, including David Garrick and Baz Luhrmann). Their conversation puts personal pain at the heart of the tragedy. With excruciating irony Marius Junior forgets the effects of the poison when he sees the reawakened Lavinia: 'Ill Fate no more, *Lavinia*, now shall part us, / Nor cruel Parents, nor oppressing Laws.'[5] But ecstasy is swiftly undercut as Marius's sense of being lifted out of torment turns out to be the experience of dying, and Lavinia is left to lament. Where Juliet wakes to speak to an ultimately ineffective Friar, another horror interrupts Lavinia's final moments: Marius Senior enters and kills her father Metellus. Violent factionalism thus even splits apart the lovers' death scene; Rome has no space for their private love. The patriarchal nature of the political structure means there is no differentiation between public and domestic realms.[6]

The focus on names in *Caius Marius* is primarily a concern with familial identity rather than, as in *Romeo and Juliet*, a larger linguistic tension between *verbum* and *res* (see Chapter 5 below). When Lavinia exclaims 'O *Marius, Marius*! wherefore art thou *Marius*?', she is focused, unlike Juliet, on the specific problem of the patronym.[7] Asked in the final scene if she is Lavinia, the bereaved wife and daughter confirms only 'Once I was.' Yet loss of name does not mean liberation from constrictive social roles but is rather a symptom of the system imploding, as the political chaos obliterates all the bonds by which Lavinia knows herself. And moments later she reasserts: 'I am *Lavinia*, born of Noble Race.'[8] Indeed, through her suicide Lavinia defines herself by the relationships that have been destroyed: 'You have my Father butcher'd', 'The Gods have taken too my Husband from me.'[9] Shakespeare's Juliet is completely fixed on Romeo when she kills herself with his dagger, but Otway's Lavinia repeats her father's death (using the 'Sword yet reeking with my Father's Gore') and then transfers her woes to humanity itself ('let Rage, Distraction and Despair / Seize all Mankind').[10] Thus as Lavinia finally defies her father-in-law, she is emphatically the victim of external forces. Where Shakespeare consoles us with a (perhaps uneasy) Capulet–Montague truce, Otway's ending offers little in the way of reconciliation. *Caius Marius* concludes with its 'Mercutio', the dying Sulpitius, pronouncing 'A Curse on all Repentance! how I hate it!'[11] Having refused to engage with the meaning of the political chaos, Otway's bleak tragic vision offers no solutions to its destructiveness.

*Caius Marius* supplied the place of *Romeo and Juliet* on the stage for over half a century, between 1680 and 1735. Even though Shakespeare's star was rising in this period, audiences and theatrical professionals saw his plays as in need of correction. Otway's play did this job by intensifying the emotion, ironing out the comic interruptions and 'improving' the language with a more standard blank verse. *Caius*

*Marius* had a lasting critical impact on the reception of *Romeo and Juliet*. It is the earliest response to insist so strongly on the unambiguous victimhood of the young lovers at the hands of a corrupt older generation. This becomes a popular reading of *Romeo and Juliet* itself, and remains so in the public imagination of the twenty-first century. Away from the stage and its adaptations, the eighteenth century sees the birth of editorial work on Shakespeare. In the study, as in the theatre, the notion of the young lovers as tragic scapegoats obtains.

## NICHOLAS ROWE (1709)

With his edition of the *Works of Mr. William Shakespear*, Nicholas Rowe may be seen as the first modern editor of Shakespeare's plays. In his prefatory essay to the collection, Rowe exculpates Shakespeare for not adhering to the unities of time and place that neoclassically minded eighteenth-century writers regarded as basic precepts for good drama. The editor argues that literary standards were very different in the Renaissance, when Aristotle's dictums on tragedy were not well known:

> ■ as *Shakespear* liv'd under a kind of mere Light of Nature, and had never been made acquainted with the Regularity of those written Precepts, so it would be hard to judge him by a Law he knew nothing of. We are to consider him as a Man that liv'd in a State of almost universal License and Ignorance. There was no establish'd Judge, but every one took the liberty to Write according to the Dictates of his own Fancy.[12] □

In fact, some early modern writers (including Philip Sidney and Ben Jonson) did see disregard for the unities as a dramatic weakness, but Shakespeare was not one of them. Rowe urges the appreciation of different talents when considering Shakespeare, especially convincing and nuanced characterization. Indeed, character is seen to determine plot: 'his Design seems most commonly rather to describe those great Men in the several Fortunes and Accidents of their Lives, than to take any single great Action, and form his Work simply upon that'. However, *Romeo and Juliet* (together with *Hamlet* and *Othello*) stands out as a play 'where the fable is founded upon one Action only'. For Rowe, the meaning of this single movement is obvious: 'The Design in *Romeo and Juliet*, is plainly the Punishment of their two Families, for the unreasonable Feuds and Animosities that had been so long kept up between 'em, and occasion'd the Effusion of so much Blood.' Here Rowe takes as the main message of the play, the moral lesson seized on by the Prince at the end (5.3.291–5). But emotional impact is also seen as one of the most significant features of the play: 'In the management of this Story, he has shewn something wonderfully Tender and Passionate in the Love-part, and very Pitiful in the Distress.'[13] Didactic purpose and, more emphatically, sentiment and feeling, remain central themes when *Romeo and Juliet* returns to the theatre in place of Otway's adaptation.

## DAVID GARRICK (1748–53)

In this period, the theatre, perhaps even more than works of scholarship, was a venue for the kind of interpretation we might now associate with literary criticism. Between 1748 and 1753 the actor and theatre manager David Garrick produced a version of *Romeo and Juliet* which would remain the standard theatrical text of the play for the next hundred years. While Garrick certainly helped to shape eighteenth-century tastes, he also responded to them, being well matched, through his naturalistic and energetic acting style, to the emerging preference for the emotional over the heroic. It is not surprising that *Romeo and Juliet* – a play in such an obviously emotional key – should prove so popular at this time. But the play enjoyed by eighteenth-century audiences was significantly different from Shakespeare's early modern script. In streamlining the play for performance, Garrick removed the Prologue, Chorus and the part of Lady Montague. He also cut the text to 'clear' what he calls 'the Jingle and Quibble', that is, rhyme and wordplay.[14] In the eighteenth century the use of puns in tragedy was frowned upon, and Garrick's shorter version of the play cuts out a good number of these supposedly indecorous distractions from the emotions of the plot. (As Chapter 5 of this Guide will show, language will remain a particularly controversial aspect of the play into the twentieth and twenty-first centuries.) Garrick's cuts intensify the focus on the two protagonists (as less prominent characters lose out to the lovers) and alter the texture of the language of the play and its rhetorical themes.

Take, for example, the lovers' first meeting. In Shakespeare's play Romeo and Juliet first speak a dialogue that takes the form of a sonnet (1.4.206–19); Garrick halves the number of lines so that the poetic structure is removed. The metaphorical complexity and logic of Shakespeare's text is vastly reduced as Romeo kisses Juliet a bare two lines after first speaking to her; in the earlier text Juliet proves herself more than a linguistic match for her wooer, and the first kiss provides the climax of the full sonnet. Garrick's Romeo has the upper hand, whereas the Shakespearean first meeting depicted strikingly and innovatively mutual lovers (the critics discussed in Chapter 6 below argue that in having Juliet join in the sonnet Shakespeare smashes the Petrarchan convention of the beloved lady's silence).

Garrick's further alterations in his 1750 version of *Romeo and Juliet* create extra disparity between the lovers. Having removed Rosaline from the text, Garrick portrays Romeo as in love with Juliet from the beginning. Romeo attends the Capulet ball knowing Juliet's full name and determined to disguise his own from her; it is only Juliet who falls in love innocent of her beloved's identity. Romeo is both cleansed of his fickleness and given a stronger sense of initiative than in Shakespeare's play. The cutting of 'Quibble' also subtly changes Juliet's role. While Garrick's Juliet still questions the value of a name, her linguistic philosophizing is less searching than that of Shakespeare's heroine. And the later Juliet does not equivocate with her mother, whereas the sixteenth-century protagonist pretends to want vengeance against Tybalt's murderer but really speaks her desire for Romeo (3.5.81–102). Shakespeare's lines record Juliet's linguistic versatility, her conscious distance from her mother and her frank understanding of her sexual passion. Garrick interprets a Juliet who is still passionate but more innocent and less alert to the moral and linguistic complexities of her situation.

Not all Garrick's changes are cuts, however. In a bid to outdo John Rich's Covent Garden production in 1750, Garrick copied that company's addition of a funeral scene for the not-yet-dead Juliet.[15] In Shakespeare's text the highly stylized Capulet lamentations border on the ridiculous (especially because they are misplaced), and their mourning is further undercut by a short comic scene featuring musicians struggling to adjust to the turn of events (4.4); Garrick cuts the musicians and validates the Capulet grief with a solemn spectacle. The eighteenth-century text is therefore more uniformly tragic, whereas the Renaissance play flirts with comedy even at the edge of Act 5's disaster.

But Garrick's hand is most evident in the tomb scene. Like Otway, Garrick revives Juliet in time to engage in a fairly lengthy conversation with her dying lover. Most of the 65-line addition is Garrick's invention, though he borrows a handful of Otway's lines. This scene, the very moment of the catastrophe, provides the clearest indication of how Garrick understood the tragedy. He presents the two lovers as its pathetic victims. Their confusion emphasizes their innocence: in stark contrast to Shakespeare's Juliet, who wakes into perfect comprehension ('I do remember well where I should be' [5.3.149]), Garrick's Juliet is disoriented and frightened ('Where am I? defend me!'); Garrick's Romeo is so overjoyed to see Juliet alive that he forgets that he has just killed himself.[16] There is no ambiguity about the nature of the disaster: Garrick's Romeo has time to explain the plot developments Juliet has missed and to deliver a straightforward moral that identifies the cause as the parental feud (by contrast, later critics will question both the severity of the feud and the extent of the older generation's investment in it). The dialogue between Romeo and Juliet in the tomb is a further instance of Garrick concentrating on an intimate relationship rather than a broader social upheaval: his lovers, though dying one after the other, effectively (and affectively) share a death scene, whereas Shakespeare's die alone.

Garrick presented *Romeo and Juliet* as a sentimental tragedy of two innocent lovers. Action focuses on the protagonists, who are themselves simplified and idealized. Tragic feeling overwhelms, while tragic meaning is didactically delivered to the audience in the Prince's final (altered) couplet: 'From private feuds, what dire misfortunes flow; / Whate'er the cause, the sure effect is WOE.'[17] Off the stage, however, methodological innovations were taking place that saw increasingly rigorous research into Shakespeare's writing practices. For Charlotte Lennox, such study built up a rather less favourable image of Shakespeare than the one Garrick promoted.

## CHARLOTTE LENNOX (1753)

One of the first female 'critics' of Shakespeare was the writer and magazine editor Charlotte Lennox, best known for her novel *The Female Quixote* (1752). However, Lennox's *Shakespear Illustrated* (published in three volumes between 1753 and 1754) is more important for its advances in critical methodology than for the gender of its author. This work is one of the first attempts at an extended investigation of Shakespeare's use of sources. Lennox provides a series of translations of what she regards as the 'original' sources of Shakespeare's plays and commentaries analyzing the dramatic significance of the differences between source and play. The work on *Romeo and Juliet* (including a translation of the story as found in Bandello's *Novelle* [1554]) is found in the first volume.

Unlike later genre critics of the play, Lennox describes *Romeo and Juliet* as 'one of the most regular of all [Shakespeare's] Tragedies.'[18] Nevertheless, she sees it as flawed in its departures from Bandello's 'beautiful Original' version of the story.[19] She contends that Shakespeare never read Bandello's version, but instead worked with either Pierre Boaistuau's French translation of Bandello (1559), or William Painter's translation of Boaistuau in *The Palace of Pleasure* (1567). While Lennox's identification of Bandello's novella as an important text in the 'Romeo and Juliet' tradition is sound, her designation of it as 'the Original' is problematic. The story has been found as far back as the fifteenth century, in Masuccio Salernitano's *Novellino* (1476), and in a variety of texts thereafter.[20] Furthermore, her assumption that Shakespeare would have recognized Bandello's tale as superior in quality to Boaistuau or

Painter is based primarily on her own literary tastes. What she regards as Boaistuau's poor translation of Bandello can instead be seen as a deliberate alteration that fits the tale to the culture of a different readership. Lennox is on safer investigative ground when she points out details shared by the French/English sources of the tale and Shakespeare's play, but not found in Bandello: Juliet briefly railing against Romeo on learning of Tybalt's murder, the Friar being detained in Verona rather than Mantua, the inclusion of the apothecary who sells poison to Romeo. It is highly likely that Lennox is right in claiming that Shakespeare did not read Bandello's version of the story, but most critics now believe that Shakespeare's immediate source was Arthur Brooke's *The Tragicall Historye of Romeus and Iuliet* (itself a translation of Boaistuau) rather than Boaistuau or Painter.

As far as Lennox is concerned, Shakespeare's lack of access to Bandello explains and exposes weaknesses in *Romeo and Juliet*. Her criticism focuses on the way Shakespeare handles the lovers' deaths: 'The plain and simple Narration of that melancholy Event in *Bandello* is more natural, more pathetic, and fitter to excite the Passions of Pity and Terror, than the Catastrophe of the Tragedy, as managed by *Shakespear*, who has kept close by the Translator.'[21] An eighteenth-century privileging of sentiment and neoclassical sensibilities (evident in the Aristotelian concern for 'Pity and Terror') determines Lennox's preference for Bandello. She draws attention to supposedly unrealistic behaviour in Shakespeare's conclusion that is more naturally presented in Bandello's narrative. She complains that in Shakespeare's play:

> ■ There appears so much Contrivance and Method in *Romeo*'s Design of buying Poison, and going to *Verona* to drink it in the Monument of his Wife, that he might expire near her, that we can hardly suppose it to be the spontaneous Effect of a sudden and furious Transport of Grief.[22] □

Far better, she declares, is Bandello's description of Romeo's reaction upon hearing the news of Juliet's supposed death: overcome with emotion, Bandello's Romeo tries to kill himself on the spot, and only after being prevented by his servant does he resolve calmly to die in the tomb with Juliet. She praises such behaviour as 'beautifully pathetic and consistent with that violent Passion he had for [Juliet] when living', again invoking another Aristotelian idea that the characterization of tragic protagonists must be consistent.[23] Crucially, the death scene itself is different in Bandello's narrative and Shakespeare's play, with Bandello's poisoned hero surviving long enough to realize his error and speak to his awakened lover. Lennox is rapturous about the scene this enables: 'How pathetically does he complain of his miserable Destiny! With what tender Extasy does he congratulate her Return to Life! With what affecting Sorrow lament his approaching Death, which must tear him from her!'[24] The numerous exclamation marks emphasize the sentimental impact Lennox celebrates. Her important discovery is used by Garrick in the aforementioned 'Advertisement' to his 1753 edition of the play, where the explanation that Shakespeare did not have access to the supposedly emotionally superior source serves to license the alteration of the death scene.

Like Garrick, Lennox sees the intervention of 'flawed' translations between Bandello and Shakespeare as explaining the play's faults. The differences she cites between *Romeo and Juliet* and Bandello's tale are all first found in Boaistuau and Painter. However, for Lennox this source use qualifies rather than protects any sense of Shakespeare's genius. She quotes Pope's distinction between Shakespeare and other poets – '"*Shakespear's* Characters are Nature herself"' – only to push Shakespeare off his pedestal, pointing out that source study reveals Shakespeare's indebtedness to literary predecessors. In *Romeo and Juliet*, she argues, Shakespeare is one with the other poets Pope attempts to distinguish him from: '"His Picture, like a mock Rainbow, is but a Reflexion of a Reflexion."' Lennox's work is thus liberated from an assumption (prevalent in much of the source studies scholarship that followed) that Shakespeare always improved upon the material he used. Her research and commentary model the interpretative opportunities available through a careful comparison of Shakespeare and his sources.

However, Lennox does not herself capitalize on all of these opportunities. Her analysis is restricted to an assessment of how Bandello's tale is superior in sentiment to Shakespeare's play. She does not remark on the linguistic and characterological changes Shakespeare makes to the story. Even so, Lennox's pioneering research paves the way for the study of Shakespeare that situates the drama in the context of its literary inheritance. In her own time some readers disliked Lennox's focus on Shakespearean weakness. Indeed her friend Samuel Johnson, while equally ready to acknowledge Shakespeare's faults, made more effort to pinpoint his strengths when he came to edit the works in 1765.

## SAMUEL JOHNSON (1765)

Samuel Johnson was one of the most important Shakespeare scholars of his age. In his annotated critical edition of 1765 he celebrates Shakespeare as 'the poet of nature; the poet that holds up to his readers a faithful mirrour of manner and life'.[25] For Johnson, this ability to show us our humanity absolves Shakespeare from his failure to adhere to the unities of time and place so important to neoclassical critics. But where Lennox criticized *Romeo and Juliet* as a flawed reflection of a weak translation, a work less completely 'natural' than one might wish, Johnson regards it as a favourite:

■ This play is one of the most pleasing of our Author's performances. The scenes are busy and various, the incidents numerous and important, the catastrophe irresistibly affecting, and the process of the action carried on with such probability, at least with such congruity to popular opinions, as tragedy requires.[26] □

Nevertheless his praise is tempered by a dislike for the play's linguistic artifice: 'His comick scenes are happily wrought, but his pathetick strains are always polluted with some unexpected depravations. His persons, however distressed, *have a conceit left them in their misery, a miserable conceit.*'[27] Here Johnson adapts Dryden's criticism of Ovid's wordplay to complain about the characters' unrealistic habit of speaking in knotty poetry when supposedly overwhelmed by emotion. Shakespeare's verbal trickery was a particular bugbear for Johnson; he famously declared: 'A quibble was to [Shakespeare] the fatal *Cleopatra* for which he lost the world, and was content to lose it.'[28] Examples of such lethal language in *Romeo and Juliet* include Romeo's rhetorical reaction to the opening street fight: 'Why then, O brawling love, O loving hate' (1.1.172). Johnson grumbles: 'Of these lines neither the sense nor occasion is very evident. He is not yet in love with an enemy, and to love one and hate another is no such uncommon state as can deserve all this toil of antithesis.' Romeo's mannered formality continues to provoke critics across the centuries (see especially Chapters 5 and 6 below). But Johnson's linguistic grievances also include some of Juliet's responses. Glossing Juliet's deliberately ambiguous replies to her mother following the death of Tybalt (3.5.81–102), Johnson protests: 'Juliet's equivocations are rather too artful for a mind disturbed by the loss of a new lover.'[29] Like the actor Garrick, the scholar Johnson has little time for Shakespeare's 'quibble'.

In looking to Shakespeare for wisdom about humanity, Johnson had a keen awareness of the potential moral implications of the plays. He is frequently disappointed by tragic plots that fail to impart an ethical lesson. For example, Johnson sees the killing of Cordelia in *King Lear* as an offence against 'natural justice' (though later commentators see this death as more precisely natural *because* of its lack of justice). *Romeo and Juliet* is less troublesome than other tragedies in this respect. Johnson observes: 'Juliet plays most of her pranks under the appearance of religion: perhaps *Shakespeare* meant to punish her hypocrisy.'[30] Failings on the part of the protagonist make the tragedy tolerable in terms of justice. A more existential insight is drawn from Romeo's misplaced 'cheerful thoughts' (5.1.5) just before he is brought the news of Juliet's 'death': 'Why does *Shakespeare* give *Romeo* this involuntary cheerfulness just before the extremity of unhappiness? Perhaps to shew the vanity of trusting to those uncertain and casual exaltations or depressions which many consider as certain foretokens of good and evil.'[31] Another way of looking at this moment might be in terms of the play's generic and tonal hybridity between tragedy and comedy, ecstasy and despair. But Johnson wants to look past the artifice in Shakespeare for deeper philosophy. While he enjoys the affecting tragedy of *Romeo and Juliet*, it would be the Romantic critics who we meet in the next Chapter who would find true profundity in the play.

# CHAPTER THREE

# Righteous Kisses and Dateless Bargains: Romantics and Victorians

The late eighteenth and early nineteenth centuries were a time of tremendous upheaval. Political revolutions in America and France, together with rapid colonial expansion, changed the international balance of power, while industrial revolution in Britain reconfigured the lives of ordinary people. The literary world was equally dynamic, as writers came to rethink and reject the rules so important to intellectuals a generation before. Enthusiasm for Shakespeare reached religious heights in some quarters, and the criticisms of the Restoration commentators are more or less shaken off. Nevertheless, this period also sees the bowdlerizing of editions of *Romeo and Juliet*, its explicit sexuality being deemed distasteful by some moralists. Commentators, including one of the earliest feminist critics of Shakespeare, Anna Jameson, dismiss such prudery, and appropriate the play for an alternative political agenda. But the Romantic age starts with a less explicitly contentious commentary, with the lectures of August Wilhelm von Schlegel.

## AUGUST WILHELM VON SCHLEGEL (1797)

In his lectures on Shakespeare, the Romantic critic Schlegel celebrated the plays for their unity; the weaknesses identified by eighteenth-century critics are rationalized as part of a poetic whole. Thus where Charlotte Lennox (see Chapter 2 above) had regarded Romeo's dealings with the destitute Apothecary as an 'Absurdity', Schlegel sees Romeo's 'bitterness against the world' in this scene as containing 'something of the tone of Hamlet'.[1] Similarly, the murder of Paris – so disliked by Lennox – exemplifies for Schlegel the tension at the heart of the play:

■ That Romeo must meet Paris at Juliet's grave, is one of the many juxtapositions of common life with the altogether peculiar, self-created existence of the lovers, whereby Shakespeare renders the infinite interval

> that separates them apparent, and at the same time makes the wonderful in the story credible, by surrounding it with the well-known course of events.[2] □

Paris's presence helps bring the couple's rarefied love into real life and into relief. Such a character is happily expendable in the Romantic vision: 'How calmly he strews his flowers! I cannot therefore ask: was it necessary, that this honest soul should be made an additional sacrifice?'[3] The imperatives of passion are of far greater moment to Schlegel than mundane morality, so that he views even the murder as an opportunity to underline Romeo's attraction: 'Romeo's nobleness breaks forth here also like a sunbeam from dark clouds, as he speaks the last words of blessing over him who is made his brother by misfortune.'

Schlegel regards the play as dealing in absolutes. Hence he describes Juliet as an emotional and spiritual abstraction: 'As Juliet's whole being is love, so is truth her virtue.' As noted in Chapter 2 above, Thomas Otway adapted the story to characterize the tragedy of Juliet/Lavinia as a division in loyalties between parent and lover. Schlegel points out that no such concerns afflict Juliet:

> ■ The tyrannical violence of her father, the vulgarity in the behaviour of both parents is very offensive; but it saves Juliet from the struggle between love and daughterly feeling, which here would not have been at all in its place; for love is not here to be deduced from moral relations, nor to be represented as at war with duties, but in its original purity as the first command of nature.[4] □

Schlegel sees *Romeo and Juliet* as dealing with the raw matter of the universe, and thus puts its tragedy on an elemental scale.

But in addition to trumpeting the love of the young couple, Schlegel also displays a warm affection for the Nurse: 'every thing about her has a speaking truth.... She belongs to the souls in whom nothing cleaves fast but prejudices, and whose morality always depends upon the change of the moment.'[5] This analysis embodies Schlegel's admiration for Shakespeare's characterization, which he takes to be a major talent. Again, a sense of 'unity' pervades the interpretation, as Schlegel praises the character's vividness and human wholeness. This is a theme taken up by the Romantic poet Samuel Taylor Coleridge.

## SAMUEL TAYLOR COLERIDGE (1811–12)

Dismissing the importance of unities of time and place, Samuel Taylor Coleridge hails Shakespeare as a genius in creating unity of action. In stark contrast to the firmly qualified praise of commentators discussed in the previous chapter, Coleridge claims Shakespeare

> ■ never introduces a word or a thought in vain or out of place: . . . He never wrote at random, or hit upon points of character and conduct by chance; and the smallest fragment of his mind not unfrequently gives a clue to a most perfect, regular and consistent whole.[6] □

Thus *Romeo and Juliet* is populated with characters such as Capulet and Tybalt who are 'contrasting, yet harmonized' with one another.[7] Nevertheless, although Coleridge finds much to admire in the play, he struggles to maintain a case for its perfect unity. Commenting on the scene where the Capulets lament Juliet's apparent death, he muses:

> ■ It is difficult to understand what *effect*, whether that of pity or laughter, Shakespeare meant to produce – the occasion and the characteristic speeches are so little in harmony: e.g., what the Nurse says is excellently suited to the Nurse's character, but grotesquely unsuited to the occasion.[8] □

Such moments of comic and tragic hybridity trip up arguments about harmonious unity. Elsewhere Coleridge identifies *Romeo and Juliet* as an early tragedy that contains 'specimens' of the 'excellencies' which appear more perfectly in later plays, but which are as yet 'not united with the same harmony'. Even so, he insists that *Romeo and Juliet* contains 'passages where the poet's whole excellence is evinced, so that nothing superior to them can be met with in the productions of his after years'.[9] This is a rather more favourable assessment than in later criticism that emphasizes the play's supposed immaturity.

Coleridge thinks that the disharmonies of *Romeo and Juliet* – where they exist – are a symptom of the 'poet' not being 'entirely blended with the dramatist'. Hence Capulet and Montague 'talk a language only belonging to the poet' rather than dialogue appropriate to their character and situation.[10] Elsewhere Coleridge sees Montague's ornamental language ('Many a morning hath he there been seen, / With tears augmenting the fresh morning's dew, / Adding to clouds more clouds with his deep sighs' [1.1.127–9]) as evidence that Shakespeare 'meant' the play 'to approach to a poem'.[11] This notion of *Romeo and Juliet* as conceived in a deliberately lyrical fashion is further developed by later critics of the play's language and Petrarchan poetry (see Chapters 5 and 6 below). Coleridge shares some of the uneasiness of seventeenth-century critics with the verbal artificiality, as exemplified by Romeo's rhetorical rant in the aftermath of the street brawl (1.1.171–7). But unlike his predecessors, Coleridge 'dare[s] not pronounce' such lines 'absolutely unnatural': a newly emergent reverence means the Romantic considers Shakespeare 'a much better judge' and Coleridge sees in the dense catalogue of oxymora a character struggling to express an unnameable idea.[12] He even strives to justify the puns so loathed by earlier commentators, naming them the 'lowest' but 'the most harmless kind of wit', and recognizing their appeal in the sixteenth century.[13] But he concedes that such incursions of Renaissance taste 'detract sometimes from [Shakespeare's] universality as to time, person and situation'.[14]

Coleridge is more comfortable when talking about the play's characterizations. His commentary on Juliet points to an important feature of her idiosyncrasy. Responding to Juliet waiting for Romeo on her wedding night ('Come night, come Romeo, come thou day in night; / For thou wilt lie upon the wings of night / Whiter than new snow upon a raven's back' [3.2.17–19]), Coleridge exclaims: 'The imaginative strained to the highest. What an effect on the *purity* of the mind!'[15] Juliet's poetic creativity is here recognized, and though he does not quite spell it out, Coleridge importantly sees her sexual enthusiasm as a form of purity (though later in the century the passage will be cut from editions of the play). He also approves of the supposedly feminine distinctiveness of her character: her boldness in swallowing the sleeping potion is moderated, with 'the finest decencies', by her terror as she hallucinates Tybalt's ghost (4.3.54–7).[16] Similarly he praises the gendering of the lovers whereby Romeo but not Juliet is seen to change affections: 'The difference in this respect between men and women – it would have displeased us that Juliet had been in love or fancied herself so.'[17]

Mercutio is identified by Coleridge as central to the structure and meaning of the play. He defines the character's linguistic style thus: 'Mercutio is a man possessing all the elements of a poet: the whole world was, as it were, subject to his law of association.' Furthermore, he has a definitive place in the plot: 'upon the death of Mercutio the whole catastrophe depends; it is produced by it'.[18] This important observation has a long legacy in the critical history of the play; Mercutio's death is now nearly always recognized as a crucial turning point in the drama. In celebrating Shakespeare's gift for characterization Coleridge is at pains to stress that the talent is not mere mimicry but imagination. Characterizations such as that of the Nurse illustrate the argument: 'Let any man conjure up in his mind all the qualities and peculiarities that can possibly belong to a nurse, and he will find them in Shakespeare's picture of the old woman: nothing is omitted. This effect is not produced by mere observation.'[19] The Romantic conception of Shakespeare delights in an idea of original creativity, a unique imagination that captures both individuality and typicality. While Coleridge may find elements of *Romeo and Juliet* uneven, he nevertheless regards it as an important example of what was increasingly being seen as Shakespeare's genius.

## WILLIAM HAZLITT (1817)

As the title makes clear, William Hazlitt's *Characters of Shakespear's Plays* (1817) develops the Romantic argument about the definitive significance of Shakespeare's individualized characters. With regard to *Romeo and Juliet* he counters the objection that the couple's immaturity disqualifies their tragic love – that they 'have had no experience of the good or ills of life' and that their 'raptures or despair must be therefore equally groundless and fantastical'.[20] For Hazlitt, the protagonists' youth makes their love all the purer. Shakespeare

> ■ has given a picture of human life, such as it is in the order of nature. He has founded the passion of the two lovers not on the pleasures they had experienced, but on all the pleasures they had *not* experienced. All that was to come of life was theirs. . . . They were in full possession of their senses and their affections. Their hopes were of air, their desires of fire. Youth is the season of love, because the heart is then first melted in tenderness from the touch of novelty, and kindled to rapture, for it knows no end of its enjoyments or its wishes. Desire has no limit but itself. Passion, the love and expectation of pleasure, is infinite, extravagant, inexhaustible, till experience comes to check and kill it.[21] □

In this argument pure love is possible because the lovers have not been corrupted by experience; they do not think back to a past that teaches them about the failure of love. Hazlitt's theory also strikes a challenging philosophical note. As Philip Davis suggests: 'the heaven that lies about the lovers is not for Hazlitt some neoplatonic memory of a mystical pre-existent state from which we grow away in time, . . . on the contrary, it is a world new to the young not through knowledge of the past but ignorance of the future'.[22] Indeed, it is imagination rather than memory (or 'experience') that facilitates love.

The imaginative substance of the play therefore makes its passion. Hazlitt announces:

> ■ Romeo is Hamlet in love. There is the same rich exuberance of passion and sentiment in the one, that there is of thought and sentiment in the other. Both are absent and self-involved, both live out of themselves in a world of imagination. Hamlet is abstracted from every thing; Romeo is abstracted from every thing but his love, and lost in it.[23] □

The comparison with Hamlet marks how seriously Hazlitt takes Romeo's passion and imaginative abstractions. Few of the later genre critics would be prepared to credit Romeo's passion with such value.

## ANNA JAMESON (1832)

Criticism takes a political turn in the work of Anna Jameson. Originally named *Characteristics of Women: Moral, Poetical, and Historical* when first published in 1832, Jameson's book was retitled *Shakespeare's Heroines* after the author's death in 1860. This double title signals what Jameson's twenty-first-century editor describes as the text's 'hybrid genre'.[24] The work is both a piece of literary criticism and a conduct book featuring commentary on exemplary female characters from Shakespeare's plays. Jameson explicitly sets her text against a contemporary culture that defined the female role as one of submissive domesticity: 'the education of women, as at present conducted, is founded in mistaken principles, and tends to increase fearfully the sum of misery and error in both sexes'. Women could serve society better by bringing their particular gifts to the public as well as the private world, and it was imperative that they were properly schooled in their emotional resources. In *Characteristics of Women* Jameson aimed to provide a panoply of female examples from Shakespeare that would form part of such training. As such, Jameson's readings centre on female characters as moral personality types rather more than as literary constructions. Nevertheless, her references to writers such as Schlegel and Hazlitt see her consciously engaging with an interpretative tradition and her focus on female characters offers a new critical perspective on the plays, anticipating the work of later feminists (see Chapter 8 below). It proved a very popular formula: by 1905 Jameson's text had been reprinted twenty times.

Jameson places Juliet in the section on 'Characters of Passion and Imagination', turning to her 'not without emotion'.[25] The commentary includes a number of observations about character traits. For example, commenting on Juliet's attack on Romeo when she learns of Tybalt's death and her hasty defence him when the Nurse joins in, Jameson points out that 'quick transitions of feeling' are characteristic of Juliet. Interestingly, she also suggests that 'With Juliet, imagination is, in the first instance, if not the source, the medium of passion; and passion again kindles her imagination.' Thus her speech in the window scene is 'one rich stream of imagery; she speaks in pictures; and sometimes they are crowded one upon another':

■ I have no joy of this contract tonight:
It is too rash, too unadvised, too sudden,

> Too like the lightning which doth cease to be
> Ere one can say 'It lightens' . . . .
> This bud of love, by summer's ripening breath,
> May prove a beauteous flower when next we meet. □
>
> (2.1.160–5)[26]

By contrast, Romeo only learns 'concentrated, earnest, rapturous' language after falling in love with Juliet cures him of his more laboured poetry.[27] Both lovers are totally absorbed in each other: they 'speak of themselves only; they see only themselves in the universe, all things else are as an idle matter'.[28] Indeed, the couple are put in pointed – and for Jameson, idealized – contrast to the world around them: 'all harmony, surrounded with all discord; all pure nature, in the midst of polished and artificial life'. Romeo and Juliet are again the innocent victims in the tragedy. In line with earlier Romantic critics, Jameson insists on overarching unity: 'in this vivid impression of contrast, there is nothing abrupt or harsh'.[29]

However, Jameson's sense of the character is somewhat larger than the textual evidence; she has a tendency to supply extra details not found in the play-text itself. Thus Juliet suddenly appears in surprising visual detail in Jameson's prose:

> ■ Juliet, like Portia, is the foster child of opulence and splendour; she dwells in a fair city – she has been nurtured in a palace – she clasps her robe with jewels – she braids her hair with rainbow-tinted pearls; but in herself she has no more connexion with the trappings around her, than the lovely exotic transplanted from some Eden-like climate has with the carved and gilded conservatory which has reared and sheltered its luxuriant beauty.[30] □

Elsewhere Lady Capulet struts into the commentary 'with her train of velvet, her black hood, her fan, and her rosary'.[31] Jameson's methodology here is evidently shaped by a literary culture dominated by the realist novel. Like a nineteenth-century novelist she seeks to understand a character by thinking about their back-story (Juliet's metropolitan upbringing), and with that she fleshes out a vivid present-tense picture. However, the generic differences between theatrical and narrative characters mean that this technique is not without its problems. Philip Davis suggests that Jameson effectively removes characters from their dramatic setting and fits them to her own alternative narrative.[32]

Indeed, for all Jameson decorates her character study with imagined visual details, she also views Juliet in abstracted terms:

> ■ All Shakespeare's women, being essentially women, either love or have loved, or are capable of loving; but Juliet is love itself. The passion is her

state of being, and out of it she has no existence. It is the soul within her soul; the pulse within her heart; the life-blood along her veins 'blending with every atom of her frame.' The love that is so chaste and dignified in Portia – so airy-delicate and fearless in Miranda – so sweetly confiding in Perdita – so playfully fond in Rosalind – so constant in Imogen – so devoted in Desdemona – so fervent in Helen – so tender in Viola – is each and all of these in Juliet. All these remind us of her; but she reminds us of nothing but her own sweet self[.][33] □

Jameson here betrays an 'essentialist' understanding of gender, whereby men and women are thought to be not only anatomically different, but also psychologically distinct. However, Jameson's modern-day editor Cheri Larsen Hoeckley claims that this proto-feminist writer is unusual in seeing 'essentialism as liberating, rather than limiting'.[34] Thus where social orthodoxy saw women as essentially weaker than men, Jameson saw the essential traits of femininity as virtues that recommended the capacity of women as socially useful. As 'love itself', Juliet encompasses a canonical range of Shakespearean virtues, from Portia's dignity to Viola's tenderness. Yet however polemically necessary this catalogue of qualities is, it does fail to address some of the more challenging characteristics that might have disturbed Victorian readers, such as Juliet's disobedience and deceptiveness. Even so, Jameson's analysis grants Juliet the individual integrity she craves when she fantasises an existence unencumbered by names: 'she reminds us of nothing but her own sweet self'. And Jameson later puts Juliet's potentially censorious behaviour in emphatically and unconventionally positive terms. Jameson writes that in the scene when Juliet confronts her father's rage at her refusal to marry Paris and is let down by the Nurse's pragmatic recommendation of bigamy, 'The fond, impatient, timid girl, puts on the wife and the woman: she has learned heroism from suffering, and subtlety from oppression.' With palpable irritation she continues: 'It is idle to criticise her dissembling submission to her father and mother; a higher duty has taken place of that which she owed to them; a more sacred tie has severed all others.' Defining Juliet's filial disobedience as 'heroism', Jameson makes a claim[35] for female autonomy in patriarchal society (implicitly associated with 'oppression').

Jameson also strongly rejects the censoring and censuring of Juliet's excited anticipation of her wedding night in the 'Gallop apace, you fiery-footed steeds' soliloquy (3.2.1–31):

■ Let it be remembered, that, in this speech Juliet is not supposed to be addressing an audience, nor even a confidante; and I confess I have been shocked at the utter want of taste and refinement in those who, with coarse derision, or in a spirit of prudery, yet more gross and perverse, have dared to comment on this beautiful 'Hymn to the Night,' breathed out by Juliet in the silence and solitude of her chamber. She is thinking aloud; it is the young heart 'triumphing to itself in words.' In the midst of all the vehemence with which she calls upon the night to bring Romeo to her arms, there is something so almost infantine in her perfect simplicity, so playful and fantastic in the imagery and language, that the charm of sentiment and innocence is thrown over the whole; and her impatience, to use her own expression, is truly that of 'a child before a festival, that hath new robes and may not wear them.'[36] □

Philip Davis objects that in apparently defending Juliet's passion, Jameson fails to acknowledge its full sexuality: she does not quote most of the speech, and in talking of 'sentiment and innocence' being 'thrown over the whole' she uses 'the language of veils and drapes'.[37] Certainly this metaphor wrongly implies that Juliet's sexual enthusiasm is here decorously covered over, when the soliloquy more provocatively makes innocence integral to frank and eager sexuality. Even so, Jameson's insistence on the necessity of the soliloquy should not be dismissed. While she may attempt to exonerate Juliet from charges of indecency by pointing out the speech's private nature, she nevertheless recognizes desire as a key facet of Juliet's (exemplary) character.

More contentious is Jameson's sentimental assessment of the final disaster of the tragedy:

■ We behold the catastrophe afar off with scarcely a wish to avert it. Romeo and Juliet *must* die: their destiny is fulfilled: they have quaffed off the cup of life, with all its infinite of joys and agonies, in one intoxicating draught. What have they to do more upon this earth? Young, innocent, loving and beloved, they descend together into the tomb: but Shakespeare has made that tomb a shrine of martyred and sainted affection consecrated for the worship of all hearts, – not a dark charnel vault, haunted by spectres of pain, rage and desperation. Romeo and Juliet are pictured lovely in death as in life; the sympathy they inspire does not oppress us with that suffocating sense of horror which in the altered tragedy makes the fall of the curtain a relief; but all pain is lost in the tenderness and poetic beauty of the picture.[38] □

Jameson here prefers Shakespeare's staging of the suicides to the 'altered tragedy' where the couple manage conversation as Romeo dies. For her Shakespeare's version is more pleasingly aesthetic – a beautiful 'picture'. Her sanitized view of tragedy edits out any complexity, presenting paradox ('lovely in death') without any sense of the tensions within it. She sees the play as leaving audiences satisfied (there is no desire to 'avert' the fatal end), but not challenged. In this reading not only is the young couple's love totally idealized, but tragedy itself is prettified.

## EDWARD DOWDEN (1875)

Another very popular book-length study of Shakespeare appeared in 1875 with the publication of Edward Dowden's *Shakspere: A Critical Study of His Mind and Art*. Based on a series of lectures given by Dowden as Chair of English at Trinity College, Dublin, this work marks the increasingly academic nature of writing on Shakespeare. Rather than responding to individual plays in isolation, Dowden scans the canon of Shakespeare's plays, formulating a narrative about how the writing develops. He classifies *Romeo and Juliet* as Shakespeare's early tragedy, a label that holds (though later critics expand the category to include *Titus Andronicus* and *Richard III*).

As the titular reference to '*Mind and Art*' promises, Dowden's analysis speculates (somewhat assertively) about Shakespeare's creative motivations and decisions. Thus he reads the two extant early quartos of *Romeo and Juliet* as evidence that Shakespeare was 'Dissatisfied' with his first attempt at the play and came to rewrite and enlarge it (for a discussion of the problems of hypothesizing about the status of these texts see Chapter 1 above).[39] In an even larger leap he declares that the experience of writing *Romeo and Juliet* made Shakespeare aware of his literary limitations: 'he considered his powers to be insufficiently matured for the great dealing as artist with human life and passion, which tragedy demands'.[40] Supposedly also cowed by the theatrical dominance of Christopher Marlowe's tragedies, Shakespeare turned to other genres. Interesting as these suggestions are, it is impossible to know the contents of Shakespeare's mind; and it is also worth noting that Shakespeare did continue to experiment with tragic material in *Julius Caesar*. However, Dowden's narrower definition of tragedy does prompt him to make a connection (like Hazlitt) between *Romeo and Juliet* and what he regards as Shakespeare's next tragedy, *Hamlet*. On the one hand the plays contrast with one another: where passion dominates *Romeo and Juliet*, meditation governs *Hamlet*; southern Europe is replaced by northern Europe; the witty prankster Mercutio is succeeded by the grave Horatio; the requited passion of Romeo and Juliet is followed by the thwarted desire of Hamlet and Ophelia. But on the other hand Dowden finds a crucial similarity between Romeo and Hamlet: 'the will in each is sapped'.[41]

A substantial portion of Dowden's analysis is devoted to the characters of the two protagonists. Like Coleridge, Dowden lauds Shakespeare's retention of the Rosaline plot, since it enables Shakespeare to trace Romeo's emotional development. When in love with this absent woman Romeo shows 'the abandonment to emotion for emotion's sake'.[42] This is love as a performance: 'Romeo nurses his love; he sheds tears; he cultivates solitude; he utters his groans in the hearing of the comfortable friar; he stimulates his fancy with the sought-out phrases, the curious antithesis of the amorous dialect of the period' ('Feather of lead, bright smoke, cold fire, sick health' [1.1.176]).[43] Although Romeo loses some of this affectation in his love for Juliet, 'there remains a certain clinging self-consciousness, an absence of perfect simplicity and directness'. By contrast, Juliet's 'direct unerroneous passion . . . goes straight to its object, and never broods upon itself'.[44] Thus in the orchard scene Romeo remains distracted by the poetic 'atmosphere' of the scene ('Love goes toward love as schoolboys from their books, / But love from love, toward school with heavy looks' [2.1.202–3]), while Juliet worries about the practical dangers he faces in an enemy household and is wary of sophisticated oaths ('farewell, compliment. / Dost thou love me? I know thou wilt say "Ay" ' [2.1.132–3]). Dowden sees in this distinction a larger point about Shakespeare's male and female characters: 'the natures of women are usually made up of fewer elements than those of men, but . . . those elements are ordinarily in juster poise, more fully organized, more coherent and compact; and . . . consequently, prompt and efficient action is more a woman's gift than a man's'.[45] For this reason Shakespeare is said to find male characters more interesting than female characters. In the case of *Romeo and Juliet* Dowden notes that Juliet acts with greater purpose than Romeo: she proposes marriage and is more collected in her response to disaster than her husband (Romeo bawls on the floor at the news of banishment; Juliet calmly makes for Friar Laurence when she learns she is to be married to Paris). Yet Dowden is impressed by Romeo's maturation and sees the tragic conclusion as marking the character's emphatically masculine fulfilment:

> ■ The moment that Romeo receives the false tidings of Juliet's death, is the moment of his assuming full manhood. Now, for the first time, he is completely delivered from the life of dream, completely adult, and able to act with an initiative in his own will, and with manly determination. Accordingly, he now speaks with masculine directness and energy[.][46] □

How this 'manly determination' and 'masculine directness and energy' differs from the determination, directness and energy said to have been displayed by Juliet is unexplained. Dowden's analysis characterizes Romeo as heroic in his final actions. The fixed resolutions of 'Is it e'en so? Then I deny you stars!' (5.1.24) and 'Well, Juliet, I will lie with thee tonight' (5.1.34) are felt to improve on the densely figurative language earlier in the play. Even Romeo's murder of Paris (which Dowden points out is an addition to the source material) is described in approving terms. He is said to speak with 'gentleness' and 'authority', emphasized by references to Paris's newly distinguished youth: 'Good gentle youth' (5.3.59); 'I beseech thee, youth' (5.3.61); 'Then have at thee, boy!' (5.3.70).

Other commentators (before and after Dowden) have been troubled by the apparently unnecessary murder of Paris, but Dowden sees no problem with this. Indeed he explicitly rejects as overly simplistic readings that attempt to draw any moral from the tragedy. In particular he derides the German writer Gervinus for suggesting that the play's fatal end stands as a warning against a lack of moderation: 'What! Did Shakspere then mean that Romeo and Juliet loved too well? That all would have been better if they had surrendered their lives each to the other less rapturously, less absolutely?'[47] This incredulity exposes the crudity of readings that attempt to fit neat lessons to the play. But Dowden goes a stage further to celebrate the tragedy itself as positive:

■ Shakspere did not intend that the feeling evoked by the last scene of this tragedy of Romeo and Juliet should be one of hopeless sorrow or despair in the presence of failure, ruin, and miserable collapse. Juliet and Romeo, to whom Verona has been a harsh step-mother, have accomplished their lives. They loved perfectly. Romeo had attained to manhood. Juliet had suddenly blossomed into heroic womanhood. Through her, and through anguish and joy, her lover had emerged from the life of dream into the waking life of truth.... And as secondary to all this, the enmity of the houses is appeased... Shakspere in this last scene carries forward our imagination from the horror of the tomb to the better life of man, when such love as that of Juliet and Romeo will be publicly honoured, and remembered by a memorial all gold.[48] □

Like Jameson, Dowden feels no final trauma in the ending; but he argues for something profounder than the sentimental beauty she praised. In Dowden's view this tragedy becomes the means by which Romeo and Juliet achieve their full potential as human beings.

## HELENA FAUCIT, LADY MARTIN (1885)

Helena Faucit (who became Lady Martin when her husband was knighted in 1880) was one of the most popular actresses of her day. Her book *On Some of Shakespeare's Female Characters* (1885) originated in a series of letters written to friends and then serialized in *Blackwell's Magazine*. It takes the form of autobiographical reflections on the experience of playing various Shakespearean roles, including Juliet, Ophelia, Portia, Desdemona, Imogen and Rosalind. The editor of the *Variorum Shakespeare*, Horace Howard Furness, extolled it as 'the finest [book] that has ever been written on Shakespeare', preferring it to Jameson's *Shakespeare's Heroines*: 'Mrs. Jameson looks at the characters as a highly intelligent sympathetic nature would look at them. Lady Martin is the character itself, and interprets to you its every emotion.'[49]

Furness's praise captures something of Faucit's mode of writing, whereby she necessarily inhabits the part and becomes 'the character itself'. As an actress she needs to flesh out each role not only at the physical level of the body, but in a psychological sense. Thus her discussion of the part of Juliet imaginatively elaborates on textual details. Discussing the lovers' first meeting, she comments that the words themselves are 'few' and dwells on the physical realization of the scene: 'The beseeching eyes, the tremulous voice full of adoration and humility – have these not spoken? The heart's deepest meanings rarely find utterance in words.'[50] Later she describes an emotional and physiological context for the window scene: 'Her throbbing pulse, the flush of the heated ball-room, make the cool moonlight air most welcome.'[51] More significant from the perspective of literary criticism are Faucit's practical insights. For example, she notes that when Juliet parts with Romeo after their wedding night and views him 'so low, / As one dead in the bottom of a tomb' (3.5.55–6), it is the last time that she will see him; and that Lady Capulet wishes her daughter dead just as the tragic disaster is set in motion: 'I would the fool were married to her grave!' (3.5.139).

Faucit talks of the part of Juliet as a deeply personal attachment: 'all my young life seems wrapped up in her. You can see, therefore, how difficult it must be to divest myself of the emotions inseparable from her name sufficiently to write of her with critical calmness.'[52] And certainly Faucit's partiality is sometimes superlative without being critically specific. Juliet is said to have achieved 'heroism of the highest type', though the nature of this 'type' is not explained.[53]

Similarly, Juliet is thought to experience 'a love in which her whole being should be merged, and by which her every faculty and feeling should be quickened into noblest life'; but precisely what makes Juliet noble (rather than say, rash and melodramatic) is not spelled out.[54] Nevertheless, with a certain wryness Faucit acknowledges the particular appeal the play had for her in childhood: 'To most young minds, I suppose, the terrible and the tragic are always the most alluring.'[55] This conjecture, though not here pursued, anticipates later psychoanalytical interpretations of the young couple themselves.

Despite her somewhat impassioned language, Faucit takes care to identify the play as more than a romantic tale. Upon reading 'the real Shakespeare instead of the imperfect copy adapted and condensed for the stage', she comes to a realization:

■ It was no longer only a love-story, the most beautiful of all I had ever read, but a tale where, as in the Greek dramas of which I had seen some glimpses, the young and innocent were doomed to punishment in retribution for the guilt of kindred whose 'bloody feuds' were to be expiated and ended by the death of their posterity.[56] □

In this assessment the feuding parents bear responsibility for the tragedy and the young couple are innocent victims. Indeed, likening them to Iphigenia (the ancient Greek mythological heroine who was sacrificed by her father Agamemnon), Faucit writes of the need for the lovers to be 'a worthy sacrifice'.[57] This 'purpose' is evident, she contends, in the declaration of the Prologue ('Whose misadventured piteous overthrows / Doth with their death bury their parents' strife' [Prologue 7–8]) and the Prince's final judgement ('Capulet, Montague, / See what a scourge is laid upon your hate, / That heaven finds means to kill your joys with love; / And I, for winking at your discords, too, / Have lost a brace of kinsmen. All are punished' [5.3.291–5]). For the tragedy to function in this way Romeo and Juliet must be understood as guiltless victims; a view Faucit presents energetically.

However, Faucit is most illuminating in her commentary on the details of particular speeches. She writes that one of the speeches she found most difficult was the passage in the window scene where Juliet admits her embarrassment at being overheard ('Thou knowest the mask of night is on my face, / Else would a maiden blush bepaint my cheek' [2.1.128–9]), invites Romeo to match her declaration of love ('Dost thou love me?' [2.1.133]), asserts her integrity ('I'll prove more true / Than those that have the coying to be strange' [2.1.143–4]) and asks to be forgiven for all of it ('Therefore pardon me' [2.1.147]). Faucit enthuses:

■ Women are deeply in debt to Shakespeare for all the lovely noble things he has put into his women's hearts and mouths, but surely for nothing more than for the words in which Juliet's reply is couched. Only one who knew of what a true woman is capable, in frankness, in courage, and self-surrender when her heart is possessed by a noble love, could have touched with such delicacy, such infinite charm of mingled reserve and artless frankness, the avowal of so fervent yet so modest a love, the secret of which had been so strangely stolen from her. As the whole scene is the noblest paean to Love ever written, so is what Juliet now says supreme in subtlety of feeling and expression, where all is beautiful. Watch the fluctuations of emotion which pervade it, and you will understand what a task is laid upon the actress to interpret them, not in voice and tone only, important as these are, but also in manner and in action. The generous frankness of the giving, the timid drawing back, fearful of having given too much unsought; the perplexity of the whole, all summed up in that sweet entreaty for pardon with which it closes.[58] □

The gushing gratitude may not be to modern critical taste, but Faucit is perceptive about the nuances of Juliet's characterization and the careful balance struck between frankness and reserve. Similarly, she is alert to the particularities of Juliet's situation, regarding Romeo as 'fortunate' in having more 'sympathetic' parents than his beloved. Holding particular disdain for the 'cruel' Nurse, Faucit (like Jameson) sees the scene in which this confidante advises Juliet to marry Paris as a moment of sudden maturation: 'Alone she must face the future – a future steeped in gloom. The child's trust in others falls from her... She is henceforth the determined woman.'[59] This change is central to the tragic dynamic; the play is about growing up: 'she is transfigured into the heroic woman just as Romeo, when possessed by a genuine passion, rises from the dreaming youth to the full stature of a noble manhood'. But it also, for Faucit, has a larger, moralistic 'purpose'. Since the play ends not with the lovers' death, but with a final admonition and reconciliation, Faucit finds a 'lesson of amity and brotherly love'. This form of tragedy deals in clarity rather than complexity: 'never could the lesson be more emphatically taught... There is in this play no scope for surmise, no possible misunderstanding of the chief characters or of the poet's purpose, such as there are in *Hamlet* and *Macbeth*.'[60] The certainty Faucit has in the play's clear-cut moral message is eroded in twentieth-century critical interpretation. In becoming a firmly established 'discipline', criticism diversifies into different methodological and ideological schools, as the next five chapters, which are organized thematically rather than chronologically, will show.

# CHAPTER FOUR

# Excellent and Lamentable Tragedy? Genre Criticism

The professionalization of literary criticism in the twentieth century transformed the discipline. No longer just the leisure activity of well-informed amateurs, English Literature acquired a new status as an academic discipline that could be studied at university and researched by trained academics. The more specialized attention of a wider group of professionals made possible the methodological, political and philosophical diversification of literary criticism that is particularly evident from the later twentieth century onwards. In order to keep track of this variegation, this Guide now switches from a chronological to a thematic organization. We begin with genre Criticism, since this directed the approach of the first major professional critic, A. C. Bradley.

Securely located in the 'Tragedies' section of the Folio and (unlike, for example, *King Lear*) labelled as a tragedy in both its early quarto editions, *Romeo and Juliet* has nevertheless provoked much critical debate about whether it can be considered a 'real' tragedy. Many scholars agree with only the second term in the sales pitch of the 1599 quarto title page, which markets the play as an 'excellent and lamentable tragedy'. But the play has also been recognized as a radical generic experiment: translating novella into drama, comedy into tragedy, and, for the first time on the English stage, giving 'household' romance a tragic form. This chapter explores how critics have engaged with the generic shiftiness of the play, and examines the reasons for the discomfort with its tragic label.

## A. C. BRADLEY (1904)

One of the first literary scholars to earn a living from his profession also became one of the most influential – and contentious – critics of the twentieth century. A. C. Bradley's *Shakespearean Tragedy* (1904) is a book-length study made up of a series of lectures delivered at the University of Oxford in 1901, when Bradley was elected Professor of Poetry.

It communicates complex philosophical analysis in accessible prose that reached beyond a university readership to the wider public. Claiming to define the fundamentals of Shakespearean tragedy, the study cast a long methodological shadow that subsequent critics worked hard to avoid.

*Romeo and Juliet* barely features in *Shakespearean Tragedy*. Bradley describes the play as 'a pure tragedy', but also 'an early work, and in some respects an immature one',[1] and he confines himself to a few snatched remarks on the drama. Instead, *Hamlet, Othello, King Lear* and *Macbeth* occupy the bulk of his attention, each play having individually formed the focus of two separate lectures. While it may therefore seem odd to consider Bradley in a Guide devoted to *Romeo and Juliet*, the omission of this play from one of the most important pieces of twentieth-century Shakespeare criticism is itself illuminating. Why should *Romeo and Juliet* fail to make Bradley's selection of 'great' tragedies? Since Bradley sets the agenda for genre criticism for many years to come, this is an essential question.

Like commentators before and after him, Bradley has fixed ideas of what tragedy is, or at least should be. Aristotle's *Poetics* dominates his thinking. Just as the Greek theorist understood plot to be the fundamental basis of tragedy, Bradley insists on a basic tragic structure which centres on an individual whose deeds determine the final outcome. However, in making character the focus of his analysis, Bradley produces a major shift in emphasis: Aristotle regarded character as expendable, valuing it only as a vehicle for plot. Ultimately, the action of tragedy should produce a 'catharsis' in the audience. Here Bradley adopts an ambiguous Aristotelian term which translates as 'rebalancing' or 'purging', and is more specific about its role than Aristotle himself (in the *Poetics* it is unclear whether catharsis happens on stage as an experience of the characters or actors, and/or offstage in the audience). Thus terms which give the illusion of fixed standards across time in fact register new interpretative priorities.

But Bradley's theory is not merely a Victorian adaptation of Aristotle: he synthesizes supposedly ancient ideas with newer German philosophy, in particular the work of Hegel (and is the first English critic to do so). Hegel understood existence as a struggle between two opposing forces; tragedy occurred at the moment of confrontation between these two forces. Bradley recognizes such conflict as the key dynamic in Shakespearean tragedy; it is present in *Romeo and Juliet* in the opposition between the 'love of Romeo and Juliet' and 'the hatred of their houses'.[2] This larger sense of an elemental clash credits the feud with a momentousness that other critics will question. Its importance for Bradley is determined by his sense of the moral structure of the universe. For Bradley, 'good' and 'evil' are not relative or abstract concepts; they are absolutes that have a material force in the world. The universe strives towards moral perfection but produces evil nonetheless; the moment of 'convulsion' when this evil is spat out is tragedy:

> ■ In Shakespearean tragedy the main source of the convulsion which produces suffering and death is never good: good contributes to this convulsion only from its tragic implication with its opposite in one and the same character. The main source, on the contrary, is in every case evil; and, what is more . . . it is in almost every case evil in the fullest sense, not mere imperfection but plain moral evil.[3] □

A 'good' character such as Othello loves Desdemona, but his good love is corrupted into evil by sexual obsession and jealousy. In the 'convulsion' both Othello and Desdemona are consumed, and our sense of waste and our realization that a good person in implicated in evil produces Aristotelian pity and terror (definitive responses to tragedy according to the *Poetics*). Tragedy is therefore analytical and morally instructive: audiences are shown how good can be perverted into evil and are made aware of the 'possibilities of human nature' even when witnessing wretchedness.[4] Suffering is celebrated by Bradley, because tragedy itself is more than just the experience of waste, but rather about that larger movement towards good. The horrors of the First World War would soon make Bradley's triumphant vision of tragedy very difficult to sustain, but in its interrogative attention to evil it is not as glib as later commentators frequently imply.

The stress on moral issues inevitably makes character the central consideration of Bradley's criticism. Indeed it was mainly his attention to character that exerted such long-lasting critical influence – and attracted derision. Bradley announced that 'The centre of the tragedy' could be said 'to lie in action issuing from character, or in character issuing in action.'[5] Characters had to be responsible in some way for the tragic fate that befell them. Again, evident here is a Victorian conditioning of an Aristotelian idea: Bradley insists on a degree of moral culpability absent from Aristotle's pre-Christian idea of 'error'. Striving to identify 'characteristic deeds' draws out the best and worst in Bradley, as he undertakes a rigorous analysis of why characters behave the way they do. His philosophical training (his undergraduate degree was in Classics, Philosophy and Ancient History) enables him to assess abstract motivations, but he lacks the sophistication later critics (beneficiaries of recently available degrees in English) had in analysing the language of the text. Bradley treats characters as if they are real people rather than literary and theatrical constructions.

The focus on character also helps to explain Bradley's lack of interest in *Romeo and Juliet*. Where Shakespearean tragedy 'is pre-eminently the story of one person, the "hero" ', with its central ' "hero" and "heroine" '

*Romeo and Juliet* is unusual in its dual focus and attention to a female protagonist.[6] This makes the play, according to Bradley's reasoning, a not particularly illustrative anomaly. But perhaps just as problematic is the nature of the characters found in *Romeo and Juliet*. Bradley notes that Shakespearean heroes, particularly those found in the later tragedies, are 'torn by an inward struggle'; however, Romeo (like other 'early' heroes) 'contends with an outward force, but comparatively little with himself'.[7] The teleological view of Shakespeare's canon imagines that Shakespeare worked to perfect a particular mode of characterization and achieved this in a 'mature' tragedy such as *Macbeth* or *King Lear*. If we want our characters to provide a rigorous, psychological self-scrutiny then Hamlet is a much richer portrait than Romeo. But character does not, and certainly did not, always aim to communicate a sense of interiority. A search for that version of depth may overlook what is present.

Even though Bradley paid little attention to *Romeo and Juliet*, the legacy of his work had a lasting impact on the criticism of the play. Having set the terms in which tragedy was to be understood, Bradley's *Shakespearean Tragedy* made it difficult to see *Romeo and Juliet* as anything other than an early tragedy, interesting only as evidence for the seeds of later greatness. For much of the twentieth century, subsequent genre critics tend to be locked into patterns of acknowledging the play's weaknesses and apologetically defending its value.

## H. B. CHARLTON (1948)

Reusing Bradley's title, in *Shakespearian Tragedy* H. B. Charlton gave a fuller assessment of the tragic status of *Romeo and Juliet*. For Charlton, the play's tragic form marks a crucial 'departure' from the English dramatic traditions of its time; it is a 'comprehensive experiment'.[8] Shakespeare has looked to the Italian writer and generic theorist Giraldi Cinthio (himself influenced by the ancient Roman dramatist Seneca). Where other English tragic drama of the period was rooted in stories from classical mythology or national history, *Romeo and Juliet* was sourced from contemporary fiction. Charlton believes this untypical choice of subject matter is motivated by a Cinthio-inspired desire to connect with the audience: 'It must therefore reflect a range of experience and base itself on a system of values which are felt by the audience to be real.'[9] The stories of ancient heroes and monarchs are too removed from an audience's life experience to engage them with the urgency necessary to tragedy. Almost by accident, love becomes the subject of Shakespeare's tragic experiment. Charlton argues that this topic follows as an 'inevitable consequence' of turning to modern fiction (which focuses 'almost exclusively on love'), thereby defining Shakespeare's interest in the love story as one of technical craftsmanship.[10]

By recognizing innovation Charlton opens out important new critical ground. But for him (just as for Bradley), 'tragedy' invokes a standard against which the play must be judged, and is not simply a genre that Shakespeare is free to manipulate in the service of his story. Charlton identifies an experiment in order to question its success. In Charlton's terms, tragedy needs 'universality', 'momentousness' and 'inevitability', all of which were harder to generate after the 'anarchist's gesture' of putting an ordinary boy and girl at the tragedy's centre.[11] But while the cast of characters and subject matter was decidedly modern, the other facet of the innovation was much older:

> ■ he was experimenting with a new propelling force, a new final sanction as the determinant energy, the *ultima ratio* [last argument] of tragedy's inner world; and though *Romeo and Juliet* is set in a modern Christian country, with church and priest and full ecclesiastical institution, the whole universe of God's justice, vengeance and providence is discarded and rejected from the directing forces of the play's dramatic movement. In its place, there is a theatrical resuscitation of the half-barbarian, half-Roman deities of Fate and Fortune.[12] □

It is through this invocation of an ancient, Senecan paradigm that Shakespeare makes Romeo and Juliet worthy of tragic attention. The force of (an anachronistic) Fate is realised through the operation of the feud, which Charlton takes to be central to the play's tragic dynamic and to the success or failure of the generic experiment. Curiously, he also sees the joint operation of Fate and feud as a way for Shakespeare to 'disown' responsibility, a 'plea for exculpation' and even a 'bribe'.[13] Here Charlton touches on, without fully confronting, the darker implications of why tragedies give writers and audiences pleasure. Rather than interrogating this tragic attraction (as the critics discussed in Chapter 7 below do), Charlton half acknowledges a guilt, buried deep within the genre, about its sadistic satisfaction in fatal plots.

Far more attention is given to the nature of the generic role of Fate and feud. But having identified what he takes to be Shakespeare's tragic structure, Charlton finds it to be rather weak. The feud fails to live up to the importance Shakespeare (or perhaps Charlton) has attached to it: the heads of the warring households are 'almost comic figures' rather than 'fierce chieftains'; mutual friends are shared between the two sides; when in love with the Capulet Rosaline, Romeo is unconcerned by her familial identity; the Montague youths confidently sneak into the Capulet party protected only by masks; and old Capulet happily tolerates the gatecrashers rather than spoil a dance. All in all, prior to

Mercutio's death, the quarrel seems almost spent.[14] Practically a 'dead letter', the feud thus proves to be a poor vehicle for Fate, so that the protagonists' fearful premonitions lose their plausibility and the story lacks inevitability.[15] The disjunctive combination of modern circumstance and pre-modern Fate finally short-circuits the tragedy: 'Fate was no longer a deity strong enough to carry the responsibility of a tragic universe; at most, it could intervene casually as pure luck, and bad luck as a motive turns tragedy to mere chance. It lacks entirely the ultimate tragic *ἀνάγκη* [necessity].'[16] Charlton's use of Greek here tellingly indicates the limits he puts on Shakespeare's tragic experiment. While he may applaud the artistic innovation in *Romeo and Juliet*, he insists that certain generic standards must be maintained, and the Greek word implies that these standards are timeless.

Nevertheless Charlton is not comfortable criticizing Shakespeare, and his objections to the play are precisely framed as technical ones: 'as a pattern of the idea of tragedy, it is a failure.' His bardolatry takes the sting out of this criticism. Backing away from the implications of his argument, he claims that it 'may seem not only profane but foolish' to regard *Romeo and Juliet* as 'an unsuccessful experiment'.[17] Having decided that *Romeo and Juliet* fails to meet the objective-sounding generic standards he set, Charlton rescues the play by more abstract praise that points to a literary essence beyond the scope of analysis: 'the achievement is due to the magic of Shakespeare's poetic genius and to the intermittent force of Shakespeare's dramatic power rather than to his grasp of the foundations of tragedy'.[18] Later critics will do more to identify the mechanics of this 'magic'.

## FRANKLIN M. DICKEY (1957)

Like Charlton, Franklin M. Dickey sees the genre of *Romeo and Juliet* as its interpretative key. Indeed, insisting on the drama's tragic credentials emerges as a means of defending a play that 'sometimes embarrasses critics'.[19] Dickey thus carefully builds a case for *Romeo and Juliet* as a 'true tragedy', a category he understands in terms of a Christianized reading of Aristotle. Thus it becomes essential to recognize the characters as exercising ethical judgement that shapes their plot.[20]

Much of Dickey's discussion centres on the way in which Shakespeare 'improves' on his source: 'Shakespeare has taken from Brooke what he needed to make an effective tragedy and has discarded the rest.'[21] This allows Dickey to celebrate Shakespeare's technical skill without putting the drama in an unfavourable comparison with more established tragedies. Shakespeare gives us a newly 'mature' (though younger) Juliet, who 'constantly' displays 'more courage and good sense than Romeo'; a Romeo who is far too passionate to be tamed by 'the Friar's consolations of philosophy'; and a Friar whose sermons are raised above the source's 'platitude'.[22] Indeed Dickey's moralizing reading of the tragedy places a great deal of significance on Friar Laurence, who 'unlike Brooke's is a true chorus whose words give the necessary moral base from which to judge the tragedy'.[23] Thus where Charlton saw institutional religion as the mere backdrop for an action alternatively determined by a pagan Fate, Dickey hears an instructive Christian voice in the play and regards it as central to the audience's response. It is telling that he should describe this 'moral base' as 'necessary', since not all theories of tragedy require moral judgement (in fact, Dickey's Christian morality would have been totally alien to Aristotle's way of thinking). He explicitly rejects the instrumentality of Fate: 'Shakespeare does not let us forget that disregard of the Friar's reasonable counsel rather than the turning of fortune's wheel dooms Romeo's love.'[24] According to Dickey, tragedy depends upon the culpability of the protagonists; allowing Fate a hand would remove that culpability and dissolve the tragedy.

This reading has the virtue (to stick with moral terms) of recognizing and addressing characterological complexity. Insisting on Romeo's moral capacity de-sentimentalizes the play. The most striking evidence that Shakespeare invites us to think critically about Romeo's behaviour is the scene of Paris's murder, an incident Shakespeare has deliberately added to the story found in his sources. The desperate Romeo begs Paris: 'Put not another sin upon my head / By urging me to fury' (5.3.62–3). The religious vocabulary is all the more pointed since Paris himself does not want to fight, but rather to bring Romeo to law: 'I do defy thy conjuration, / And apprehend thee for a felon here' (5.3.68–9). Dickey therefore interprets the scene 'as another of the signposts which Shakespeare has given us to help make the tragedy a real tragedy in which the catastrophe depends not upon fate but upon the passionate will of Romeo'.[25]

These signposts direct an understanding of the suicidal climax of the play: 'the Elizabethan audience would have realized that in his fury Romeo has committed the ultimate sin'.[26] Nevertheless Dickey does not regard the play as a sermon or moral exemplum; the tragedy causes its audience to recognize fault without provoking outright condemnation. Indeed Dickey's reading carefully calibrates a sense of Christian culpability against an Aristotelian reaction: 'Romeo's death is not the cold-blooded action of a mortal sinner though, and it should inspire us with both pity and terror.'[27] This commentary sensitively draws out some of the ambiguity of the play's conclusion, whereby we recognize fault in a character with whom we also sympathize. But Juliet is somewhat edited out of this moral vision, for all Dickey earlier recognized her greater maturity. Her suicide is a mere side effect of Romeo's sin, acknowledged in a secondary clause: 'and her suicide may be thought of as the direct result of his'.[28] In defending the play as a tragedy, Dickey implicitly draws on a traditional generic structure that is determined by a single (male) protagonist, even though his own analysis of the 'catharsis' produced by Juliet's death invites a fuller consideration of her role and proactive decisions.[29]

Moral choice is absolutely definitive for Dickey; it underpins the most fundamental distinction between comedy and tragedy. Like countless critics before and after him, he recognizes the comedic potential of the play that is killed off with the death of Mercutio. Dickey contends that this generic crux turns on an ethical decision:

> ■ It would certainly have spoiled the play for Romeo to have waited for the law to punish Tybalt, but the fact remains that this reasonable action would have turned tragedy into comedy. In this choice between reasonable and passionate action lies one great difference between the genres. Forgiveness produces the happy ending of comedy; revenge produces the catastrophe of tragedy.[30] □

This observation valuably pinpoints an ethical difference between comedy and tragedy (though like many generic descriptions, it is not completely watertight: revenge proves very comic in *The Merry Wives of Windsor*, for example). The broader stress on moral choice usefully shows the serious nature of this tale of young love. But there is perhaps something a little too confident in the judgements that Dickey assumes that he, the audience and the play all share. He cites Robert Burton (discussed in Chapter 1 above) to show that Renaissance audiences would have understood the physical and mental dangers of love. He thus laudably reminds us of our historical distance from Shakespeare and his audiences. But the single reference to Burton does not clear up the complicated problem of the Elizabethan understanding of suicide (valorized in classical literature and condemned in Christian doctrine). Dickey's criticism thus does much to rehabilitate the tragic status of the play, but its greater value lies in the questions it opens as much as those it answers.

## JOHN LAWLOR (1961)

John Lawlor's essay on *Romeo and Juliet* forms part of an anthology dedicated to *Early Shakespeare*, and is a concerted effort to rescue the play's critical reputation. As in other criticism, the terms of his defence implicitly indicate the play's assumed weakness. This, it is claimed, is

Shakespeare's 'first major incursion into tragedy'.[31] However, Lawlor recognizes that the play's 'alleged shortcomings' are themselves determined by 'certain assumptions about the tragic', and he introduces his analysis with a discussion of the different modes of tragedy that he believes other scholars have confused or misrepresented.[32] He draws a distinction between medieval '*tragedie*' in which Fortune or Fate is operative, and a tragedy of character. In his view, *tragedie* had been misunderstood as cruel and arbitrary, when it actually encourages the audience to look beyond 'inexplicable suffering to a happiness beyond time's reach'.[33] This medieval tragic vision thus has a Christian dimension that is inscrutable in its operations, but which necessarily points beyond earthly mortality. In carefully distinguishing two separate ideas of tragedy, Lawlor insists: 'The important consideration is that the one is not an imperfect form of the other; where causal connection interests the Greek, what absorbs the medieval mind is the absence of a rationale in any terms less than an unsearchable Divine wisdom.'[34]

This identification of alternative conceptions of tragedy usefully indicates the way in which different cultural circumstances inform the structure and meaning of the genre; judging Shakespeare only by the supposed rules of Greek tragedy risks missing the true tragic design of his play. Though he deems it important to recognize separate strands of tragic thinking, Lawlor claims that good tragedy (like *Romeo and Juliet*) draws on both modes: 'The centre of attention in any serious drama must be the over-burdened human figure who is yet an *agent*. In Elizabethan terms this must mean one who achieves an end which does not minimize, much less cancel, Fortune's power, but which denies her an entire victory.'[35] Thus the action of the tragic protagonist can have some influence over his/her destination, but Fortune remains a determining (though not all-powerful) force. This more detailed understanding of tragedy is put in the service of a positive, if not triumphalist, reading that is not all that different from some of Bradley's celebratory interpretations of the 'big' tragedies. The influence of *tragedie* sees *Romeo and Juliet* demonstrate that 'out of evil comes not good merely but a greater good' in which life is 'regenerated'.[36]

This morally optimistic reading tends to rely on an assertion about *tragedie* rather than a detailed analysis of Shakespeare's tragedy itself. Lawlor does reject specific claims made by earlier critics that supposedly account for the play's weakness: for example, he denies that the feud is a dead letter, noting that the comic potential of old Capulet and Montague is balanced by the serious involvement of the servants, as well as Tybalt and Mercutio.[37] But his own line of interpretation is a little selective in its use of evidence. For Lawlor, the young lovers are kept apart from the Veronese society they inhabit: there is a 'decisive turning, in both Romeo and Juliet, away from the "mature" viewpoints of all around them, to a new thing'.[38] This reference to an abstract 'new thing' is typical of Lawlor's argument, which claims transcendence for the play and its two protagonists. He is referring to the couple's 'love', which he regards utterly alien to the world of Verona, but a purifying force. The lovers' youth gives them an innocence that transforms into an alternative form of wisdom, so that even as they reject the 'maturity' of their feuding families, Romeo is said to 'grow' to 'a final maturity which outsoars all else in the play', and the pair achieve a paradoxical 'premature "estate" '.[39] Yet this argument requires Lawlor to absolve the couple of any responsibility for the suffering experienced in the play. He tackles this in generic terms by denying the relevance of character 'flaws' and 'causal connection' between character action and tragic consequence.[40] Such a contention usefully moves away from anachronistic readings of the play that presume Shakespeare was trying and failing to meet some Victorian understanding of Aristotelian prescriptions for tragedy. It allows him to ignore the less 'pure' aspects of the action (for example, Romeo's murder of Paris). But while Lawlor's refusal to attribute blame may capture the popular sympathy audiences feel for the couple, it does gloss over the emotional as well as the moral complexity of the play. Similarly, his ecstatic reading of the play's fatal end responds to only part of the tragic experience: 'The love of Romeo and Juliet is in fact to transform the world they live in ... That Death has no final power over the lovers is the great truth to which we are directed by their own rapturous hyperboles and by the central fact of their love.'[41] But the nature of the 'transformation' achieved by the suicidal pair is not fully interrogated, and it is not clear why we should accept their 'hyperboles' rather than notice the disjunction between the 'soaring' lyricism and the material presence of dead bodies. Lawlor's reading of this 'early' tragedy returns us to the transcendence of the Romantic vision (discussed in Chapter 3 above). It is not surprising, then, that he should see in the play the seeds not of Shakespeare's later tragedies, but of his miraculous and reconciliatory romances.[42]

## NICHOLAS BROOKE (1968)

Nicholas Brooke's chapter on *Romeo and Juliet* in his book *Shakespeare's Early Tragedies* refines the critical commonplace that sees the drama as apprentice work: 'this is not simply, or so much, an immature play, as a very highly organized play about (among other things) immaturity'.[43] Brooke also liberates himself from previous attempts to legitimize the text in terms of perceived rules of what a tragedy should be; identifying the play's tragic scale as 'almost domestic', he simply accepts that scope as valid and turns his attention to the particular (and peculiar) impact of the play.[44] Like Charlton, he finds in *Romeo and Juliet* the curiosity of an artist consciously experimenting with genre and form. This fits a pattern of exploration in the first stages of Shakespeare's career (where *Titus Andronicus* and *Richard III* represent two additional, alternative approaches to tragedy). Brooke characterizes *Romeo and Juliet* in rather unpromising terms as 'a formal exercise in romantic tragedy'.[45] But if this description makes the play sound drily academic, the argument behind it unlocks the provocative energy of the play.

Brooke finds more meaning in the variety of generic excursions within the tragedy than previous commentators. *Romeo and Juliet* is situated not only in a group of 'early tragedies', but also in a period of comedic writing (which produced *The Two Gentlemen of Verona, A Midsummer Night's Dream* and *Love's Labour's Lost*). This canonical proximity reveals Shakespeare's tendency to pose similar questions in different generic modes. In *Romeo and Juliet* Shakespeare realizes, paradoxically, 'the nearness and oppositeness of a comic and a tragic sense of love'. Additionally, the play explores 'the world of the love sonnet' (see also the readings in Chapter 6 below), so that a range of different literary discourses are put in dialogue within one tragic framework. Where other critics had regarded such generic crossbreeding as an aspect of the drama's weakness (or at least inconsistency), Brooke makes a convincing case for the play as meaningfully integrating different ideas in order to interrogate them. Thus the play tests alternative literary conceptions of love ('the rank bawdry of the servants, the warm earthiness of the Nurse, and the witty cynicism of Mercutio', together with the romance of the sonneteering lovers).[46] But in doing so it also poses still more searching questions about the relationship between literature and reality. The lyrical hyperboles (celebrated as truth by Lawlor) stand in a contrast to more deflationary passages that forces us to ask which is truer to experience, and whether there might be dangers in soaring poetry.

The poetic structure of *Romeo and Juliet* is therefore integral to Brooke's understanding of a play in which content and form are mutually illuminating. Close attention to shifts between poetry and prose, varieties of metre and rhyming patterns allows him to address rather than gloss over or condemn the tonal disjunctions disliked by earlier critics of the play's tragedy. In fact, he argues that the play 'develops round a series of paradoxes'.[47] These are produced not only by the oxymora within individual speeches, but through contrasts between characters. Mercutio (a figure of Shakespeare's invention) is centrally important in this respect. His mocking of Romeo's romantic pretensions sharply contradicts the straight-faced amorous poetry of the lovers. But as Brooke smartly observes, Mercutio's cynicism is slightly off target: not only is Romeo no longer, as his friend assumes, infatuated with Rosaline, but the play's romantic extremes are not quite of the quality Mercutio ridicules. The first meeting between Romeo and Juliet is formally framed as a sonnet (14 lines of their dialogue concluding with a rhyming couplet [1.4.206–19]). But this formality produces an appropriate sense of ritual, of 'betrothal' that culminates in the physical connection of a kiss and is counterbalanced by Juliet's preventing Romeo overextending the metaphors after the sonnet is complete:

ROMEO: Sin from my lips? O trespass sweetly urged!
Give me my sin again.
*He kisses her*
JULIET: You kiss by th' book.

(1.4.222–3)

The sonnet here functions as poetic, a 'formal embodiment of valid feeling in distinction from sonneteering as mere attitudinizing'.[48] So when Mercutio comically exposes the absurdity of the rhetoric of courtly love in the Queen Mab speech, or bawdily mocks Romeo for 'groaning for love' (2.3.83–4), he derides a romantic pretension that Romeo has moved beyond. Even so, the combination of different attitudes to love – and, crucially, ways of expressing these attitudes – invite the audience to contemplate the authenticity and value of each.

If his criticisms do not quite hit the mark, Mercutio is nevertheless central, almost literally, to the tragedy. Brooke regards Mercutio's death in Act 3, and not the romantic suicide, as potentially 'The most moving scene in the play'.[49] Like Coleridge, Brooke sees this death as a generic and thematic hinge: up to this point the play proceeds comically with tragic foreboding; afterwards, the play turns tragic with increasingly dark moments of comedy. Similarly, where sex dominated the first half of the play, death overwhelms the second. But Mercutio's death is not only significant as a structural marker; Brooke contends that 'The whole play is challenged and re-directed by this scene.'[50] After receiving his death wound Mercutio makes jokes in prose (Brooke argues that his death speech itself should be printed as prose rather than verse) and reproves Romeo for having inadvertently caused his death ('Why the devil came you between us? I was hurt under your arm' [3.1.102–3]). What is excruciating here is the banal realism of accidental death. There is a sharp 'sense of actuality as Mercutio dies the way men do die – accidentally, irrelevantly, ridiculously; in a word, prosaically', so that 'the fanciful world of poetic romance which is fulfilled by a poetic death is reproved by a prosaic one; as poetry is apt to be reproved by life'.[51] Thus Brooke brilliantly uncovers the way in which this drama self-consciously reflects on its own mode and qualifies the romantic extremes it articulates.

The play's interrogative attitude to romance is also evident in the presentation of the love of Romeo and Juliet itself. Juliet, in particular, has a frank understanding of the necessary immodesty of sexual love: 'O, I have bought the mansion of a love, / But not possessed it; and though I am sold, / Not yet enjoyed' (3.2.26–8). Brooke claims that Juliet herein discovers 'that in most wanting her true love with Romeo she must experience the wish to be a whore in the fullest sense'.[52] While this analysis adeptly reveals a paradox within the notion of 'true love', it fails to attend to another important paradox, whereby Juliet is buyer and possessor as well as 'whore'. But the fuller point that youthfulness does not simply mean innocence (as in Lawlor) marks a significant critical development. This play 'diagnoses' the association of love and death as a symptom of youthful feeling, so that the couple can only conceive of their passion as 'lightning before death'.[53] Juliet's elated apostrophe to 'night', as she waits for her new husband to arrive, emphatically links sex with death ('Give me my Romeo; and when I shall die, / Take him and cut him out in little stars' [3.2.21–2]), and omits any reference to growth or fertility. This 'leaves the love-death conjunction without division or alternative'.[54] Romeo and Juliet thus produce an inevitably tragic end for themselves, but not because of a limiting sense of 'character flaws'. Rather, the play questions not only their attitudes, but also the way the literary expression they use shapes them. Even their death 'is not, perhaps, very real. It is far more obviously the beautiful consummation of the unfulfilled love, and its place as climax of the formal structure is very strongly felt: it is moving as part of the formal dance to which I compared the play, rather than as the shock of death in the living world, which Mercutio's was.'[55] The counterpoint between the different kinds of death maintains the self-reflection of the innovative tragedy. In an article for the journal *Essays in Criticism*, Susan Snyder also assesses the play's generic experimentation, though for her, the relationship between comedy and tragedy drives the drama.

## SUSAN SNYDER (1970)

In a short but significant article of 1970 Susan Snyder resolves some of the problems raised by earlier genre criticism. She reads *Romeo and Juliet* not as a substandard tragedy, but rather as a unique manipulation of generic form: 'it becomes, rather than is, tragic'.[56] What had previously been read as weaknesses in Shakespeare's tragic structure is explained as a deliberate design whereby the play starts out entirely differently, as a comedy, and shifts into tragedy. Underlying Snyder's compelling argument is an expansive sense of the function and form of genre. Instead of restricting tragedy to a fixed set of ingredients, she probes more deeply at the way genre organises human experience:

> ■ Comedy and tragedy, being opposed ways of apprehending the real world, project their own opposing worlds. The tragic world is governed by inevitability, and its highest value is personal integrity. In the comic world 'evitability' is assumed; instead of heroic or obstinate adherence to a single course, comedy endorses opportunistic shifts and realistic accommodations as means to an end of new social health.[57] □

This distinction between tragic inevitability and comic 'evitability' or possibility offers an insight into the drama's tonal disjunctions.

Understood as a comedy, the play's first half (up to the ever important death of Mercutio) makes more sense. Comedic conventions are found in abundance. Young lovers intrigue to maintain a relationship in defiance of parental obstacles; the dramatis personae are taken from the domestic world of the minor aristocracy (and their servants) rather than from the high politics of the monarchy; Friar Laurence and the Nurse act as go-betweens who assist the comic marriage plot through their 'opportunistic shifts'; this same movement towards marriage promises not just a union between the young lovers, but also wider social harmony for the whole community. This analysis goes a long way to answering the objections of earlier criticism. Snyder specifically remakes Charlton's point that the feud has a 'comic aspect', and shows that rather than failing to 'plant the seeds of tragedy' Shakespeare is instead 'playing on *comic* expectations'. As a social division with a long-forgotten cause, perpetuated by bawdy servants and impotent old men, the feud seems to be a problem that is set up to be surmounted. In this reading, Tybalt's frustrated attempt to apply the feud's violent code at the Capulet ball serves as further evidence that the play, in its first scenes, is governed by 'festive accommodation', as old Capulet patiently tolerates the Montague interlopers.[58] It is Tybalt, as the one character to have thoroughly internalized the law of the feud, who is generically out of place; he alone appears tragic. Romeo himself displays 'classic comic adaptability' when he switches his affections from the uninterested Rosaline to the enthusiastic Juliet (making him comparable with Proteus in *The Two Gentlemen of Verona*, Demetrius in *A Midsummer Night's Dream*, Phoebe in *As You Like It* and Olivia in *Twelfth Night*).[59] Furthermore, awareness of a comic sensibility qualifies the sense of foreboding and obsessive connection of sex and death (identified by Brooke). Fatalistic images of lightning flashes are complemented by alternative ideas of hazard and seizing opportunity: 'I am no pilot, yet wert thou as far /As that vast shore washed with the farthest sea, /I should adventure for such merchandise' (2.1.125–7). Such rhetoric implies that the narrative might be able to evade a fatal end; risk might reap reward.

But the death of Mercutio transforms the generic landscape. As for Brooke, though for different reasons, the point is not only structural: 'Shakespeare makes the birth of a tragedy coincide exactly with the symbolic death of comedy', since Mercutio is himself 'the incarnation of comic atmosphere'. Mercutio's comic credentials are fundamentally linguistic: his dialogue is saturated with puns that see him flirt with the multiple meanings of words and continually switch the direction of conversations. He is a linguistic opportunist and as such is emphatically comic. Killing him kills the 'evitability' principle he embodies, and fate takes hold of the play. With the generic shift the role played by time changes cast. Comic time opens out space for the correction of misunderstandings and for reconciliation; tragic time rushes past opportunity to destruction. Bad news reaches Romeo before Friar John can convey the happier truth. Clinging to his comic calling, Friar Lawrence hastens to the tomb to save the couple, but 'The onrushing tragic action quite literally outstrips the slower steps of accommodation before our eyes.'[60]

Perhaps surprisingly, Snyder does not develop the implications of this analysis – what it means for comedy and tragedy to be shown in close proximity with one another, and even compete (to extend Snyder's athletic metaphor) to define the play. She does suggest that a consequence of the dual structure is the externalization of the tragedy; that is, the fatal events are not determined by the central characters themselves, but by the outside force of fate. The swift movement from comedy to its generic opposite confirms the lack of control characters have over events. Nevertheless, Snyder underplays the perseverance of comic elements in the latter half of the play: think, for example, of the ludicrous lamentations of the Capulet household over the sleeping Juliet, of the musicians' deflationary response to this grief, and the use of the 'feigned death' device, which as Snyder notes, is a trick Shakespeare uses in the comedies *Much Ado About Nothing*, *All's Well that Ends Well*, *Measure for Measure* and *The Winter's Tale*. Furthermore, Snyder does not consider how the comic possibilities of the first acts are qualified by the Prologue's inevitably tragic script (printed in Quarto 1 and Quarto 2, though not the Folio). However, her brilliant observation of comedic convention opens the play out to this very analysis, as we shall see when we look at the work of Martha Tuck Rozett. Before we get to her, however, we meet a critic whose close reading introduces a new generic intervention in the play.

## GARY M. MCCOWN (1976)

Gary M. McCown's article, '"Runnawayes Eyes" and Juliet's Epithalamium' concentrates on a relatively brief moment in the play:

Juliet's monologue at the start of 3.2. But the consequences of this work resonate beyond its immediate intervention into close textual analysis and literary history, to genre and (implicitly) gender criticism.

McCown argues that Juliet's speech is 'a dramatized version of the epithalamium', a lyric poem sung at weddings.[61] In the first section of the three-part article, he explains the history of the form. The revival of the classical genre in the Renaissance – probably prompted by the discovery of a manuscript by Catullus which contained two epithalamia – saw the lyric flourish across Europe. In England Latin epithalamia were sung at royal weddings and English poems were composed by poets as influential as Philip Sidney, Edmund Spenser, George Chapman, John Donne and Ben Jonson. McCown asserts that it would be odd for Shakespeare to have been ignorant of the genre and speculates that his manifest interest in lyric poetry in the years 1592–94 extends into his subsequent writing of *Romeo and Juliet*.

The monologue itself is situated at exactly the moment at which an epithalamium might be sung: at dusk, after the wedding ceremony and banquet, but before the consummation. Similarly, plea for day to give way swiftly to night is typical of epithalamia. And in syntax and structure the soliloquy also adheres to the conventions of epithalamium:

■ Perhaps the most striking feature of Juliet's speech is its peculiar reliance upon the second person address and the imperative mode of the verbs. Within thirty lines Juliet employs no fewer than eleven imperatives: 'Gallop . . . Spread . . . come . . . learne . . . Hood . . . Come . . . come . . . Come . . . Give . . . Take . . . cut.'[62] □

This lyrical exhortation bespeaks Juliet's passion, but just as Brooke noted the formal qualities of the couple's first conversation (a sonnet), McCown shows this ardour is realized through a poetic structure.

Recognition of the lyrical form enables McCown to resolve a long-standing textual problem. Lines 5 to 7 prove enigmatic to the modern reader and viewer: 'Spread thy close curtain, love-performing night, / That runaway's eyes may wink, and Romeo / Leap to these arms, untalked of and unseen.' Who is the rather obscure 'runaway'? In the second section of the article McCown rejects earlier suggestions of Phoebus, Phaethon and night, and identifies the runaway as Cupid:

■ First, Cupid played an important role in epithalamia going back at least to Silver Age poetry. Second, through countless imitations of Moschus' original Idyl, the epithet 'runaway' or 'fugitive' became a permanent part of the lore surrounding the god. Third, Tasso's *Aminta*, which used Moschus' legend to introduce pastoral drama, was especially effective in popularizing the idea of Cupid as 'runaway' in the late sixteenth century. Finally,

> the number of English versions published in the early 1590s indicates unusual interest in the story at precisely the time when Shakespeare was composing most of his lyric poems, as well as the play *Romeo and Juliet*.[63] □

This careful research makes a convincing case for Cupid as the mysterious 'runaway', and neatly explicates a difficult passage.

However, the larger implications of the generic revelation are still more important. Most telling is the way that Shakespeare departs from the conventions of the genre he clearly uses. In speaking an epithalamium, Juliet breaks with a tradition which saw a male poet voice the celebratory lyric. Her utterance associates her, as McCown points out, with an 'ominous' set of literary precedents: the grieving Hecuba and the mad Cassandra also reverse the conventions of the form by speaking it. The flouting of generic norms underlines the novel gendering of Juliet's character: where epithalamia represented brides as fearful of sex, given a violent aspect in the metaphor of battle, Juliet eagerly anticipates what is to come: 'learn me how to lose a winning match, / Played for a pair of stainless maidenhoods' (3.2.12–13). War is ameliorated to a game; Juliet's sexual eagerness is sharply drawn. But where feminist critics might celebrate a radical depiction of female sexual agency, McCown argues that the breaks with generic convention serve to intensify our sense of foreboding. For one thing, 'The absence of any social context for this epithalamium spoken in solitude alerts us to an ominous undertone.'[64] Though McCown does not make the point, evident here is another generic movement from the social community of comedy to the isolation of tragedy. Furthermore, Juliet's imagery reworks that of traditional epithalamia in a 'shocking' manner:

> ■ Come gentle night, come loving black-browed night,
> Give me my Romeo; and when I shall die,
> Take him and cut him out in little stars,
> And he will make the face of heaven so fine,
> That all the world will be in love with night,
> And pay no worship to the garish sun. □
>
> (3.2.20–5)[65]

Rather than call for lamps to light the longed-for night, as was traditional, Juliet desires absolute darkness. The funereal gloom is all the more portentous given the dangers associated with night in classical and Renaissance literature (raised in numerous epithalamia). The generic inversion works to characterize Juliet's bold passion and awaken the audience's 'pity and pathos' for a heroine who 'inauspiciously invokes' night, 'unaware' that it is 'kin to that amorous death'.[66] Once again then, *Romeo and Juliet* proves to be a play in which generic innovation produces meaning.

## MARTHA TUCK ROZETT (1985)

In Martha Tuck Rozett's article, 'The Comic Structures of Tragic Endings: The Suicide Scenes in *Romeo and Juliet* and *Antony and Cleopatra*', we return to the larger generic problem of the relationship between comedy and tragedy. Like Dickey, Rozett defines the play as a tragedy of love, set apart from other tragedies driven by revenge or ambition. This subject matter has major structural implications for the tragedy: 'two lovers theoretically have equal claims on the role normally reserved for a single protagonist'.[67] In particular, this gives untypical prominence (at least among Shakespeare's tragedies) to female characters, and establishes a cross-genre link with the comedies, where women are much more central to the action. Rozett determines that this connection with comedy is not coincidental, but speaks to a pattern of comic devices inherent in the tragedy's organization.

The identification of comic material in *Romeo and Juliet* is familiar from the work of Snyder. But Rozett advances on the earlier argument by locating comedy not only prior to the death of Mercutio, but also after it. Central to her thesis is the comic nature of the 'false death' device (found also, as Rozett demonstrates, in *Antony and Cleopatra*; my discussion concentrates on her analysis of *Romeo and Juliet*). The trick's theatrical heritage is instructive:

> ■ the dangerous adventure of feigned death and promised resurrection was one of the oldest and most popular comic traditions on the English stage. The resurrection of a seemingly dead character was the central event in the mummers plays, for example, which celebrated the miracle of seasonal renewal by dramatizing the death of the old year and the birth of the new. And once drama ceased to be so closely linked to religious ritual, the resurrection motif continued to appear in comic plots. As an ironic reversal of expectations, it constituted a moment of festive triumph over the inevitable exigencies of time and death, for characters and audience alike.[68] □

Feigned death thus represents an assertion of optimism in the very face of death; comedy defeats tragedy at its most definitive moment. The depth of the comic theatrical tradition reveals the jarring shock of Shakespeare's generic redefinition. Certainly, as Snyder noted, when Shakespeare uses the device elsewhere in his drama, it also fulfils a comic function. *Romeo and Juliet* raises generic expectations only to confound them.

It is not only the false death that tropes comedy in the final acts of the play. Rozett regards the numerous errors and accidents that cause Romeo's fatal misunderstanding as comic in nature: a letter that never arrives, a misinformed servant, a slow-footed friar. As in Snyder's reading, old evidence of malformed tragedy is here alternatively understood as deliberately redeployed comic material – mistakes that arguably weaken tragedy are the essence of comic plots. Even Romeo's death speech, Rozett asserts, is comic in its self-direction: 'Eyes, look your last. / Arms, take your last embrace' (5.3.112–13). She claims that the theatricality of these instructions recalls the ineptly self-conscious performance of the players in the Pyramus and Thisby scene in *A Midsummer Night's Dream* (see Chapter 1 above). This looser connection perhaps overstretches the potential for humour in Romeo's death. But other observations of comedy are more persuasive. Certainly, the emphasis on revelation (Friar Laurence has a 41-line speech that re-narrates what the audience has already seen) and reconciliation more typically belongs to comedy.

One of the key reasons why this comic potential degenerates (or, if generic hierarchies are to be accepted, elevates) into tragedy is the attitude of the young lovers themselves. Rozett believes that they are unable to follow their comic cues. For example, 'In a comedy the challenge posed by Juliet's dilemma [of being commanded to wed Paris after her marriage to the banished Romeo] would rouse the heroine to new heights of ingenuity.' Instead 'it reduces Juliet to suicidal desperation, and she places herself in the hands of the Friar'.[69] It is not so much fate or character flaws as a lack of comic capacity that produces tragedy. In any case, while comedy may persist after the deaths of Mercutio and Tybalt, those deaths mean that it can never succeed. For Rozett, the conversion of comic strategy to tragic resolution lacks any sense of final 'triumph' (which she detects in *Antony and Cleopatra*), because of the 'irrevocable losses and the burden of guilt that confront the survivors'.[70] Although she does not elaborate, her evidence of raised comic expectations usefully supports this point: an audience bombarded with comic hope is all the more sensitive to the wasted potential of the suicides. Awareness of generic interaction within the play thus gives us a fuller understanding of its tragic impact.

The genre criticism of Bradley up to Rozett reveals the heavy critical baggage attendant on the idea of 'tragedy'. For many critics, tragedy is felt to be a peak to be scaled rather than a (pragmatic) literary category. But the variations between different theories of tragedy should caution us against setting too much store by the textual hierarchies they generate. Genre is both a useful and a problematic interpretative tool. When understood flexibly, genre provides a means of identifying how

Shakespeare engages with his audience – how he takes us by the hand, and how he sometimes does so only to run off in another direction. Conceived as a strict set of rules, genre can obscure what is most innovative, playful and challenging in a text. The next chapter focuses on a different critical topic, where *Romeo and Juliet* is thought to show Shakespeare on surer ground: language.

# CHAPTER FIVE

# What's in a Word? Language and Deconstruction

Juliet's famous question, 'What's in a name?' (2.1.86), articulates the linguistic self-consciousness of *Romeo and Juliet*. This chapter surveys readings that pay close attention to the play's language, and also its investigation *of* language. Critics of the early and mid-twentieth century usefully identified recurrent images and patterns in the text; later, more theoretical criticism looks at how language functions. In recent years *Romeo and Juliet* has been seen to pose the question, 'do we shape language or does language shape us?', prompting debates of far-reaching linguistic and philosophical importance which have shown the play to be of much greater significance than 'early' context for the 'mature' tragedies that followed.

## CAROLINE SPURGEON (1935)

Caroline Spurgeon's book *Shakespeare's Imagery and What It Tells Us* (1935) played a key role in making language the primary concern of literary criticism. Published just over thirty years after Bradley's *Shakespearean Tragedy*, Spurgeon's work represented the newly specialized critical skills of the evolving discipline. Her central contention is that 'recurrent images' in Shakespeare's drama are crucially important in 'raising, developing, sustaining and repeating emotion'.[1] She demonstrates this point by carefully scrutinizing the texts and collating groups of connected words and images. The use of charts and tables in the appendices indicate the almost scientific approach she takes to the project. Nevertheless, the literary claims for this argument are significant. Image patterns demonstrate the 'terms' by which Shakespeare 'sees and feels the main problem or theme of the play, thus giving us an unerring clue to the way he looked at it, as well as a direct glimpse into the working of his mind and imagination'.[2] Language is the means through which one might unlock the meaning of a given play; it gives access to the process of creativity.

Spurgeon finds images of light and darkness to be the dominant pattern of *Romeo and Juliet*. Lying behind this imagery is a suggestion of the transformative power of love: 'the beauty and ardour of young love are seen by Shakespeare as the irradiating glory of sunlight and starlight in a dark world'.[3] Thus Romeo's first words on seeing Juliet are infused with light:

> ■ O, she doth teach the torches to burn bright!
> It seems she hangs upon the cheek of night
> As a rich jewel in an Ethiop's ear[.] □
>
> (1.4.157–9)

Similarly, he later figures her as the sun: 'what light through yonder window breaks? / It is the east, and Juliet is the sun' (2.1.45–6); Juliet subsequently complements this image, apostrophizing Romeo as 'day in night' (3.2.17). Both lovers depict each other as ablaze with a light so bright that it outshines day. Thus Romeo muses what would happen if Juliet's eyes were to switch places with stars:

> ■ The brightness of her cheek would shame those stars
> As daylight doth a lamp; her eye in heaven
> Would through the airy region stream so bright
> That birds would sing and think it were not night. □
>
> (2.1.62–5)

Juliet's treatment of this theme is still more adventurously imaginative:

> ■ Give me my Romeo; and when I shall die,
> Take him and cut him out in little stars,
> And he will make the face of heaven so fine,
> That all the world will be in love with night,
> And pay no worship to the garish sun. □
>
> (3.2.21–5)

The language of the young couple's love glitters and gleams; though Spurgeon does little to analyse the details of these descriptions.

Spurgeon's most exciting insight is that such rhetoric is not merely decorative but rather integral to the tragic problem itself: 'Shakespeare saw the story, in its sweet and tragic beauty, as an almost blinding flash of light, suddenly ignited, and as swiftly quenched.'[4] This smart observation has been accepted as a basic critical truth about the play (compare the way Nicholas Brooke – featured in Chapter 4 – sees this attitude to love as part of the couple's youthful and tragic pathology). Images of exploding brightness certainly abound. Juliet worries that her betrothal:

> ■ Is too rash, too unadvised, too sudden,
> Too like the lightning which doth cease to be
> Ere one can say 'It lightens'. □
>
> (2.1.161–3)

Likewise, the Friar warns:

> ■ These violent delights have violent ends,
> And in their triumph die like fire and powder,
> Which as they kiss consume. □
>
> (2.5.9–11)

Similes and metaphors of ignited gunpowder capture the frantic passion. Romeo imagines that the sound of his name, 'Shot from the deadly level of a gun' (3.3.102), murders Juliet as she grieves for her murdered cousin. The Friar reproves Romeo that his wit, 'Like powder in a skilless soldier's flask, / Is set afire by thine own ignorance' (3.3.131–2). And the suicidal Romeo later seeks a poison that will drive breath from his body 'As violently as hasty powder fired / Doth hurry from the fatal cannon's womb' (5.1.64–5). These images of blasted brightness are matched by a rapidly compressed time structure: the story which lasts nine months in the source is squeezed into a mere five days. While language forms the basis of Spurgeon's investigation, the argument itself is larger; Shakespeare emerges from the study as a careful craftsman, who strategically matches words, action and meaning. The text is seen to operate as a finely balanced unity, and will continue to seem so throughout the period of New Criticism's intellectual dominance in the early and mid-twentieth century.

Although Spurgeon's approach has some similarities to that of American New Criticism, she does not engage in the rigorous close analysis that would become the hallmark of the practice. To be sure, the book is underpinned by an essential analytical idea (image patterns are the key to Shakespeare's meaning), and she certainly has a brilliant eye for detail. But she says little about how those details are constructed, and analysis sometimes slips into simple appreciation. For example, the conventionality of the play's language is defended with little else but enthusiasm:

> ■ The intensity of feeling in both lovers purges even the most highly affected and euphuistic conceits of their artificiality, and transforms them into the exquisite and passionate expression of love's rhapsody.[5] □

Since 'intensity of feeling' is communicated through the 'highly affected and euphuistic conceits', it is unclear how the language transforms itself. As an account of image patterns, the book is more suggestive in the identification, rather than the interpretation, of those patterns. Spurgeon implies that the brightness that shines out of the play's amorous discourse symbolizes love's real, if brief, glory; later critics who look closer at the drama's linguistic structures will question this reading. Nevertheless, Spurgeon's major excavation of images established patterns which today's critics and editors still find to be of structural importance to the play's design.

## M. M. MAHOOD (1957)

In the chapter on *Romeo and Juliet* in her book *Shakespeare's Wordplay*, M. M. Mahood describes the drama as 'one of Shakespeare's most punning plays'.[6] Commentators from Garrick onwards had regarded this linguistic playfulness as stylistic weakness; but Mahood revels in the intellectual and emotional complexity she believes the puns produce. At the outset of the chapter, she roundly rejects the critical line that calls the play and its author immature: Shakespeare was over 30 when he produced *Romeo and Juliet* and had already gained diverse experience writing a range of drama. Mahood is therefore confident in describing the wordplay not as the flash of a naive writer, showing off his linguistic agility, but rather as fully 'functional'. Words are not only the vehicles through which the action is communicated; but the experience of comprehending their ambiguity is one of the ways the audience experience the different facets of the tragedy. On one (important) level words convey the protagonists' emotions, but their double and triple meanings also strengthen the play's dramatic irony. More importantly, the sense of different meanings straining against one another is itself at the heart of the tragic conflict. As far as Mahood is concerned, worries about whether the tragedy is generated by fate or character flaw are an irrelevant critical dead-end. These questions (which bedevilled a number of the critics discussed in Chapter 4) are a merely academic enterprise that ignore and distort the 'dramatic experience' of the play. Instead the ambiguity of the language produces the central tragic problem, which is itself a form of uncertainty: 'is its ending frustration or fulfilment?'[7]

Mahood's subtle argument depends upon a finely tuned ear for the dialogue's counterpointing connotations. The discussion brilliantly draws out the scope of the tragedy's exploration of love. She recognizes that the language of the early scenes is strained in its conventionality. Romeo's infatuation with Rosaline is a form of posturing that

Romeo himself already realizes to be foolish. He dutifully recites popular Petrarchan clichés: love is sickness ('A sick man in sadness' [1.1.198]), religious worship (hence puns on 'bliss' and 'despair' [1.1.218]), war and conquest ('th'encounter of assailing eyes' [1.1.209]). Yet the density and exaggeration of these tropes suggest they are not to be taken seriously, especially since they are undercut by Romeo's decidedly unromantic concern for his stomach: 'Where shall we dine?' (1.1.169). (For further discussion of the meaning of Petrarchism, see Chapter 6.)

It is on seeing Juliet that Romeo's language gains subtlety. He describes 'Beauty too rich for use, for earth too dear' (1.4.160). Mahood regards this line as profoundly suggestive:

■ When we recall that *use* means 'employment', 'interest' and 'wear and tear' that *earth* means both 'mortal life' and 'the grave', that *dear* can be either 'cherished' or 'costly' and that there is possibly a play upon *beauty* and *booty*..., the line's range of meanings becomes very wide indeed. Over and above the contrast between her family's valuation of her as sound stock in the marriage market and Romeo's estimate that she is beyond all price, the words contain a self-contradictory irony. Juliet's beauty is too rich for use in the sense that it will be laid in the tomb after a brief enjoyment; but for that very reason it will never be faded and worn. If she is *not* too dear for earth since Romeo's love is powerless to keep her out of the tomb, it is true that she is too rare a creature for mortal life. Not all of these meanings are consciously present to the audience, but beneath the conscious level they connect with later images and quibbles and are thus brought into play before the tragedy is over.[8] □

The expansive commentary in this passage exemplifies the rigorousness of Mahood's approach: various strands of meaning are teased out, so that puns are shown to cue the tragedy.

Like Spurgeon, Mahood regards the image of exploding gunpowder as deeply significant, but she gives it a new depth. As quoted above, the Friar likens 'violent delights' to fire and gunpowder: 'Which as they kiss consume' (2.5.9–11). Since *consume* means 'to reach a consummation' as well as 'to burn away, be destroyed', it functions as a pun that encapsulates the paradox of the tragedy: love is blissfully achieved and totally annihilated. Mahood insists that this does not mean that the young lovers have a death wish. Their desire for a married future together repudiates such a reading. The driving ambivalence of the play lies not so much in their passion as in the tragedy it produces (an idea which perhaps explains something of the critical uneasiness with the drama – it designedly avoids giving us a clear-cut sense of how to interpret the catastrophe). Connecting the images that Spurgeon merely enumerated, Mahood reveals the contradictory messages the play gives us about the love story: self-consuming sparks and flashes would seem to signal wasted defeat, but they are matched by images of Romeo and Juliet as permanent fixtures in the heavens, triumphantly stellified – turned into stars (2.1.62–5 and 3.2.21–5, quoted above). This paradox is painfully present at the moment of tragic climax when Romeo kills himself: 'O true Apothecary, / Thy drugs are quick. Thus with a kiss I die' (5.3.119–20). The word *true* records both the Apothecary's honest description of the poison's effectiveness and his truth to his profession in providing a cure for Romeo's malady. In connoting both 'speed' and 'life', *quick* creates a sharper paradox, as the means of Romeo's death is figured as life-giving.

The tragedy itself functions, in this analysis, much like a pun: different, even conflicting, meanings are held in tandem. Mahood describes the emotional impact as neither 'satisfaction' nor 'dismay'; we witness 'a tragic equilibrium which includes and transcends both these feelings'.[9] This sensitive account of the play's ambivalence seems a more accurate and productive interpretation of the play's tragedy than those generated by scholars working with somewhat reductive conceptions of genre at a similar point in the twentieth century (see Chapter 4). While subsequent critics will find further complexities in the tragedy's wordplay and others will problematize the textual unity she presumes, Mahood remains a valuable starting point for close textual analysis of the play (as is evident in her place in the glosses of modern editions).

## HARRY LEVIN (1960)

Levin opens his article on 'Form and Formality in *Romeo and Juliet*' by quoting Juliet's awareness of violated convention: 'Fain would I dwell on form, fain, fain deny / What I have spoke; but farewell, compliment' (2.1.131–2). Blushing in the dark at the realization that Romeo has overheard her private thoughts voiced at the window, Juliet raises an issue Levin sees as central to the play's linguistic and generic structure. Juliet's 'form' refers to social practice (that which prevents a young girl from announcing her passion to the one she loves); but Levin argues that the drama's concern with 'form and formality' is much more comprehensive than that. Standards of social decorum (formality) are associated with linguistic, literary and dramatic convention (form) in *Romeo and Juliet*. Shakespeare stages various contraventions of convention (Romeo overhears Juliet's soliloquy having broken into the Capulet garden), and also contextualizes the action in a world saturated with formal artifice (as when the couple meet in the ceremonious conditions of the Capulet ball and formalize their first conversation in the shape of a sonnet). Just as Mahood reconceived of Shakespearean wordplay as functional rather than frivolous, Levin opens up the artificiality of the play to an assessment of its purpose.

When Juliet asks 'What's in a name?' (2.1.86), Levin claims that her meditation is far-reaching: 'She calls into question not merely Romeo's name but – by implication – all names, forms, conventions, sophistications and arbitrary dictates of society, as opposed to the appeal of the instinct directly conveyed in the odor of a rose.'[10] For the first time in its critical history, the play is here recognized as philosophically serious, not only in its exploration of the nature of love, but also in its interrogation of supposedly civilizing forces of society. Language, in particular, is under investigation, as the dialogue of the lovers stands in revealing contrast to that of other characters in the play. Although she is conscious of Romeo's dangerous breach of social decorum, Juliet does not protect herself with formally expressed censure, but voices frank monosyllabic concern: 'I would not for the world they saw thee here' (2.1.117). Similarly, Romeo abandons his infatuation with 'verbal embellishment' (as well as Rosaline) once his affections are fixed on Juliet.[11] This rejection of linguistic formality distinguishes the couple from, for example, Paris, who speaks a sestet at Juliet's tomb and who earlier had to be dismissed by Juliet in the terms of his own highly rhetorical stichomythia (4.1.18–36). The play's imagery also illustrates Paris's formal features. Lady Capulet uses a textual metaphor to describe his face:

■ This precious book of love, this unbound lover,
To beautify him only lacks a cover.
The fish lives in the sea, and 'tis much pride
For fair without the fair within to hide. □

(1.3.89–92)

The rigidity of the couplets enhances the dustiness of the depiction. In contrast to such artificiality, the young lovers' frequently monosyllabic language has a striking immediacy and intensity. Their metaphors also repeatedly speak a 'recoil from bookishness' (2.1.202–3; 5.3.81–2).[12] Nevertheless the opposition is not absolute since formal digressions index the emotional twists and turns of the relationship. Thus Juliet reuses the book metaphor on learning that Romeo has murdered her cousin: 'Was ever book containing such vile matter / So fairly bound?' (3.2.83–4). The intellectualizing distance of the image (how can a beautiful man perform an ugly deed?) is of a piece with the catalogue of wooden oxymora which precede it: 'Beautiful tyrant, fiend angelical, ... honourable villain' (3.2.75–9). Levin argues that the apparent inconsistency in Juliet's expression indicates moments where she temporarily loses faith in Romeo and with it authentic utterance. But the opposition between different forms of verbal expression helps to produce our sense of the couple's love as precious: 'at every level, the mutuality of the lovers stands out, the one organic relation amid an overplus of stylized expressions and attitudes. The naturalness of their diction is artfully gained . . . through a running critique of artificiality.'[13] Shakespeare strategically counterbalances different linguistic styles, both to characterize his protagonists and to invalidate overly conventional form.

Citing Charlton and Dickey (see Chapter 4), Levin stresses the experimental nature of *Romeo and Juliet* as a tragedy. For him, this generic innovation starts with language. The first quarto describes the play as '*an excellent conceited Tragedie*'; since 'conceited' could mean 'witty' in Elizabethan English, the drama is predicated on 'one of those contradictions in terms which Shakespeare seems to have delighted in resolving'.[14] Where later genre critics such as Snyder spot structural features of comedy in the tragedy, Levin views the play as an exploration and ultimate rejection of the verbal artifice found in comedy. Even so, figuration connects closely with the tragic theme, even at a formal level. Antithesis is a dominant figure in the play: the oppositions between light and dark, youth and age encapsulate for Levin (unlike Mahood) the concerns of the *Liebestod* myth, whereby love is associated with death. Contrast also serves a broader structural function: verbal paradoxes are supplemented by oppositions between scenes, as the private setting of Acts 2 and 4 are offset by the public bustle of the rest of the play. A similar friction is evident in what happens to the two protagonists. Untypically double as this play's tragic focus might be, generic impulses separate the lovers: 'Tragedy tends to isolate where comedy brings together, to reveal the uniqueness of individuals rather than what they have in common with others.'[15] Even if their story focuses on their union, each protagonist dies alone. And yet this individuation is itself superseded by the antithetical movement of the play, as the social world takes over again (though curiously, Levin locates this movement in the earlier commotion of the grieving Capulet household in Act 4, rather than in the re-entry of the community in the final scene).

As we shall see, later critics who adopt a theoretical approach will explore in more depth aspects of an idea first raised by Levin – what it means, for example, to question all 'form', even words themselves. However, Levin's new critical approach astutely identifies this as a problem posed by the play. In connecting language with social behaviour he successfully integrates an aesthetic appreciation of the drama's poetry with a searching interpretation of what the poetry means for the action of the play.

## JAMES L. CALDERWOOD (1971)

James L. Calderwood's analysis of *Romeo and Juliet* puts the problem of form into a more theoretical perspective. Like Levin, he recognises Juliet's reflection on words as articulating the play's linguistic interests:

■ 'Tis but thy name that is my enemy;
Thou art thyself, though not a Montague.
What's Montague? It is nor hand nor foot,
Nor arm nor face, nor any other part
Belonging to a man. O be some other name!
What's in a name? That which we call a rose
By any other word would smell as sweet;
So Romeo would, were he not Romeo called,
Retain that dear perfection which he owes
Without that title. Romeo, doff thy name,
And for thy name, which is no part of thee,
Take all myself. □

(2.1.81–92)

Calderwood gives Juliet's attitude an academic designation: 'verbal nominalism' (i.e. the belief that words are only arbitrarily connected to the things they represent and have no inherent meaning). He claims that it is related, in Juliet's outlook, with 'a kind of social personalism':

■ in her anxiety to circumvent the opposition of their relatives Juliet would reject all relations and find ultimate truth in the haecceity, thisness, or as she puts it 'dear perfection' of a totally unaffiliated Romeo. In the same way nominalism rejects the family or tribal relations of words in their more universal and abstract forms and situates verbal truth in the concrete and particular terms that seem most closely tied to the unique, unrelated, and hence true objects of which reality is composed.[16] □

In other words, the problem of the feud provokes Juliet to disclaim familial allegiance and see Romeo as a wholly independent person, unshaped by any outside influence; at the same time she denies that words bring any associative meaning to the things they describe. Once again, *Romeo and Juliet* is likened to comedy, as Juliet's argument is also found in *Love's Labour's Lost*, an early (and extremely 'wordy') comedy in which a group of lords attempt to close themselves off from the linguistic corruption of the wider world. But the comparison reveals the extremity of Juliet's desire: she would remove language itself and strip Romeo of his name.

Calderwood's linguistically sensitive Juliet consciously works to train Romeo out of his old stylistic habits. She twice interrupts him when he slips into rhetorical tricksiness, instructing him not to swear by 'th'inconstant moon' (2.1.152) and then simply 'do not swear' (2.1.159). In refusing to hear vows, Calderwood argues, Juliet demonstrates a desire for linguistic purity that language cannot achieve, since words can never fully capture the essence of the things to which they refer: 'Seeking an ideal communion of love at a level beyond idle breath, Juliet would purify words quite out of existence and reduce dialogue to an exchange of intuition and sheer feeling – a marriage of true minds accomplished without the connective medium of language.'[17] This yearning is also found at times in lyric poetry (Calderwood quotes Milton's 'Lycidas', Keats's 'Ode on a Grecian Urn' and Hopkins's 'The Habit of Perfection'), where poetry seeks to purify itself of the discordant conditions of the world and achieve a 'melody' or even 'a point beyond sound' – a 'stillness'.[18] Yet this is a self-destructive desire for a poet, whose art *is* words, not ideas. Shakespeare, Calderwood contests, is alive to the potential absurdity of the nominalist, lyrical position, and *Romeo and Juliet* therefore critiques the intimate language of the lovers. Indeed, the linguistic opposition is not, as Levin saw it, between a formal and an instinctive style, but rather between a public language shared by everyone in Verona, and an attempt at a private language stripped of inessential external associations.

Juliet's nominalist pretensions are swiftly undermined by her practical need to use names. In the same scene in which she disparaged names, she finds herself needing to call back 'Romeo', who can only be hailed with a name; her volte-face is underlined by her longing for a louder voice that would make Echo hoarse 'With repetition of my "Romeo"' (2.1.209). Furthermore, names are not only necessary to communication, but are also the poetic subject of love. Romeo exults:

■ It is my soul that calls upon my name.
How silver-sweet sound lovers' tongues by night,
Like softest music to attending ears. □

(2.1.210–12)

And Juliet later avers: 'every tongue that speaks / But Romeo's name speaks heavenly eloquence' (3.2.32—3). Juliet's contradictory attitude thus proves to be 'in keeping with a play that seems founded on the principle of oxymoron: she wants, it seems, a "nameless naming"'.[19]

Perhaps more damningly, the lovers' linguistic seclusion helps generate some of the tragic difficulties they face. Marriage gives private love public endorsement; while Romeo and Juliet consolidate their love with a formal bond, in keeping the marriage secret they are never supported by public recognition. And there is a telling imbalance between the purchase of their private words and that of public words. While the words of their clandestine marriage ceremony have no impact on Verona, the Prince's word 'banished' (repeated 19 times) drastically reshapes the plot of their love story (Juliet bemoans the word's force at 3.2.122–6). In fact, as Calderwood shrewdly observes, the vaunted 'purity' of the lover's discourse can only be sustained when kept private, and therefore denuded of public significance. But living by an independent code of language is still more actively dangerous, as the departure scene at 3.5 demonstrates. By renaming the 'lark' as a 'nightingale' (3.5.2) and the 'sun' as a 'meteor' (3.5.13), Juliet seeks to linger in a timeless lyric moment (framed in the conventional terms Levin thought she had surpassed). But she quickly realizes that living by this new language would bring death to Romeo, who has to obey the sharp public sentence of the banishment.

Calderwood contends that Shakespeare's goal in *Romeo and Juliet* is to achieve a 'viable poetic purity' – a lyrical mode that captures the essence of things, uncorrupted by, but meaningful in, the world. But it is not clear, as Calderwood suggests, that the 'structure of the play' necessarily reveals this intention. Shakespeare 'did not complete the journey' to workable purity 'in satisfactory style'.[20] As we have seen, linguistic failure is tied up with the tragic fall; Calderwood makes this tragically necessary failure of the protagonists a symptom of Shakespeare's failure as a writer. But if we follow the logic of Calderwood's interpretation, had Romeo and Juliet achieved functional stylistic purity there would be no tragedy. The larger metadramatic narrative of Calderwood's book (Shakespeare uses his drama to reflect on the processes of producing drama) overwrites the analysis of this particular play. Having identified a failed stylistic project, Calderwood also finally finds fault with the project itself, since it generates unsatisfactory tragedy. Romeo and Juliet, in their romantic and stylistic isolation, lack the 'complexity' that comes with interaction in the world, and also 'self-division' and 'self-perceptiveness', so that 'they become a study in victimage and sacrifice, not tragedy.'[21] Once again we are returned to a Bradleian conception of tragedy that requires protagonists to demonstrate fraught inner lives.

The nearest *Romeo and Juliet* comes to resolving Calderwood's 'linguistic dilemma' is through symbolism rather than poetic style. In the statues of the lovers promised by Capulet and Montague, the couple finally arrive at a 'lyric stasis' that is 'publicly available'. Significantly, these statues are *'artistic form'*.[22] Herein lies Shakespeare's discovery in this play: 'with men as with poems uniqueness resides in the form or contextual organization of non-unique qualities – a form sufficiently complex in its internal relations to defy reductive abstraction'.[23] Workable poetic purity is thus to be found in form itself, rather than in its obliteration or in a world without words and names. This, like earlier passages of close analysis, is a perceptive interpretation. While

Calderwood's larger argument is not fully convincing, his strenuous investigation of details and readiness to explore the larger linguistic implications of the play mark an important critical development.

## MICHAEL GOLDMAN (1972)

In *Shakespeare and the Energies of Drama,* Michael Goldman provides a suitably lively account of the verbal dynamics of *Romeo and Juliet.* Like other critics, Goldman recognizes the play's affinity with comedy in its concern with wordplay and young love; but the 'Theatrical Experience', as his chapter heading puts it, is tragic.[24] Once again genre is seen to function through the play's linguistic structure. As Goldman incisively contends: '*Romeo and Juliet* is a tragedy of naming, a tragedy in which at times Romeo's name seems to be the villain.'[25] Where Juliet fantasizes about a world without names, declaring them to be without essential significance, Romeo is attuned to their danger. Learning that Juliet, grieving for her murdered cousin, collapses and calls 'Romeo', he cries:

■ As if that name,
Shot from the deadly level of a gun,
Did murder her, as that name's cursèd hand
Murdered her kinsman. O tell me, Friar, tell me,
In what vile part of this anatomy
Doth my name lodge? Tell me, that I may sack
The hateful mansion. □

(3.3.101–7)

Romeo's speculation exposes the flaws in Juliet's linguistic theory. The problem with names is not that they accrue unfortunate associations for which the bearers are not responsible, but that they carry the real meaning of a person's history and crimes. Seeking to cut out his name, Romeo gives it a 'peculiar substantiality': it has an agency (it murders) and physical presence (it can be cut out and killed). The image resonates with a prevailing linguistic mood in which 'words themselves take on a namelike intensity':[26]

■ Say thou but 'Ay',
And that bare vowel 'I' shall poison more
Than the death-darting eye of cockatrice.
I am not I if there be such an 'I',
Or those eyes shut that makes thee answer 'Ay'.

That 'banishèd', that one word 'banishèd',
Hath slain ten thousand Tybalts. □

(3.2.45–9, 113–14)

Goldman suggests that this repetition of words strips them of their meaning, so that they seem to have an independent force, like names. As these examples suggest, names and name-like words have a violent energy that directs (or misdirects) the plot. Thus the right naming of the 'lark' in 3.5 forces the lovers to part.

Like Mahood, Goldman also addresses the particularly heavy concentration of puns in *Romeo and Juliet*. Puns are inherently violent: meanings are split apart and usually unrelated objects are forced together. Goldman deftly relates this linguistic dynamic to the action of the tragedy:

> ■ Romeo and Juliet themselves are like the components of a particularly good pun – natural mates whom authority strives to keep apart and whose union is not only violent but illuminating, since it transforms and improves the order it violates, though it is necessarily impermanent.[27] □

Furthermore, the playful nature of the pun draws on our innocence, our delight in temporarily reshaping the world according to our own design. We see this idea in action when the young lovers themselves briefly pretend that day is night. But the energy of puns is also dangerous: the play opens with puns provoking a brawl that quickly escalates into a more serious public disturbance. As Goldman perceptively remarks, there is a perilous frisson between the disorderly nature of puns and the strictures of Veronese society, where names have a fixed significance. It is also a play which (as many critics have complained) is full of mistakes: Benvolio tries to quell the street fight, but only intensifies it; Capulet gives his Capulet-only guest list to a servant who cannot read, so that Montagues come to learn of the ball; Romeo tries to save Mercutio by intervening between him and Tybalt, bringing about his death; and Romeo's suicidal attempt to reunite himself with Juliet is, of course, founded on error. In Goldman's reading these mistakes are part of the play's static electricity: like puns, each 'backfiring gesture . . . subverts its manifest intention.'[28]

Goldman is similarly more sympathetic to the drama's depiction of tragic selfhood than many other critics. In his view, *Romeo and Juliet* presents for the first time in Shakespeare's canon the 'tragedy of the unsounded self' (by which he seems to mean a 'self' with a private interiority that is at odds with the imperatives of the outside world).[29] The isolating effects of tragedy are painfully evident in this love story, where the lovers are constantly being separated (even the romantic games about the 'lark' and the 'nightingale' form a departure scene). The physical arrangement of the action emphasizes the strained nature of their union: Romeo has to climb a wall and gaze upwards at Juliet's window, a rope ladder is necessary to his escape in 3.5, and he needs a crowbar to break into her tomb. They finally die alone. In recognizing the tragic deaths as individual events, Goldman pays more heed to the impact of Juliet's fatal end than many earlier twentieth-century critics:

■ Shakespeare follows his source, Brooke's *The Tragical History of Romeus and Juliet*, in having Juliet commit suicide with Romeo's knife. But his Juliet, unlike Brooke's, first canvasses other ways to die – the poisoned cup, a kiss. These deaths, like Romeo's, are elegant, leave no mark upon the body, and have the comforting theatrical import of an easy transcendence of death – but they are not available to her; the impulsive pace of the action will not allow it. The watch is heard. She reaches for the dagger instead... The death is messy, violent, sexual. It is interesting that Romeo's is the more virginal, and that Juliet's is the first in the play that has not been immediately caused by a misunderstanding.[30] □

This sensitive reading of Juliet's difference from Romeo anticipates the focus of later feminist criticism. The detail of the physical messiness usefully points to the ambiguity of the tragic conclusion, which collapses transcendence with physical limit.

Goldman's chapter on *Romeo and Juliet* offers rewarding close textual analysis of some of the play's verbal action, though it does not produce any new insights into its larger meaning. Goldman does not always take the time to test the limits of his richly suggestive associations (e.g. the central relationship as a form of pun). But in some respects this very ludic quality is advantageous: Goldman's rapid analysis captures something of the experience of the frenetic tragedy, where the plot rushes past us before we have time to ponder the deeper questions it raises. Still more provocative is the somewhat gnomic reading of Jaques Derrida, whose work exemplifies one major aspect of the theoretical turn of literary criticism in the later twentieth century.

## JACQUES DERRIDA (1986)

French philosopher Jacques Derrida wrote 'Aphorism Countertime' to accompany the Paris production of *Romeo and Juliet* by Daniel Mesguich in 1986. Even though it is an 'occasional piece', it speaks to Derrida's broader intellectual concerns. Derrida originated the practice of deconstruction whereby the mechanics of a text or idea are revealed in a way that manifests their paradoxical nature. This process challenges 'logocentric' notions of language that presume that ideas exist independently of the words used to describe them. Obviously, we are now some considerable distance away from Spurgeon's 'image patterns' and Mahood's 'wordplay'. Where earlier criticism sought to identify the effects of language, Derrida's theory explores how linguistic function determines those effects. The title 'Aphorism Countertime' announces the work's subject matter and its mode of expression. Thus 'Aphorism', as the first sentence obliquely puts it, 'is the name'; the main focus of the discussion is the problem of naming.[31] But aphorism (a definition and a concise statement) is also the structural unit of Derrida's prose. In contrast to a traditional essay, in which a single argument is logically sequenced through one narrative, this piece is broken down into short, numbered aphorisms. Accordingly, Derrida also engages in the 'countertime' he discusses. His editor, Derek Attridge, explains: '*contretemps*, [is] a word which in French can mean both "mishap" and "syncopation", while the phrase *à contretemps* suggests both "inopportunely" and, in a musical sense, "out of time" or in "counter-time" '.[32] Derrida thus appears to be turning his attention to those untimely mistakes that have so irritated early critics of the play; but in fact, this reading of untimeliness looks past the mishaps of the plot to the temporal disjunctions of the play's linguistic condition, in particular, its names.

In some respects, Derrida's written style (which uses puns to fuse meanings together) and methodology (which exposes the moments of paradox in ideas) are well suited to *Romeo and Juliet*, a play built on wordplay and oxymoron. His approach is different from the literary critics we have looked at earlier in this chapter, who work to give a fuller picture of the text by drawing out nuances other scholars have missed. Derrida's 'criticism' (if we can call it that) instead enters into a kind of conversation with literature. Rather than 'clarifying' (and effectively overwriting) the text, Derrida puts us in the middle of the difficulties or paradoxes he has found there. (It might therefore be argued that attempting to 'explain' Derrida's work somewhat misses its point.) These paradoxes are not the rhetorical figures articulated by the play's characters (explained and analysed by the close readers above), but are instead the deeper conditions of the play, and the problems of naming that it stages.

Taking Derrida at his word when he says that each aphorism 'can come before or after the other',[33] it is helpful to start with an aphorism that comes towards the end of the essay, which makes a connection between 'countertime' and naming:

> ■ I am not my name. One might as well say that I should be able to survive it. But firstly it is destined to survive me. In this way it announces my death. Non-coincidence and contretemps between my name and me, between the experience according to which I am named or hear myself named and my 'living present.' Rendezvous with my name. *Untimely*, bad timing, at the wrong moment.[34] □

Following Juliet, Derrida recognizes that the name is inessential to the person it identifies – s/he could live without it. Except that our names outlast us after we die. Names consequently highlight our impermanence, the fact that we will die. Thus there is a 'countertime' inherent in being a named individual: our mortality puts us in a different time frame from our more durable names. It is a disjunction that is extended by the paradoxical 'inhumanity' or 'ahumanity' of names ('It is nor hand nor foot, / Nor arm nor face, nor any other part / Belonging to a man' [2.1.83–5]) which are nevertheless definitively human (no animal names itself).[35] Juliet's musings are the occasion of philosophical investigation for Derrida. He is less concerned with the specific action of this 'tragedy of names' (to reuse Goldman's description) than with its broader revelations for linguistic understanding.

Nevertheless, the context of the love story is meaningful to Derrida. The specific narrative manifests the structural relationship between lovers: 'Since there is neither desire nor pledge nor sacred bond (*sacramentum*) without aphoristic separation, the greatest love springs from the greatest force of dissociation, here what opposes and divides the two families in their name.'[36] Although he does not quote it, this point deconstructs the fundamental problem of the play, as articulated by Juliet: 'My only love sprung from my only hate' (1.4.251). At this first moment of realization, Juliet is appalled by what she takes to be a contradiction. But Derrida finds a broader logic in the particular situation: for love to be love, it is directed outwards, to a being wholly separate from ourselves ('I love because the other is the other', Derrida says), so it follows that the greater the difference, the greater the love.[37] Part of this difference is also temporal, since two lovers have individual lifespans: 'one must die before the other. One of them must see the other die.' Yet *Romeo and Juliet* addresses this structural tragedy of love with an impossible plot device: Romeo and Juliet 'live *in turn* the death of the other, for a time, the contretemps of their death.' Derrida pushes the analysis a stage further, declaring that even though the play performs what is physically impossible in reality, it does in fact manifest 'the truth' about love, since from the moment a 'pledge' is made, each lover trusts 'if you die before me, I will keep you, if I die before you, you will carry me in yourself'.[38] Shakespeare's play actualizes this abstract condition of love. Plenty of critics have claimed that *Romeo and Juliet* illustrates a 'timeless' love; Derrida makes this proposal in philosophical terms. And in his analysis timelessness is itself deconstructed.

However, what interests Derrida most is the iconic scene in which Juliet meditates on the problem of names and the protagonists pledge their love to one another (2.1). Isolating this scene from the complexities of the plot as a whole, Derrida's analysis performs another 'contretemps', but one which mirrors that produced by the scene itself, so culturally familiar even to those who have never seen or read the full play. Like Calderwood, Derrida observes the fullness of the rejection of names. It is not only a matter of distinguishing 'Romeo from Montague and Juliet from Capulet': 'in the denunciation of the name . . . they also attack their forenames, or at least that of Romeo, which seems to form part of the family name'.[39] Once again this desire is found to be unattainable, but the impossibility is more sharply drawn by Derrida, as his playful prose reveals the inextricability of onomastics (names) and ontology (existence): 'It is in his name that she continues to call him . . . and that she asks him, Romeo, to renounce his name.'[40] Names cannot be escaped; we live in and in some ways through a linguistic reality. Therefore Juliet's attempt to remove Romeo's name is fatal: 'She declares war on "Romeo," on his name, in his name, she will win this war only on the death of Romeo himself. Who? Romeo. But "Romeo" is not Romeo. Precisely. She wants the death of "Romeo". Romeo dies, "Romeo" lives on.'[41] The name 'Romeo', however inessential to Romeo's person it may appear to be, is timeless in a way that Romeo-the-person tragically is not. Furthermore, there is no life outside the name. In what has become one of the most clichéd (and timeless?) of all of the play's lines, Juliet exclaims: 'O Romeo, Romeo, wherefore art thou Romeo?' (2.1.76). Derrida points out:

> ■ She does not say to him: why are you called Romeo, why do you bear this name (like an article of clothing, an ornament, a detachable sign)? She says to him: why *are you* Romeo? She knows it: detachable and dissociable, aphoristic though it be, his name is his essence. Inseparable from his being. And in asking him to abandon his name, she is no doubt asking him to live at last, and to live his love (for in order to live oneself truly, it is necessary to elude the law of the name, the familial law made for survival and constantly recalling me to death), but she is *just as much* asking him to die, since his life *is* his name.[42] □

The paradox of the *Liebestod*, the love/death paradox, here takes on a linguistic form. Names are found to be the essence (and inessence) of the tragedy.

What is true for the protagonists is also true for *Romeo and Juliet* itself. The play's title, or name, has a meaning linked to but also separate from the text, especially since as a play it is constantly remade in performance: 'It belongs to a series, to the still-living palimpsest, to the open theatre of narratives which bear this name.'[43] Other critics have remarked on the need to see past our preconceptions of this most familiar of plays, in order to recognize its historical novelty or to revalue its tragic significance. Derrida makes a different but equally important point: the play has become its varied productions, adaptations and cultural associations, as well as the original text(s).

Some readers find Derrida's abstractions overly complex for the interpretative light they shed. Yet understood on its own terms, 'Aphorism Countertime' provides a strenuous and stimulating reflection on the play and the wider operations of naming it explores. From the 1980s onwards criticism is increasingly theoretical in nature; Derrida is an essential influence on this work. Catherine Belsey builds explicitly on Derrida's methods, synthesizing them with the theories of the French psychoanalyst Jacques Lacan.

## CATHERINE BELSEY (1993)

Catherine Belsey opens her essay, 'The Name of the Rose in *Romeo and Juliet*', by posing a question: 'Is the human body inside or outside culture?'[44] Her essay then deconstructs the opposition on which the query is predicated. After the 'Enlightenment' and under the influence of Descartes, the human being is understood as dual: body and mind. But Shakespeare's age registered no such distinction, and desire, as illustrated by *Romeo and Juliet*, 'deconstructs the opposition'.[45] Love is (paradoxically) both an essential bodily desire and the product of cultural conditioning. This is evident in the 'account' Romeo and Juliet have of their love: 'while it displays a longing to escape the constraints of the symbolic order, [it] reveals in practice precisely the degree to which it is culture that enables love to make sense'.[46] Romeo and especially Juliet long to push back the veil of language to access directly the real experience of love; but that experience of love is understood through and even produced by language. Thus in her elated epithalamium, Juliet invites night to 'Hood my unmanned blood, bating in my cheeks, / With thy black mantle' (3.2.14–15). Juliet's sexual desire is, Belsey argues, a desire to 'obscure even the signifying practices of the virgin body', with consummation figured as 'pure sensation, sightless, speechless organisms in conjunction, flesh on flesh, independent of the signifier'. Yet this fantasy of an experience beyond signification ('symbolic order') can only ever be a fantasy, as Juliet's highly figurative description shows: 'The text specifies a wish in a tissue of formally ordered allusions, comparisons and puns, which constitute a poem, the zenith of signification, self-conscious, artful, witty.'[47] Culture, through language, subsumes reality. Therefore Juliet is wrong when she claims: 'That which we call a rose / By any other word would smell as sweet' (2.1.86–7). Although there may well be nothing inherently horticultural about the sign 'rose', our familiarity with its supposed sweetness is shaped by a long Western literary tradition that relates roses and romance. Words not only convey meaning, they produce it. Earlier readings that claim for Romeo and Juliet a distinct and 'authentic' language (see Levin, for example) are hereby shown to be linguistically naive. There is no escape from 'form', only an illusion of new truth produced by switches between different forms: 'Ovid disrupts Petrarch; comic form leads to tragic denouement; choric narrative appropriates the lyric voice of the sonnet.'[48]

Belsey describes the tragedy of the play in deconstructionist terms: 'the letter invades the flesh, and the body necessarily inhabits the symbolic'.[49] The tragic problem is not merely, in this reading, a matter of being encumbered with divisive names; it is the larger problem of being predetermined by cultural language. Of course, naming is an aspect of this condition. Like other critics, Belsey remarks on the impossibility of living without names. Romeo, readily acceding to Juliet's request to 'refuse' his name (2.1.77), can only offer an alternative name, not namelessness: 'Call me but love, and I'll be new baptized. / Henceforth I never will be Romeo' (2.1.93–4). Belsey advances on earlier critics in this observation through her analysis of what it means to be named protagonists. Romeo's inability to 'doff' (2.1.90) his name registers the subject's lack of control over the signifier: we do not speak language; language speaks us. Drawing on Derrida, Belsey argues that in the same way the lovers cannot control their love: since love is expressed by words, messages and letters, it is part of the symbolic. The odd agency of signifiers is evident, she claims, in the mistimed lamentations over Juliet's 'dead' body, first in the Capulet household (4.4) and then in Romeo's suicidal grief in the tomb (5.3). In their untimely nature and prescient appropriateness, these lamentations suggest that the 'signifier [lives] a life of its own, partly but not entirely independent of the referent'.[50] What is key, then, is the slippery nature of the signifier, which is both a shaping part of the world it 'defines and differentiates' and distinct from it.[51] Even as the lovers and their love are defined and circumscribed by their language, their yearning to pass beyond words articulates a feeling that is somehow in excess of the words it cannot escape. However, the conclusion of the play sees the continuing power of the symbolic, particularly the name. The tomb in which Romeo and Juliet take their lives is a monument to the Capulet name. When approaching Juliet in that space, Romeo is distracted by the dead body of Tybalt, whose violent insistence on the law of the feud makes him a 'representative of the inherited symbolic order in all its dead – and deadly – otherness'.[52] The lovers are denied even a private death scene, as Tybalt and his symbolic order intervene yet again. Death itself then transforms the lovers into signifiers, as they are to be memorialized as golden statues. But this metamorphosis does not achieve, as in Calderwood's reading, a pure, lyrical stasis; instead the statues speak a meaning related to but different from the lovers: 'the effigies will signify concord, not desire'.[53] The last words of the play are, fittingly, the lovers' names: 'For never was a story of more woe, / Than this of Juliet and her Romeo' (5.3.309–10). The final word is, inevitably, the signifier.

Belsey's theorized reading of the play illuminates its broader cultural significance, and points to its historical specificity. In taking as a starting point the difference between pre- and post-Enlightenment conceptions of human being, she registers our historical distance from the play; though the implication of her argument is the universalizing one that Cartesian dualism misreads the relationships between body and mind, self and the world that are more accurately depicted in the play. This thesis is a rather large claim for the play, especially since Belsey concludes the essay by contemplating whether the play's enduring popularity is testament to our 'dissatisfaction with the neat Cartesian categories by which we have so diligently struggled to live'.[54] In raising the problem of historical specificity (our Cartesian difference from the play), Belsey dismisses it (the Cartesian model is unsatisfactory, and Shakespeare's play is universal after all). The full implications of historical change are yet to be explored, but it is awareness of historical specificity that provides the starting point for Kiernan Ryan, to whom we now turn.

## KIERNAN RYAN (2002)

Kiernan Ryan gives Shakespearean tragedy a political 'value'. The drama is driven by a sense of the 'contradiction between justified desires and their unjustifiable suppression'.[55] This tension both produces the tragic outcome and awakens in the audience the danger of societies that trample on individual potential. Timeliness is again at issue: not simply the local mistimings which mean Balthazar's news reaches Romeo before that of Friar Laurence; but rather the larger problem of the historical moment that the protagonists inhabit, the particular culture that dictates how things must be. In insisting on the historical specificity of the tragedy, Ryan explicitly writes in opposition to a range of critical approaches that all find in *Romeo and Juliet* a universal plight of humanity. Critics who regard the young lovers as the victims of natural law, or at the mercy of bad luck, or as self-destructively flawed, all accept (to different extents) the appropriateness of the tragedy. As we saw in Chapter 4, genre critics tend to insist that 'inevitability' is a crucial part of tragedy. For Ryan, by contrast, the tragedy of *Romeo and Juliet* is precisely that it did not have to be that way – a feeling of which the audience is excruciatingly aware. While the roles of the stars, accidents, and moral failings are each raised at different points in the play, the full impact of the tragedy is greater than any of these parts or even their sum. Similarly, as far as Ryan is concerned, even more recent psychoanalytical and feminist scholarship (discussed in Chapters 7 and 8 below) misses the real tragedy by insisting that the play reveals something universal about human subjectivity or gender difference:

> ■ What all these interpretations screen off are precisely the qualities that account for *Romeo and Juliet*'s profound hold on the hearts of generations of spectators and readers down through the centuries. The source of the play's abiding power lies in the way it foreshadows a more satisfying kind of love, freed from the coercions that continue to drive men and women apart and prevent their meeting each other's emotional needs.[56] □

For all he rejects universalizing readings the tragedy, Ryan himself universalizes the impact of the play, which is thought to please audiences in the same way 'down through the centuries'. Ryan insists that the human condition cannot be calcified into a single form, and therefore that the experience of tragedy in the sixteenth century and the twentieth centuries is necessarily different. But his thesis nevertheless makes emotional rebellion an alternative (in both senses) universal trait.

Language is once again found to be instrumental in the tragedy. The play reveals that 'the crippling constraints on the lovers are largely enforced through the language that binds them to a world with which they cannot compromise, and which they would therefore rather relinquish'.[57] Language both reveals and enforces social values. Different modes of discourse in the opening scenes of the play all express similarly unhealthy social configurations of love. Thus, pining for Rosaline, Romeo's moribund Petrarchisms conceptualize love as the experience of domination by a cruel mistress (he is: 'Shut up in prison, kept without my food, / Whipped and tormented' [1.2.56–7]); conversely, but following the same logic, Mercutio counsels violent male mastery ('If love be rough with you, be rough with love; / Prick love for pricking, and you beat love down' [1.4.25–6]); and Lady Capulet's bookish description of Paris prepares her daughter merely to provide a cover to her husband's content ('To beautify him only lacks a cover' [1.3.90]). In every instance love produces a subjugating hierarchy, itself created by the highly formalized modes of expression. There is nothing natural or universal about either the social or the linguistic formulations, Ryan asserts.

Here Ryan's 'radical' difference from Derrida and Belsey begins to emerge. All three understand language as a cultural force, but where Derrida and Belsey accord language a pre-existent power (so that our prior knowledge of words shapes the ideas expressed by them), Ryan sees an opportunity for change. He points out that Romeo and Juliet meet when Romeo is disguised by a mask and neither knows the other's name, so that they briefly experience the namelessness they later crave. Of course, this anonymity cannot last. Ryan puts the critical commonplace about the names' tragic significance in a social perspective: 'The designations "Capulet" and "Montague" fix Romeo and Juliet within a patriarchal power-structure, whose demands frustrate their self-sanctioned needs as human beings.'[58] As in Calderwood's earlier work, Ryan's Romeo and Juliet consciously strive to live by an alternative language. Metaphors of books mark their refusal of existing social scripts: at their first meeting, Juliet breaks off from a second shared sonnet by teasing Romeo: 'You kiss by th'book' (1.4.223); Romeo figures his desire as a rejection of books: 'Love goes toward love as schoolboys from their books' (2.1.202). For Ryan, the orchard scene (where Juliet interrupts artificial vows, and pointedly decides not to play the courtly part of the distant beloved) marks the lovers' awakening: 'A way of life which had seemed unquestionable is exposed as a prison-house, whose walls are built of words.' In this analysis Romeo and Juliet react against the conditions language has produced rather than against language itself. The alternative they forge for themselves is not only a matter of seclusion and an attempt to peel off the corrosive influence of words (as in Calderwood), but rather an entirely new understanding of what love means: 'it is founded on reciprocity rather than subservience'.[59] The Chorus celebrates the mutuality of their love: 'Now Romeo is beloved and loves again, / Alike bewitchèd by the charm of looks / ... And she, as much in love' (2.0.5–11) (though we might also note, as Ryan does not, that these lines remind us of the repetitive nature of Romeo's love for a Capulet woman 'again'). Romeo gives rhetorical stress to the equivalence that balances their relationship: 'one hath wounded me / That's by me wounded' (2.2.50–1); 'As mine on hers, so hers is set on mine' (2.2.59); 'Her I love now / Doth grace for grace and love for love allow' (2.2.85–6). And Juliet imagines love as an endless gift that enriches giver as well as receiver: 'My bounty is as boundless as the sea, / My love as deep; the more I give to thee, / The more I have, for both are infinite' (2.1.176–8).

Ryan's insightful observation usefully pushes past the linguistic impasse at which other critics have stopped, and also gives a fuller account of what makes the love of Romeo and Juliet distinctive (beyond better poetry). The celebration of mutuality within love is, he argues, as much a part of the play's message as the more widely recognized vindication of the 'right to love whoever one chooses, regardless of arbitrary prohibitions or prejudice'. Of course, the lovers themselves are unable to escape the fatal discourse of Verona: 'they are caged in a culture which precludes the survival of such emancipated love'.[60] As tragedy overwhelms the lovers, metatheatrical and metatextual remarks signal the presence of a social script that strips them of control: 'My dismal scene I needs must act alone' (4.3.19); 'O, give me thy hand, / One writ with me in sour misfortune's book' (5.3.81–2). Nevertheless, the force of the tragedy is to make the audience recognize that Verona's script is not universal:

> ■ by sundering the lovers from the discourse that defines them, Shakespeare shows their plight to be man-made and mutable, the local imposition of a transient culture.... In the estranged idiom of the lovers can be read the tragedy's estrangement from its era, the imprint of its commerce with futurity.[61] □

*Romeo and Juliet* is ahead of its time in its criticism of discourses that figure sexual relationships as hierarchies; it exposes the cultural specificity of these discourses to its audience, so that they might be inspired with a sense of the possibility of change. This analysis is energized by a thrilling sense that literature can intervene in society and change the world for the better; though this reading may idealize (in the terms of Ryan's own political convictions) audience responses to the play. Romeo and Juliet themselves are also celebrated in selective terms. While Ryan's point about the reciprocity of their love is astute, the privatized nature of this love rather complicates it as a force for social good. Deliberately shunning the world around them, rather than actively trying to change it, Romeo and Juliet trap themselves in the tragedy. Nevertheless, Ryan's interpretation brilliantly reconnects the play to an awareness of social context that is somewhat missing from earlier linguistic analysis. Maguire takes this a step further, by exploring a particular linguistic/social context for the play.

## LAURIE MAGUIRE (2007)

Names in *Romeo and Juliet* operate, Laurie Maguire explains, as 'a paradigm of language'.[62] However, she resists the idea that the play is a 'tragedy of names', instead pointing to the ambivalent quality of language that both harms and heals. Language's multifaceted nature is evident in the famous orchard scene (2.1). Maguire draws out the linguistic differences between the couple at this early stage in their relationship: concerned for Romeo's safety, Juliet asks straightforward questions of fact and issues clear warnings ('How camest thou hither, tell me, and wherefore?' [2.1.105]; 'If they do see thee, they will murder thee' [2.1.113]; 'I would not for the world they saw thee here' [2.1.117]; 'By whose direction found'st thou out this place?' [2.1.122]); Romeo replies with euphoric but evasive metaphors ('With love's light wings did I o'erperch these walls' [2.1.109]; 'there lies more peril in thine eye / Than twenty of their swords' [2.1.114–15]; 'I have night's cloak to hide me from their eyes' [2.1.118]; 'By love, that first did prompt me to inquire' [2.1.123]). Language both communicates and obscures information.

*Romeo and Juliet* investigates the paradoxical functions of language as part of its relentless play with verbal, generic and thematic contrast. Thus Juliet is right to view Romeo as a being independent of his linguistic definition, his name; but Mercutio is also correct when he thinks Romeo's (bawdy) wordplay reveals his real self ('Now art thou sociable, now art thou Romeo, now art thou what thou art by art as well as by nature' [2.3.84–5]). Similarly, Juliet's varied attitude to vows does not bespeak her inconsistent attitude or linguistic entrapment, so much as an exploration of language function. In the soliloquy that questions the value of names, Juliet is sceptical about the coherence between words and their referents, but after talking to Romeo she comes to place her faith in words: 'Dost thou love me? I know thou wilt say "Ay", / And I will take thy word' (2.1.133–4). In the same breath she then worries about the veracity of lovers' oaths ('yet if thou swear'st, / Thou mayst prove false' [2.1.134-5]), but soon requests a marriage vow. Marriage itself participates in the linguistic investigations of the play. Maguire argues that the framing of the marriage scene with scenes that 'ponder the question of language and the relationship between personal names and selfhood, nouns and quiddity' (the orchard scene and the naming of the lark/nightingale) is 'no accident': 'Marriage is, in Christian tradition, the gaining of an identity while losing an identity.' Conventionally, a woman sheds her family name to take on that of her husband, though in *Romeo and Juliet* the gender distinction is erased: 'Deny thy father and refuse thy name; / Or if thou wilt not... I'll no longer be a Capulet' (2.1.77–9). This is, Maguire stipulates, 'not onomastic reciprocity or equality so much as accommodation'.[63] And such linguistic accommodation ties together the play's focus on love and on language.

In Maguire's argument, 'Love... means learning to speak the language of the beloved.'[64] This thesis identifies a different linguistic dynamic from those encountered in the criticism discussed above. Neither an obstacle to be overcome nor an idealistically authentic poetry, language is here important as a process that unites the two lovers. Maguire figures the lovers' language games as translation, a transformation that works as 'interpretation and adaptation'.[65] In 3.5, when Juliet attempts to keep Romeo from going she does so by recasting the world in her own language: 'It was the nightingale, and not the lark' (3.5.2). Romeo not only agrees to stay, but also learns to speak Juliet's language: 'I'll say yon grey is not the morning's eye: / 'Tis but the pale reflex of Cynthia's brow; / Nor that is not the lark whose notes do beat /

The vaulty heaven so high above our heads' (3.5.19–22). Juliet quickly switches to Romeo's language: 'It is the lark that sings so out of tune, / Straining harsh discords and unpleasing sharps' (3.5.27–8). The accommodating adaptation of 'bilingualism' provides, in Maguire's terms, a 'positive metaphor for a relationship'.[66]

Translation within the play is further illuminated by a translation of the play. The second part of Maguire's chapter discusses the French/English *Romeo & Juliette,* co-directed by Robert Le Page and Gordon McCall in Canada in 1989–90. Featuring six English speakers and six French speakers, the production used a script where 20 per cent of the dialogue had been translated into French. Language patterns underscored and produced the cultural tensions between Capulets and Montagues:

■ the Capulets automatically spoke English to anglophones; the anglophones, by contrast, were consistently monolingual, apart from Mercutio, who offered Tybalt a few incendiary French taunts, and Romeo, who falteringly tried to communicate with Juliette, and, after his marriage, with his new kinsman Tybalt, in French.[67] □

Without explicitly drawing on it, this production was performed in a context of cultural-linguistic controversy in Canada, when the Meech Lake accord failed to produce a constitutional agreement to preserve and promote Québec's francophone identity. The tragic feud thereby resonated with national dispute. Yet Maguire's analysis does more than simply indicate the play's adaptability to modern culture. Reporting the way in which the Canadian production spliced French and English dialogue, Maguire reveals the divisive and conciliatory possibilities of language. Where Romeo's attempt to address Tybalt in French shows an attempt to pacify him, Tybalt's switch from French to English clarified the violence of his intentions: 'turn and draw' (3.1.66); elsewhere Mercutio's satirical use of French gained newly derisory force: 'Signor Romeo, *bonjour*: there's a French salutation to your French slop' (2.3.42–2). Maguire's reading of a specific production uncovers – more vividly, perhaps, than in the theoretical abstractions of Derrida and Belsey – the depth of cultural significance (and difference) encoded in language. Linguistic clashes are cultural clashes, precisely because language is tightly bound up with personal, familial and historical identity.

Yet in this optimistic reading of the play, language contains within it the salve for its own malady. Wordplay that ignites division from the opening street brawl also has alternative potential: 'The pun is a sign not simply detached from its signifier but reattached to multiple signifiers. Thus, like the paradoxes and oxymoron in *Romeo and Juliet,* it is a linguistic model of coexistence, for Verona and for Canada.'[68] Romeo and Juliet may be unique among their families in choosing bilingual accommodation, but the play's final words offer hope:

> ■ Go hence to have more talk of these sad things;
> Some shall be pardoned and some punishèd.
> For never was a story of more woe
> Than this of Juliet and her Romeo. □
>
> (5.3.307–10)

The Prince here expresses faith in the reconciliatory power of language and the story is finally defined as a tale of individuals, 'Juliet' and 'Romeo', rather than as a patronymic Montague/Capulet feud. Even as Maguire's work outlines the magnitude of cultural baggage that freights linguistic difference, it also rehabilitates language as a means of pushing past tragedy.

From broadly conceived language struggles, we turn now to a narrower form of discourse that was of special importance in the Elizabethan period: Petrarchism.

## CHAPTER SIX

# Kissing by the Book: Reading Petrarchism

In a bid to tease his friend back to sociability, Mercutio labels Romeo a stereotypically Petrarchan lover: 'Now is he for the numbers that Petrarch flowed in' (2.3.37–8). Some of the most invigorating criticism of *Romeo and Juliet* has examined the play's place in a Petrarchan tradition and paid attention to the very conceits that earlier criticism had condemned. Francesco Petrarca, or 'Petrarch', was a fourteenth-century Italian poet whose work was profoundly influential in early modern England. Petrarchan discourse was the dominant Renaissance idiom of love (and even had a political application in Elizabeth's court), so fluency in the Petrarchan poetic is essential to an understanding of both *Romeo and Juliet* and its cultural context. Inaugurating a new strand of critical investigation, Leonard Forster pointed out that the play is predicated on a Petrarchan situation: 'The enmity of Montague and Capulet makes the cliché of "dear enemy" into a concrete predicament.'[1] Although he did not explore the implications of this insight, this chapter shows how a range of critics have debated whether the play adheres to or explodes a strictly Petrarchan design. 'Traditional' attention to details such as metre and rhyme can serve, as these critics demonstrate, a variety of ideological and cultural perspectives.

### ROSALIE L. COLIE (1974)

*Romeo and Juliet* is hidden in Rosalie L. Colie's book *Shakespeare's Living Art* within a chapter named for *Othello*. The earlier tragedy serves, according to this argument, as a trial run for working through problems Shakespeare will properly master in *Othello*. Even though teleological readings sometimes depreciate the independent value of *Romeo and Juliet*, Colie's analysis provides essential insights into the play. She connects *Romeo and Juliet* with *Othello* because in both plays Shakespeare unconventionally turns the subject of love into tragic matter. Colie's sensitivity to generic form clarifies the particular difficulties of putting love in tragedy, which was not just a matter of challenging expectations. Love's instability made it fitter for the perturbations of farce and romantic comedy than for tragedy. In non-dramatic literature love was most often found in romance (which shared structural conventions with stage comedy), and, more significantly, in love lyrics. The influence of the sonneteering tradition on *Romeo and Juliet* is, as we have seen, widely recognized; but Colie's fluency in Petrarchan discourse means that she is particularly attuned to its generic function in *Romeo and Juliet*. Sonnets and sonneteering language help translate love into a tragic mode: sonnets provide 'a vast reservoir of *topoi* of self-inspection' and 'opportunities for deep and faceted self-examination'; furthermore, 'the sonnet-sequence honors the profound seriousness' of love.[2] In this reading the play's purple Petrarchism enables rather than detracts from tragic meaning.

Colie's willingness to read Petrarchism on its own terms also flushes out subtleties in characterization. She agrees with other critics who regard Romeo's Petrarchan idioms as rote-learned, but also points out what is sometimes overlooked – how adept he is at adopting this poetic persona:

■ Love is a smoke made with the fume of sighs,
Being purged, a fire sparkling in lovers' eyes,
Being vexed, a sea nourished with loving tears.
What is it else? A madness most discreet,
A choking gall and a preserving sweet. □

(1.1.186–90)

Romeo neatly defines love with a *blason* (poetic catalogue), easily running through a range of oxymora that convey an aptly ambivalent tone. His verse is so formally correct that Rosaline, whom he ostensibly describes, is kept invisible:

■ she'll not be hit
With Cupid's arrow, she hath Dian's wit;
And in strong proof of chastity well armed,
From love's weak childish bow she lives uncharmed.
She will not stay the siege of loving terms,
Nor bide th'encounter of assailing eyes,
Nor ope her lap to saint-seducing gold.
O she is rich, in beauty only poor,
That when she dies, with beauty dies her store. □

(1.1.204–12)

Rosaline (dis)appears as a combination of classical allusions. Romeo's thinking is of a piece with the *carpe diem* (seize the day) logic of so many love lyrics, and more specifically, with the generative arguments of Shakespeare's non-dramatic *Sonnets*. Colie concludes with other critics that Romeo's poetic posturing is too conventional, but her closer analysis of its details more effectively establishes the interrogative tone of the play, which does not totally reject Petrarchism.

Similarly, Colie also corrects the critical commonplace (which emerged in the criticism considered in Chapter 5 above) that pitches Juliet's language against Romeo's as less artificial. Colie maintains that Juliet is as proficient in Petrarchan conventions as Romeo, as seen in her ability to split a sonnet with him, taking up the second quatrain after Romeo speaks the first and then sharing the sestet. Like Romeo, Juliet has a way with rhetorical contrast: 'lie upon the wings of night / Whiter than new snow upon a raven's back' (3.2.18–19). She also readily elaborates on conceits:

> ■ when I shall die,
> Take him and cut him out in little stars,
> And he will make the face of heaven so fine,
> That all the world will be in love with night,
> And pay no worship to the garish sun. □
>
> (3.2.21–5)[3]

Colie herself elaborates:

> ■ Juliet's metaphoric daring is greater than Romeo's: she solves the sun-stars problem firmly and defiantly in favor of her image, while his imagery was less committed, less precise, and less extreme: he speaks, more than she, by the book. Her conceit of 'little stars,' which shall translate Romeo to classical immortality in a constellation, sends us back to his likeness of her to the sun. Her language honors the darkness in which her love is conceived, and its ugliest, most forceful image ('cut him out in little stars') forebodes that love's violent end.[4] □

Juliet therefore outstrips Romeo in figurative creativity; her language does not function as a plain or 'authentic' corrective to his poetic flights of fancy. Indeed when, on learning of Tybalt's murder, Juliet attacks the absent Romeo as a 'serpent heart' with a 'flow'ring face' (3.2.73) and recites a list of related oxymora, she is not, Colie suggests, speaking completely out of character. While the extreme nature of the rhetoric registers her passion and confusion, the images themselves connect back to earlier images used in loving poetry: 'fiend angelical, / Dove-feathered raven' (3.2.75–6). Petrarchan idioms consolidate the play's dialogue. In Colie's view, the important distinction is between embellishment and experience; between empty Petrarchan cliché, and Petrarchan poetry where the paradoxes have been felt, where style is '*the* vehicle for amorous emotion'.[5]

Ultimately, what limits *Romeo and Juliet* – a play Colie describes as an 'apprentice' piece – is Shakespeare's failure to integrate fully poetry and drama.[6] Action stops for lyrical set pieces such as the poems of the Chorus, the lovers' sonnet, Juliet's Ovidian apostrophe to night, and various laments. Yet the most important insight of Colie's work on the play is her identification of a technique Shakespeare uses to realize (and real-ize) poetic figures in the play. She shrewdly detects a process of ' "unmetaphoring" of literary devices', whereby formal conventions take on a reality within the action.[7] Thus an *aubade* features as a literal 'dawn-song sung after a night of love, when the lovers must part', but the force of the parting is given a deeper significance because of Romeo's banishment; the biblical and amatory metaphor of the *hortus conclusus* (the virgin as a closed garden) is literalized as the virginal Juliet opens her window onto a walled orchard that her true love breaches; lyrical desire for endless night gains real urgency as night (refigured by the lovers as light) is the only safe time for their illicit love; and of course clichéd comparisons between love and war provide a plot for this couple drawn from feuding households. Colie's brilliant observation indicates the profound importance of Petrarchan poetry to Shakespeare's conception of the tragedy. While she prefers the way the later *Othello* handles the 'Problematics of Love' (as her chapter title puts it), other critics choose to dwell on the impact of Petrarchism in this play.

## RALPH BERRY (1978)

Squaring up to the critical uneasiness with *Romeo and Juliet*, Ralph Berry highlights the play's unsettling tonal change from comedy to tragedy. He diagnoses language as the ultimate source of scholarly discomfort, particularly its oft-criticized conventionalism. But for Berry, this awareness of formality prompts questions about how the language directs audience response to the tragedy, rather than providing an answer about its supposed weakness.

Taking the sonnet as 'the channel through which the play flows',[8] Berry detects a related emphasis on rhyme:

> ■ The Veronese think in rhyme, and communicate in rhyme ... But rhyme is psychologically more interesting than it looks. I discern two main varieties of the mode. With the elders, the heavy, jogging rhymes have the effect of a self-fulfilling prophecy. *Night* must follow *light* with the same inevitability that it does the day. The rhymes figure a closed system. The younger people, apt

> to confuse facility with penetration, seize on the other aspect of rhyme – that it can pick up the loose ends of a companion's speech. ... Rhyme, in sum, is inward-turning, acquiescent, reflective of social forces. It tends to codify its own categories, and insulate them against erosion.[9] □

Thus the audience first meet Friar Laurence in soliloquy, speaking in heavy rhyming couplets (for example, 'tomb'/'womb' [2.2.9–10]); the entrance of Romeo and the switch to conversation does not prise him from this rigid verbal structure. The younger Romeo uses rhyme almost playfully, so that he matches Benvolio's concern for his 'good heart's oppression' with the aurally appropriate 'Why, such is love's transgression' (1.1.180–1). After her first meeting with Romeo, Juliet glosses this trend:

NURSE: What's tis? What's tis?
JULIET: A rhyme I learnt even now
Of one I danced withal.

(1.4.255–6)

Her sonnet with Romeo is aptly associated with a 'rhyme', expressing both the reciprocity and the artificiality of the moment. Verbal conventions reveal and shape social understanding and behaviour in the play (Levin made a similar case in 1960; see Chapter 4 above).

This conventionality makes more sense in the context of the late Elizabethan literary scene. Berry situates *Romeo and Juliet* at the end of a long line of Petrarchan publications in the 1590s: Philip Sidney's *Astrophel and Stella* (1591); Samuel Daniel's *Delia* (1592); Henry Constable's *Diana* (1592; republished with additions 1594); Barnabe Barnes's *Parthenophil and Parthenope* (1593); Giles Fletcher's *Licia* (1593); Thomas Lodge's *Phillis* (1593); Michael Drayton's *Ideas Mirrour* (1594); Edmund Spenser's *Amoretti* (1595); and Barnabe Barnes's *A Divine Centurie of Spirituall Sonnets* (1595). Composed between 1594 and 1596, *Romeo and Juliet* emerges at a time when sonnet sequences and collections of poems dominated by sonnets were in fresh supply. What linked these different poetic outputs was a shared consciousness of their inheritance from Petrarch and certain key tropes (such as the cruel lady, the melancholy lover, sickness, insomnia). Detailing this range of publications, Berry usefully recharges the meaning of 'convention' from a bland sense of 'habit' to a more meaningful 'mental environment' inhabited by Elizabethan writers.[10] As far as Berry is concerned, *Romeo and Juliet* is totally subsumed in this paradigm. This is why the characters tend towards the typical, if not the stereotypical. Only young characters or old characters fit into this emphatically literary world; there is no space for the middle aged. These characters 'appear as quotations, and they speak in quotations: the cliché, of which the sonnet is exemplar, is the dominant thought-form of Verona'.[11] Petrarchism thus informs action as well as expression, character as well as poetry.

Yet as a thoroughly Petrarchan text, *Romeo and Juliet* conventionally contains within it anti-Petrarchan impulses. The more adept poets of the age self-consciously critiqued the Petrarchan role they nonetheless played. Shakespeare maintains a similar balance of attitudes in his play. The most important opposition to the drama's Petrarchan hyperbole is Mercutio, who explicitly mocks Romeo's Petrarchan posturing: 'Now is he for the numbers that Petrarch flowed in' (2.3.37–8). He also performs 'what is virtually a burlesque, rhymeless sonnet':

■ Romeo! Humours! Madman! Passion! Lover!
Appear thou in the likeness of a sigh;
Speak but one rhyme and I am satisfied.
Cry but 'Ay me', pronounce but 'love' and 'dove'[.] □

(2.1.8–11)[12]

Berry takes the reference to 'rhyme' to be especially significant, since it underscores Mercutio's stylistic and attitudinal difference from Romeo, and from everyone else in the play. Where others speak in rhyme, Mercutio opts for blank verse, and more often prose. His expression therefore challenges the Petrarchan supremacy elsewhere in the dialogue. He pointedly rebukes Romeo's Petrarchan speech and behaviour, congratulating him when he breaks from it to join in sexual banter:

■ Why, is not this better now than groaning for love?
Now art thou sociable, now art thou Romeo, now
art thou what thou art by art as well as by nature; for
this drivelling love is like a great natural that runs
lolling up and down to hide his bauble in a hole. □

(2.3.83–7)

Berry asserts that Mercutio here exposes the role-playing artificiality of Romeo's Petrarchan stance. This is a valid point, but the repetition of 'art' makes Mercutio's argument a little more complex than Berry allows: Romeo is *now* what he truly is ('art') by 'art' (artifice?) as well as 'nature'. However, Berry's larger insight into the significance of Mercutio is important: 'The gravest critical error concerning *Romeo and Juliet* is to assume that the play, more or less, identifies itself with the lovers; and the violence of Mercutio's commentary is on record to remind us of the counterforce whereby ultimate poise is achieved.'[13] Identifying Mercutio's role as providing an alternative perspective on the tragedy helpfully captures more of the emotional and intellectual complexity of the drama, which is not merely a sentimental love story. The play questions its own action.

Just as much as the other (Petrarchan) characters, Mercutio embodies for Berry a strand of Elizabethan literary culture. Mercutio's out-of-tempo language, which swaps transcendent romance for sexual explicitness, is aligned with an emerging trend for satire found in the work of Joseph Hall, John Donne and John Marston. To the many contrasts critics have found in *Romeo and Juliet,* Berry thus adds one of clashing literary modes, so instrumental to the play's dynamic as to be described as Hegelian (compare Bradley's reading of Hegel, discussed in Chapter 4 above). Of course, Mercutio's verbal challenge to the play's romantic dialogue does not last, but with his demise his realist voice is replaced by a still more forceful intrusion of the real: death.

Like most other critics, Berry marks a difference between the first and the second half of the play. Mercutio's death means that the artifice of Verona's poetic society necessarily collapses. Berry shrewdly observes that 29 of the play's 30 references to 'name' occur in the first three acts, revealing the nominalist and artificial nature of the society: 'Appearance, and form, are the realities of the Veronese. They are none the less genuine for that; but they are vulnerable.'[14] And there is a change in the last two acts, where rhyming couplets are far less frequent. However, the difference marks an inability to sustain the poetic fiction rather than changed perception. The notorious frequency of mistakes and accidents is, Berry argues, symptomatic of a lack of understanding in a 'wrong-choice society'.[15] The characters simply do not have the capacity to reach a full anagnorisis (recognition); the only character who did – the play's anti-Petrarchan spokesman – was murdered in Act 3.

Thus as much as Berry rehabilitates the value of the play's conventionality, he finally finds the tragedy wanting. In fact, the self-conscious interrogation of Petrarchism, pushed to its limits by the interruption of death, makes *Romeo and Juliet*'s closest canonical relation *Love's Labour's Lost* (where news of death postpones a happy ending for four Petrarchan lords). What we might call Berry's 'literary historicism' successfully reveals *Romeo and Juliet* as a play of its time, illuminating meanings sometimes overlooked in considerations of its 'timeless' status. As Chapter 8 below will demonstrate, queer theorists will see Mercutio as more than a stylistic foil to Romeo's Petrarchan lover. But Berry's analysis carefully alerts us to the varied texture of the play.

## ANN PASTERNAK SLATER (1988)

Ann Pasternak Slater begins her article 'Petrarchanism Come True in *Romeo and Juliet*' by spelling out some of the critical debate about the stylistic variation in the play: some regard Romeo's early speeches as an affectation that he grows out of in his love for Juliet; others spot a difference between conventional and less formulaic language, but contend that Shakespeare is not in control of the overall effect. Slater enters the fray by marshalling further evidence for a sustained Petrarchan design that unifies language and action. Her reading enlarges effectively on Forster's point that Petrarchism provides the situation of the plot, and on Colie's idea that Shakespeare 'unmetaphors' poetic devices in *Romeo and Juliet.* But Slater discerns a much more sustained trend of literary figures (Petrarchan in their paradoxical nature) becoming operational in the action. Thus Romeo's first speeches in the play, frequently dismissed by critics as meaningless Petrarchan platitudes, predict the tragic plot. Elaborating on the theme of 'brawling love' and 'loving hate' (1.1.172). Romeo appears to over-extend himself talking of 'Still-waking sleep that is not what it is' (1.1.177), yet this accurately describes Juliet's deathly appearance in the tomb in Act 5; and the reference to 'choking gall and a preserving sweet' (1.1.190) prefigures his poison and Juliet's sleeping potion. Such literalizing of Petrarchan paradoxes matches the generic fusion of comedy and tragedy. Like Forster, Slater shows that this plot itself is a realization of the clichéd love/hate paradox. But she also reveals a denser pattern of other literalized paradoxes: 'Whenever characters indulge in outrageous literary hyperbole, the plot takes them at their word. Juliet hysterically opts for any horror rather than bigamous marriage to Paris ... Done!'[16] So she is instructed to 'go into a new-made grave' and hidden 'with a dead man in his tomb' (4.1.84–5). Similarly when the distraught Romeo, just informed of his banishment, asks the Friar if he has 'no poison mixed, no sharp-ground knife', the tragedy ultimately does produce these means of suicide. Still more poignantly prescient is the actualization of Juliet's equivocal language when she talks to her mother:

■ Indeed, I never shall be satisfied
With Romeo till I behold him – dead –
Is my poor heart so for a kinsman vexed.
Madam, if you could find out but a man
To bear a poison, I would temper it,
That Romeo should, upon receipt thereof,
Soon sleep in quiet. O, how my heart abhors
To hear him named, and cannot come to him
To wreak the love I bore my cousin
Upon his body that hath slaughtered him. □

(3.5.93–102)

Juliet ambiguously hides her desire for Romeo behind an apparent desire ('satisfied') to see him killed (it is her heart that is 'dead' in his absence); she apparently wishes to prepare a poison for him while really wishing she could assuage its effects ('temper'), and her longing to give his body her love is encoded as revenge ('wreak'). Yet the deeper irony is that Juliet will in fact next 'behold' Romeo 'dead', when he will 'bear a poison' that she will 'temper' with her own suicide.

Slater argues that through this process Shakespeare makes Petrarchan discourse dramatically coherent: 'Shakespeare's manipulation of the minutiae of staging is broadly devoted to two ends: to make the verbal hyperboles traditionally associated with Petrarchan love rhetoric actually come true, and, therefore, to stage convincingly a series of incompatible and unstable paradoxes.'[17] Thus while Berry sees in *Romeo and Juliet* a critique of the Petrarchan mode, Slater finds Shakespeare rationalizing poetic exaggeration. In some respects Slater might herself seem to take Petrarchism too much at its word, assuming that in being realized as plot devices its paradoxes are shown to be 'true' rather than exposed as unrealistic. Perhaps the very nature of paradox means that these moments hover between the real and the ridiculous. Slater's analysis is most useful in its identification of a process rather than in the immediate argument drawn from it. The translation of Petrarchan paradoxes – so beautifully demonstrated in this article – might also be considered as another way in which Shakespeare tests their robustness (or even, perhaps, as a means of questioning language's influence on society). Nevertheless, the focus on paradox does open out the drama's complexity. As Slater points out, paradox resists easy moral conclusions. The Friar's first speech issues this very warning through its multiple oxymora: 'Virtue itself turns vice, being misapplied, / And vice sometime by action dignified' (2.2.21–2). Such thinking cautions us to appreciate the ambivalence of the conclusion, where the suicidal lovers have achieved tragic grandeur and committed (in traditional Christian terms) a sin, and where reconciliation is generated through annihilation.

Furthermore, Slater's theatrical sensibility means she does excellent work in recognizing the drama in the text (a facet sometimes missing from literary criticism). Situating the play on the Elizabethan stage, she observes that Shakespeare turns theatrical practicalities to artistic advantage. Acted in daylight, night-time scenes were ironically signalled through the presence of additional light in the form of torches and tapers; in *Romeo and Juliet* this visual effect manifests the verbal figures that remake night as light (compare Spurgeon in Chapter 5 above). The literalizing of paradoxes is a way for Shakespeare to stage their meaning, to show opposing concepts inhering in one another. Carefully noting the past tense of Capulet's remark that 'The curfew-bell hath rung' (4.4.4), Slater suggests that the audience would have heard the ringing during Juliet's fearful speech of what awaits her in the tomb. The bell ominously sounds a funeral for Juliet, but simultaneously signals dawn and wedding festivity for Capulet. Similarly, Juliet's wedding bed also functions as a deathbed. And at the end of the play, her 'Still-waking sleep' makes life and death, and love and death, look exactly like one another. Slater's analysis vivifies the Petrarchan discourse of the play and provides a very instructive account of the mechanics by which Shakespeare transforms poetry into drama. However, she assumes that this is a rather smooth process and does not follow up the interpretative implications of the translation. It is these very questions that Gayle Whittier addresses in an article published the year after Slater's essay appeared.

## GAYLE WHITTIER (1989)

In her article 'The Sonnet's Body and the Body Sonnetized in *Romeo and Juliet*', Gayle Whittier grapples with the exchange that takes place when Petrarchan poetry in transformed into dramatic action, studying the impact each form has on the other: 'in *Romeo and Juliet* the inherited Petrarchan word becomes English flesh by declining from lyric freedom to tragic fact through a transaction that sonnetizes the body, diminishes the body of the sonnet, and scatters the terms of the *blason du corps* [an itemization of the beloved's beautiful body parts]'.[18] The shaping pressure between the two modes is evident from the very first lines of the play, in the opening choral sonnet:

■ Two households both alike in dignity,
In fair Verona, where we lay our scene,
From ancient grudge break to new mutiny,
Where civil blood makes civil hands unclean.
From forth the fatal loins of these two foes
A pair of star-crossed lovers take their life,
Whose misadventured piteous overthrows
Doth with their death bury their parents' strife.
The fearful passage of their death-marked love,
And the continuance of their parents' rage –
Which but their children's end naught could remove –
Is now the two hours' traffic of our stage;
The which if you with patient ears attend,
What here shall miss, our toil shall strive to mend. □

(PROLOGUE 1–14)

The English sonnet structure marks a formal Petrarchan 'inheritance', but it is 'emptied of its traditional lyric treasures – the lovesick persona, dense metaphor, emotional extremity, song itself'. These features are displaced by a 'civic' discourse, so that it is the 'Two households' rather than the young lovers that open the poem. Whittier argues that this sonnet lacks a poetic purpose: briskly recounting the plot of the play in just 14 lines, it introduces the action rather than lingering on the transcendent moments and emotion of Petrarchan verse. Indeed its temporality – the carefully accounted and brief 'two hours' traffic' – is totally different from the 'liquidity of Petrarchan time'.[19] A flash of Petrarchan energy is evident in the oxymoron 'fatal loins', but the theatrical address concludes the sonnet with a lame couplet ('attend'/'mend'). Dramatic conditions (such as public narrative, chronological sequence and defined time scale) drain the sonnet form of its vital features.

Inflected by linguistic theory, Whittier's reading draws out the way in which language – specifically Petrarchan discourse – precedes and even produces the subjects who speak it. Romeo is first introduced to us as a verbal effect: in a description by his father that punningly hints at his literary essence. Montague worries that his son 'makes himself an artificial night' (1.1.136), a comment which Whittier notes sounds like 'artificial knight'. Romeo strives to play the part of courtly lover. But Whittier identifies a structural problem in Romeo's efforts: 'Beyond poetic forms, Romeo seeks to become the *author* of the persona he imitates, an artificer born out of an artefact. That is, he would create his own pre-creation, and so preempt inheritance.' Furthermore, Romeo makes a category error in trying to live a Petrarchan role:

> ■ the Petrarchan word is especially non-referential, with its obvious hyperbole, celestial compliments, and paradox. It is dangerous in that, where the word is performative, Romeo lives out its terms in a referential way, ultimately converting himself from life to 'story.' When Romeo falls in love with a story already *scripted* as otherworldy and then seeks to dramatize that script, he falls into the living power of an inherited word, which, like fleshly inheritance, bestows *both* life *and* death.[20] □

The disjunctions between lyric and life, poetry and flesh pull Romeo apart.

Juliet's relationship with language is rather different. Unlike the majority of earlier critics, Whittier believes that Juliet, as well as Romeo, linguistically matures through the course of the play. But this maturation is something like that experienced by Adam and Eve – a fall into knowledge. It is only after meeting Romeo that Juliet speaks contradiction: 'My only love sprung from my only hate, / Too early seen unknown and known too late' (1.4.251–2). Now she knows something of the paradox of love that collapses life in death. (Though Whittier does not mention it, lurking behind this contradiction is the Elizabethan pun on 'to die' as to orgasm and to experience death.) Along with this knowledge of antithesis comes an awareness of time, which governs the real, lived world and which will entrap the Petrarchan love in a tragedy. The brittle oxymora that the shocked Juliet uses to describe her murdering husband (3.2.73–85) mark for Whittier the completion of her loss of 'linguistic innocence'.[21] This analysis helpfully refigures what others have seen as temporary stylistic derangement on the part of Juliet and/or Shakespeare, or more subtly Juliet's estrangement from her husband and herself (see Levin and Colie above), as a meaningful stage in the characterization and the progression of the tragedy. Juliet's earlier nominalist innocence is painfully echoed in the Nurse's exclamation: 'O Romeo, Romeo, / Whoever would have thought it Romeo?' (3.2.41–2). Now Juliet realizes that signifiers she had thought of as arbitrary can be deceptive. At around the same time Romeo himself falls into linguistic understanding when he realizes that words cannot pacify the violent body of Tybalt (who 'hate[s] the word' peace [1.1.66]) and yet can 'banish' him. Significantly, these lessons split 'the vows (word) and the consummation (body) of their love', falling as they do between 2.5 and 3.5.[22]

Both lovers are subject to the bodily impact of the sonnet, just as their bodies impact on the sonnet. Whittier contends that Shakespeare 'risks moving a symbolic transaction from lyric concept (the sublime androgyne) to dramatic embodiment (the grotesque)'.[23] The solid presence of the actors' bodies is at odds with the fluid sexual identities figuratively produced in Petrarchan verse. This produces the indecorous scene that so embarrassed Victorian actors, where a wailing Romeo flings himself on the floor after learning that he has been banished. Both the Nurse and the Friar are alert to the inappropriateness of this behaviour: 'Stand up, stand up, stand an you be a man' (3.3.88); 'Art thou a man? Thy form cries out thou art. / Thy tears are womanish' (3.3.108–9). Other gender inversions are also more marked because physical bodies are present in the theatre in a way that they are not in poetry. Shakespeare intensifies the effect by having Juliet speak forms associated with male voices, such as soliloquy (a masculine mode in the Shakespeare canon, according to Whittier) and epithalamium (see McCown in Chapter 4 above). Whittier explains: 'The poetic forms that Juliet uses, then, draw attention to her gender, to her body; in lyric poetry, both sexes may fit "to one neutral thing," but drama embodies and temporalizes.'[24] This analysis brilliantly demonstrates the ongoing tensions between the Petrarchan mode of the play and its dramatic form; though a further complication that Whittier does not address is the fact that the theatrical body present on the Renaissance stage would have been the male body of a boy actor. Nevertheless, Juliet's presence works in telling contrast to Rosaline, who appears only as a name and lacks even a physical description.

Juliet's physical presence also disrupts an important Petrarchan trope, the *blason du corps*, whereby the beloved's bodily parts are catalogued. It is through this technique that the Petrarchan lady is usually seen, within the perspective of the male poetic voice which translates body parts into metaphors of flowers and precious materials. Tellingly, the *blason* is never used to describe Juliet, who is an emphatically physical presence, not the Platonic ideal of poetry. Indeed the form is renegotiated during the course of the play. In a typically anti-Petrarchan gesture, Mercutio inverts the usual direction of the *blason* when attempting to taunt Romeo out of hiding:

> ■ I conjure thee by Rosaline's bright eyes,
> By her high forehead and her scarlet lip,
> By her fine foot, straight lip, and quivering thigh,
> And the demesnes that there adjacent lie[.] □
>
> (2.1.18–21)

Where Petrarchan poets restrict themselves to the upper parts of the beloved's body, Mercutio gazes down from her face and then up again from her feet to focus on the place of her sexual organs. The bawdiness of this *blason* works to expose the absence of flesh in the Petrarchan discourse. Similarly, the Nurse provides a literally prosaic *blason* that denies poetic hyperbole: 'Romeo? No, not he, though his face be better than any man's, yet his leg excels all men's, and for a hand and a foot and a body, though they be not to be talked on, yet they are past compare' (2.4.38–41). And Juliet's declaration of the insignificance of names takes the form of a negative *blason*: 'What's Montague? It is nor hand nor foot, / Nor arm nor face, nor any other part / Belonging to a man' (2.1.83–5). Denying names means breaking up the body.

Only a brief moment of harmony between dramatic and poetic forces, body and sonnet, is achieved in the play. Whittier regards the lovers' 'co-created encounter sonnet' as the one place where 'voice and flesh reciprocate'. Here the narrative of falling in love and moving to a first kiss works in tandem with the figures of lyricism. Yet, she points out, 'even here, while seeming to elevate it to a religious mystery, the poetic word actually deals on behalf of the flesh'.[25] The couple work through a metaphor of pilgrimage to a shrine to arrive at a kiss: 'My lips, two blushing pilgrims, ready stand / To smooth that rough touch with a tender kiss' (1.4.208–9). Romeo playfully here asks for more intimate physical contact to purge the sin of touching. The kiss itself both concludes and breaks free from the sonnet. In a fifteenth extra line Romeo says: 'Thus from my lips, by thine, my sin is purged' (1.4.220). The resolution of the sonnet – the kiss – has to be seen, as Romeo's word 'Thus' indicates. It is a moment, Whittier suggests, that 'marks both the silencing of the poetic speaker and the *sonnet's* corruption into the world of substance and time'.[26] As this moment is dissolved, such balance between poetry and flesh also disappears.

The sonnet form takes hold of Juliet's body in her feigned death, as she embodies Petrarchan antithesis in a 'living death'. As Slater pointed out, Romeo's poetic fantasy that the corpse looks alive is literally true: 'Death . . . Hath had no power yet upon thy beauty. / Thou art not conquered; beauty's ensign yet / Is crimson in thy lips and in thy cheeks' (5.3.92–5). It is only in this state that the *blason* approaches Juliet's body, because only now does Romeo perceive her body as finite to Romeo, so he rhetorically breaks it into parts. Fittingly, he also sees his own body in a state of partition: 'Eyes, look your last. / Arms, take your last embrace. And lips . . . seal with a righteous kiss / A dateless bargain to engrossing death' (5.3.112–15). When Juliet wakes she is forced to confront the material fact of a mere body – a corpse. Finally the tensions between poetry and drama bring collapse: 'narrative structures a sonnet's body lacking a spirit, while extreme lyricism ensouls without form'.[27] The play concludes in a different register, in the public discourse of the Prince, whose forensic interests ('clear these ambiguities' [5.3.217]) turn away from the mysteries of the lovers' poetry. He wants their love retold as a narrative (a 'story' [5.3.309]) that has a clear civic reference rather than poetic transcendence.

Whittier's reading illuminates the Petrarchan ethos of the play through a theoretical framework. It exemplifies the interpretative possibilities of synthesizing different critical approaches.

## DIANA E. HENDERSON (1995)

*Romeo and Juliet* drives an introductory discussion to a much larger study of the relationship between Petrarchan discourse and theatre in Diana E. Henderson's book *Passion Made Public: Elizabethan Lyric, Gender and Performance*. Assessing the wider trend of 'lyrical' drama in the Elizabethan period, Henderson addresses what motivations lay behind the use of the private poetic form on the public theatrical stage, and the cultural and aesthetic consequences of the cross-fertilization. She demonstrates that lyric performances stage attitudes to gender. Her revealing study puts Petrarchism in its historical context.

Good and bad Petrarchan practice could be found in Elizabethan literary culture: for some poets, adapting Petrarch's verse forms and conceits enabled them to wrestle with the ontological problems of passion; others simply copied superficial stylistic features. Henderson believes that a lack of understanding about the variegated quality of Elizabethan Petrarchism has produced misinterpretations of *Romeo and Juliet*, with numerous critics using the presence of Petrarchan forms to accuse Shakespeare of creative failure. It is a misconception produced by the difference between early modern and modern taste: where humanist culture celebrated skilful *imitatio*, modern readers and audiences valorise originality and are suspicious of conventionalized expressions of emotion. Henderson's work looks closely at the details of Petrarchan language and broadly at its Elizabethan value.

Henderson gives careful attention to the sonnet shared by Romeo and Juliet at their first meeting. The dramatized poem creates for the lovers a separate linguistic space amidst the noise of the Capulet ball; it is an early example of their withdrawal from the public feud. Calderwood (discussed in Chapter 3 above) criticized this lyrical seclusion, seeing in it alienation from the real world and its meaning. However, Henderson contends that Shakespeare here remakes a Petrarchan opposition. In their interrogation of passion, lyrics often figured a conflict between desire and reason. But Shakespeare puts reason on the side of desire. Romeo and Juliet

■ rebel against the *un*reasonableness of the Veronese feud, a political backdrop of obscurely motivated violence. Here the sonnet form epitomizes Shakespeare's complicated inversion of value, elevating the lovers above Tybalt (who 'storms' to Capulet to bombast out a few lines of blank verse and some unmemorable couplets in anger at Romeo's intrusion) and Capulet (whose comically choppy blank verse dominates the exchange). In contrast, the lovers' interplay of rhymes and Neoplatonic conceits makes them sound, if not exactly serious, all the more gentle, charming, and well-matched.[28] □

This analysis smartly illuminates why an audience is drawn into sympathy with the lovers, and how the play interrogates its Petrarchan paradigm. However, the thesis is not necessarily sustainable across the play as a whole, as the young lovers' pronounced haste rather qualifies any sense of their 'reason'.

More importantly, Henderson identifies the striking innovation in Petrarchan gender roles staged by this sonnet. Petrarchan ladies were typically silent; Juliet joins in, reshaping Romeo's metaphor in order to regulate his behaviour. Romeo, in the religious imagery of a quattrocento Italian sonneteer, audaciously offers to correct the sin of touching Juliet with his hand by kissing her with his lips:

■ If I profane with my unworthiest hand
This holy shrine, the gentle sin is this,
My lips, two blushing pilgrims, ready stand
To smooth that rough touch with a gentle kiss. □

(1.4.206–9)

Juliet reciprocates in the same figurative terms, but playfully and decorously invites Romeo to think more kindly of his hand:

■ Good pilgrim, you do wrong your hand too much,
Which mannerly devotion shows in this,
For saints have hands that pilgrims' hands do touch,
And palm to palm is holy palmers' kiss. □

(1.4.210–13)

Of course the sonnet does produce a kiss, but the careful depiction of Juliet endows her with desire that is not divorced from virtue. Again her difference from the female beloved of courtly love tradition reveals the beginning of a major shift in attitudes to sexual behaviour. In earlier Petrarchan tradition desire was 'extramarital' and 'sublimated'. Juliet demonstrates the possibility of chaste but actualized desire when she subsequently rejects Romeo's poetic assurances of his love, requiring instead the validation of a marriage vow. Much has already been said about the linguistic implications of Juliet's attitude, but Henderson here perceptively reveals its significance for sexual culture. Shakespeare (like his immediate poetic forebears Philip Sidney and Edmund Spenser) is making 'normative a coincidence between female desire and the patriarchal social structure of marriage'.[29] The play participates in a social realignment of marriage, gender and sex.

Intriguingly, Henderson also spots a possible political comment in this romantic marriage plot. Petrarchan discourse was the language of the court of the Virgin Queen, Elizabeth I. In drawing upon this same sonnet tradition, Shakespeare capitalizes on a voguish literary form, but also, Henderson speculates, challenges its values. She points to Romeo's apostrophe to Juliet as the sun:

■ Arise, fair sun, and kill the envious moon,
Who is already sick and pale with grief
That thou, her maid, art far more fair than she.
Be not her maid, since she is envious;
Her vestal livery is but sick and green,
And none but fools do wear it. Cast it off. □

(2.1.47–52)

Courtly, Petrarchan discourse often celebrated Elizabeth as the moon goddess Cynthia. Shakespeare here 'seems to be creating a new goddess, in the likeness of a marriageable fourteen-year-old, to supplant the courtly worship of the aging Elizabeth'. The 'cult of Virginity' associated with Elizabeth's court, which proved to be rather a difficult standard for 'lovesick lords and ladies-in-waiting', is gently mocked, and the young lovers' married opposition to a 'hostile court culture' in Verona has Elizabethan echoes.[30] Overstating this political resonance would diminish the argument, but Henderson makes a valuable point about how the play works within its historical context.

Henderson returns briefly to *Romeo and Juliet* in the final chapter of her book, which surveys lyrical meaning in Shakespeare. Like Whittier she recognizes the *blason* in Romeo's last speeches in the play, when he ironically thinks his apparently dead wife looks alive, and when he addresses his own body during his suicide (5.3.91–6, 112–15; as quoted in the section above). But Henderson's reading of this figure counters 'feminist revisions of Freud's reading of the sadistic gaze', which detect in the descriptive partition of the body a literary dismemberment whereby the male viewer wrests control of the female form. Instead Romeo's *blason* (which after all details both viewed and viewer) brings added anguish to the scene, as the husband dwells on every feature of his loved wife, and the 'physical loss' at the heart of the tragedy is emphasized. Henderson argues that this sympathetic and tragic treatment of lyrical discourse 'redeems the rhetoric mocked in *Love's Labour's Lost*' (where the lords' Petrarchan poses prevent the communication of real love, and ultimately the communion of a happy ending).[31] But she also rejects the idea that the Petrarchan discourse is somehow at odds with the meaning and mode of *Romeo and Juliet*. In Henderson's view 'lyricism provides an essential position in the play's tragic dynamics: here the interplay between lyricism and narrative *creates* the unresolved conflict which constitutes drama'.[32] In this sense lyricism is necessary to dramatic action; it is not an artificial digression that hampers the play's tragic status, or the key to the young lovers' failings, or part of an artistically disjunctive attempt to compress two incompatible media together.

*Passion Made Public* does not provide a lengthy or sustained interpretation of *Romeo and Juliet*. However, in reconceptualizing the nexus between lyric, theatre and gender, it offers new insights into the cultural significance of the play's use of a popular lyric form, while sensitively registering its emotional charge.

In recognizing the ways in which literary discourse filters, or even shapes, emotional experience, these Petrarchan critics raise the possibility that love is culturally conditioned. This question of whether or not love is essential to all human beings across time, or is instead socially specific, is central to the psychoanalytical scholarship we consider in the next chapter.

CHAPTER SEVEN

# Death-Marked Love: Psychoanalytical Criticism

Where the critics featured in the previous chapter explored love as a literary effect, the commentators in Chapter 7 look at literature as a trace of psychological drives. Underpinning these interpretations is an interest in the unconscious impulses motivating Shakespeare and his characters. This branch of criticism thus pushes beyond the surface level of the text to reveal deeper structures. The combination of passionate love and a tragic end proves especially interesting in psychoanalytical approaches, because it bears the hallmarks of the 'death-drive', a deep-seated and supposedly universal human ambivalence in which the will to love is (paradoxically) collapsed into an urge for self-destruction. However, psychoanalytical criticism, like other modes of interpretation, changes over time, and by the end of the twentieth century, this approach is put in unexpected (and fruitful) conversation with seemingly incompatible historicist methods. In the twenty-first century, psychoanalytical theory underpins an 'aesthetic' reading of the play that separates love and death once more.

## NORMAN RABKIN (1967)

Norman Rabkin's book *Shakespeare and the Common Understanding* is guided by a psychoanalytical approach, though as mid-twentieth-century criticism it remains rooted in the principles of close textual analysis. Thus the section on *Romeo and Juliet* returns us to the ideas of Shakespeare's self-conscious interrogation of literary style (as raised by critics discussed in Chapter 5 above) and the role of Petrarchan discourse (see Chapter 6 above).

Rabkin provides a psychoanalytical reading of love: 'Shakespeare tells us that love, the most intense manifestation of the urge to life, is ineluctably linked with the self-destructive yearning for annihilation that we recognize as the death wish.'[1] In this perspective the human condition is constant across time; Shakespeare's lesson about love is as true in the sixteenth century as in the twentieth century. Rabkin's starting point is thus very different from, for example, Kiernan Ryan's (see Chapter 5 above), who argues that the point of the tragedy is its historical specificity. Building on the work of Denis de Rougemont, especially *Love in the Western World* (1939; revd edn, 1972), Rabkin sees Shakespeare as writing about one of the great themes of Western art: 'the double vision of eros [i.e. love] as the impulse to both life and death'.[2] Love is a death wish. The cultural importance of this subject matter marks out *Romeo and Juliet* as significant. Indeed Rabkin carefully defends the drama against criticism that dismisses it as immature, arguing that it suffers only by comparison with later Shakespearean plays. While accepting that it is wrongheaded to insist that Shakespeare was a flawless writer, he maintains that it is as problematic to assume that work 'we have not yet come to understand' is 'juvenile or not fully achieved'.[3]

Having identified tragic structure (the catastrophe depends on mistakes; the protagonists' adolescent failings lack the appropriate scale) and patchy style as key critical complaints against the play, Rabkin offers standard commentary that rehabilitates the varying literary quality of the dialogue as dramatically effective. Written at around the same time as the stylistically experimental *Richard II, A Midsummer Night's Dream* and *Love's Labour's Lost, Romeo and Juliet* is once again found to be self-consciously playing with modes of expression, to make the audience aware of the problem of style. Thus when the Capulet household strain their rhetorical capabilities to express their grief at Juliet's apparent death in 4.4, the situation helps to expose these wordy exercises as a form of detachment: they lament for nothing. Both Capulet and Paris allude to lines from Thomas Kyd's popular revenge play *The Spanish Tragedy*. Paris's 'O love, O life, not life, but love in death!' (4.4.84) recalls Hieronimo's 'O life! no life, but lively form of death'; and Capulet's 'O child, O child, my soul and not my child!' also echoes Hieronimo's grief. In parodying Kyd's straight-faced dialogue in a scene ironically undermined by the inappropriate nature of the laments, Shakespeare seems to be criticizing the older style. There is also a deliberate contrast, Rabkin suggests, in Romeo's reaction to Balthazar's report of Juliet's death, since rather than elaborate on his grief, Romeo simply speaks of action: 'Well, Juliet, I will lie with thee tonight' (5.1.34). Indeed, at various points the dialogue explicitly criticizes excessive verbal trickery. Friar Laurence cautions Romeo: 'Be plain, good son, and homely in thy drift; / Riddling confession finds but riddling shrift' (2.2.55–6). Similarly, Juliet stops Romeo from reciting a blazon:

■ Conceit, more rich in matter than in words,
Brags of his substance, not of ornament.

They are but beggars that can count their worth;
But my true love is grown to such excess,
I cannot sum up sum of half my wealth. □

(2.5.30–4)

This analysis usefully flags up issues dealt with more fully in other scholarship. But what is most interesting about Rabkin's piece is the way in which he translates this linguistic analysis into a psychoanalytical reading.

Like other scholars, Rabkin states that Romeo's language matures as the play progresses, but for him the maturation takes the form of a movement away from speech for its own rhetorical sake to speech as an expression of emotion. What connects the two distinguishable styles is the place of paradox. As we have seen, oxymora litter the dialogue of the early parts of the play, but the later poetry is also: 'founded on paradox. The paradoxes are not of the lovers' seeking, but tragically built into the experience to which they surrender themselves. Oxymoron is not simply a rhetorical device; it is a definition of their lives.'[4] This analysis is similar to criticism of the play's Petrarchism that saw clichéd paradoxes of poetry being actualized. But Rabkin's emphasis is different. Where Slater saw Shakespeare validating the meaning of Petrarchan contrasts, in Rabkin's argument, verbal forms are superseded by a deeper awareness of paradox inherent in experience itself. At this point his interpretation takes a psychoanalytical turn:

■ Love between the children of enemies is paradoxical; even more so is a love that finds its marriage only in death. Such paradox emerges not from the inventive mind of a sonnet-fed young man, turned in upon himself and delighting in the ambiguities of emotions simultaneously bitter and sweet, but from the actual confrontation of a reality that destroys in creating.[5] □

The death-drive is thus the central paradox of the play. It even illuminates the dramaturgical function of Mercutio. In the first half of the play Mercutio opposes Romeo's sterile courtly love for Rosaline with an earthy sexuality, a counterpoint that is no longer necessary once Romeo marries Juliet. Furthermore, Romeo comes to a deeper understanding than Mercutio in learning that the full satisfaction of his love will not be achieved in the energetic life embodied by his friend, but rather in death. Even as Shakespeare dismisses the rhetorical forms of Petrarchan paradoxes, he 'affirm[s] the existential antinomies from which Petrarch drew his true power'.[6]

Believing Shakespeare fastens on to an essential truth about the psychology of love, Rabkin hails Romeo and Juliet as heroes in their emotional perceptiveness. Their disregarding of adult warnings to go

'Wisely and slow' because 'they stumble that run fast' (2.2.94) reveals their 'wiser' understanding of desire.[7] Tragedy is the only appropriate conclusion for desire on the scale they experience it:

> ■ Only annihilation can do full justice to such longings as Romeo and Juliet share. Theirs is not a love of propagation and domestic contentment, but rather a yearning for a transformation of the world that will correspond to their inner state. Anything but death would be a betrayal of that love.
>
> Thus we feel at the end of *Romeo and Juliet* as we do at the end of every Shakespearean tragedy: We have watched not the process of nemesis, or of fortune, or of retribution, but rather the playing out of an awesome dialectic in which what is worth prizing in the hero is set complementarily against the wisdom that the world for good reason advises. The play's expressed judgment is against impetuosity and irrationality as destructive, but the valuation it implies is a judgment in favour of precisely these qualities as the foundation and essence of a transcendent love.[8] □

Overly effusive as Rabkin's endorsement of teenage suicide may be (anything else would be a 'betrayal'), this analysis captures a tension in audience response to the play: despite having been *told* that disaster follows rash passion, there is something perversely uplifting about the play's destructive end. Pulling back a little from his celebration of the lovers, Rabkin astutely observes that paradox precludes easy judgements and moralization. However, his reading requires us to accept the universal validity of a death-drive that even more cautionary audience members can thrill to, if not accept. It is certainly a compelling suggestion that goes some way to explaining the contradictory effects of the tragedy. As an early psychoanalytical account of the play, however, Rabkin's reading does little to distinguish the two lovers. Later commentary will redress this balance.

## JULIA KRISTEVA (1983)

Feminist psychoanalyst Julia Kristeva provides a longer account of the ambivalence in *Romeo and Juliet,* and makes the paradox of 'love-hatred (*amour-haine*) central. Like Rabkin, Kristeva accepts Denis de Rougemont's thesis in *Love in the Western World* of romantic love as a transgression (usually adultery). Though not adulterous, the love of Romeo and Juliet is 'outlaw love': it is opposed to the code of the Capulet–Montague feud specifically, but it also, in its clandestine nature, resists the patriarchal, symbolic order.[9] The tragic 'affirmation' of the play is that the drive for a sexual union and the attempt to legalize that passion are unsustainable and can produce 'only ephemeral happiness'.[10] Crucial to the attraction Romeo and Juliet feel for each other is their awareness of 'being within a hairsbreadth of punishment'. Kristeva elaborates:

> ■ The shadow of a third party – relatives, father, husband or wife in the case of adultery – is doubtless more present to the mind during carnal excitement than the innocent seekers of happiness together are willing to admit. Take away the third party and the whole construct often crumbles, lacking a cause for desire, after having lost some of its passional tinge.[11] □

The excitement of transgression energizes Romeo's love for Juliet, as it did his love for the Capulet Rosaline. Similarly, Juliet is wrong to describe Romeo's name as irrelevant to her love; 'quite the contrary, it determines it'.[12] There is much that is persuasive in this reading of a passion stoked by the thrill of prohibition, though Kristeva overlooks the namelessness of the 'love-at-first-sight' moment, where Romeo and Juliet exchange lyrical small-talk and even kiss. However, the larger point is that while the play might be uniquely eloquent in demonstrating the beautiful poignancy of such love, the love itself is not unique and certainly not perverse. Kristeva maintains that we are all 'constantly driven to seek the animal sources of a passion that deifies the Name to the advantage of loss of self in the flood of pleasure'.[13] Indeed, the reading is underpinned by a supreme confidence in the universality of the psychoanalytical diagnosis: 'young people throughout the entire world, whatever their race, religion, or social status, identify with the adolescents of Verona who mistook love for death'.[14] Such a grand claim cannot be substantiated, since it is not clear that love is conceptualized in the same way in different cultures and historical periods.

Responding to the imagery of the text, Kristeva identifies a 'solar love' that is idealizing and which reaches beyond time: 'It is the east, and Juliet is the sun. / Arise, fair sun, and kill the envious moon' (2.1.46–7). But trapped in time (and ambivalence) the love also 'takes refuge in blindness, in darkness':

> ■ or, if love be blind,
> It best agrees with night. Come, civil night,
> Thou sober-suited matron all in black...
> Come gentle night, come loving black-browed night,
> Give me my Romeo; and when I shall die,
> Take him and cut him out in little stars,
> And he will make the face of heaven so fine,
> That all the world will be in love with night,
> And pay no worship to the garish sun. □
>
> (3.2.9–25)[15]

These words reveal, according to Kristeva, Juliet's unconscious desire to break Romeo's body apart, an impulse produced by the hate within love. However, there is also something specifically female about the urge:

> ■ feminine desire is perhaps more closely umbilicated with death; it may be that the matrical source of life knows how much it is in her power to destroy life (see Lady Macbeth), and moreover it is through the symbolic murder of her own mother that a woman turns herself into a mother.[16] □

It is these subconscious conflicts that account for the tragedy itself far better, Kristeva suggests, than the external pressures usually cited: 'Whose fault is it? The parents? Feudal society? The Church, for it is true that Friar Laurence departs in shame? Or love itself, two-faced, sun and night, delightful, tragic tenseness between two sexes?'[17] In its ambivalent force, love (love-hatred) is unstable and cannot last. The tragedy demonstrates this in its truncated timescale and the early death of its protagonists. Indeed, no alternative ending could be 'happy' in the romantic terms established by the play. Kristeva contends that if the couple had somehow survived, their relationship would have developed in one of two ways:

> ■ Either time's alchemy transforms the criminal, secret passion of the outlaw lovers into the banal, humdrum, lacklustre lassitude of a tired and cynical collusion: that is the normal marriage. Or else the married couple continues to be a passionate couple, but covering the entire gamut of sadomasochism that the two partners already heralded in the yet relatively quiet version of the Shakespearean text. □

Ending as it does, *Romeo and Juliet* preserves a fantasy of a 'pure couple' whose innocence remains intact.[18] Audiences swoon with pity that death destroys the promise of the young love, but actually it is the tragedy that preserves it.

*Romeo and Juliet* is also an expression of its author's psyche, and Kristeva claims that Shakespeare had special reason to protect this ideal fantasy of love. She rightly dates the play as belonging to the 'second period' of his career, and not as an immature work. More contentiously, she links its conception to the death of Shakespeare's son Hamnet in 1596. Shakespeare had left his wife Anne Hathaway in Stratford to live in London 11 years earlier when Hamnet and his twin sister were born. Kristeva hypothesizes that the death of Hamnet awakened in Shakespeare nostalgia ('*nostos*-return'; '*algos*-pain') for past married love: 'Let us then think of *Romeo and Juliet*, in its idyllic tinge, as a dirge for the son's death. The father's guilt confesses in this play, along with hatred for marriage, the desire to preserve the myth of the enamoured lovers.'[19] The ambivalence of the love-hatred is in part a manifestation of Shakespeare's own feeling, provoked by a recent trauma. The play compensates for Shakespeare's guilt at marriage breakdown by creating a fantasy of a marriage where love remains eternally pure (but only through death). Kristeva similarly links the genesis of *Hamlet* with the death of Shakespeare's father and the publication of the *Sonnets* with the death of his mother. Readers will be divided on the extent to which such biographical analysis is feasible or valuable.

Kristeva's thesis of love-hatred originates in Freud's claim that hatred precedes love in human development: 'In the object relation, the relation with an other, hatred, as Freud said, is more ancient than love. As soon as an *other* appears different from myself, it becomes alien, repelled, repugnant, abject – hated.'[20] Hatred is intrinsic in our relations with others, and is therefore intrinsic even in love (compare Derrida's point that love is necessarily directed to an other; see Chapter 5 above). Romantic love is a refiguration of the child's relation with his/her mother: 'The man then finds a harbour of narcissistic satisfaction for the eternal child he has succeeded in remaining: an exquisite normalisation of regression. The woman calms down temporarily within the restoring support furnished by the mother-husband.'[21] Love returns the lover to a 'mother' figure. Even as the lovers encounter the other they do so as a way of returning, like a child, to a fantasy of wholeness, of being connected with the mother.

This analysis of hate inhering in love and of love of the other functioning as self-love can seem counter-intuitive to those not versed in psychoanalytical theory. But Kristeva's provocative account invites us to look beneath the text to a subconscious level. Perhaps the biggest challenge (and potential pitfall) of this methodology is the claim to the universality of the drives observed: we are asked to accept that this is how love works, in sixteenth-century England and in any culture now. However, Lloyd Davis offers an alternative means of addressing psychological impulses while attending to the shaping influence of historical situation.

## LLOYD DAVIS (1996)

Lloyd Davis's account of '"Death-Marked Love": Desire and Presence in *Romeo and Juliet*' is inflected by a psychoanalytical understanding of the structures of romantic love. Yet his article also challenges some of the larger assumptions of that methodology by synthesizing it with historical detail and a cultural-materialist approach. His argument is thus less problematically assertive than some of the other critics considered in this chapter. Rather than assume that *Romeo and Juliet* constitutes a model of desire applicable to all ages and cultures, he explores why that status might have been conferred on the play by looking at its situation in a transitional moment in sexual history.

Having announced the protagonists' fatal end in the Prologue, *Romeo and Juliet* is structured in a way that directs the audience to question 'less what happens than how it happens'.[22] How does desire produce tragedy? Drawing on the theories of Freud, Lacan and their followers, Davis explains that desire is constantly in negotiation with presence: predicated on a lack, desire seeks the fulfilment that would end it. But the nature and meaning of desire is not settled in *Romeo and Juliet*. The play 'stages a paradigmatic conflict between ways of representing and interpreting desire'.[23] It thus participates in its cultural moment and helps to shape it. Indeed, time is significant in a number of ways. Within the plotted action a more immediate sense of time (the breathless speed of the action and the agonizing mistimings) both enables desire and threatens it. In addition the drama puts tropes from various earlier discourses of desire – 'Platonic, Ovidian, Petrarchan, as well as popular sayings' – into play.[24] But these scripts are questioned by Romeo and Juliet, who repeatedly dismiss the words of others: 'Yet tell me not, for I have heard it all' (1.1.170); 'Thou talk'st of nothing' (1.4.94); 'And stint thou too, I pray thee, Nurse, say I' (1.3.60). They then come to doubt the adequacy of such discourse to speak to their experience: 'Thou canst not speak of that thou dost not feel' (3.3.64); 'Some say the lark makes sweet division; / This doth not so, for she divideth us' (3.5.29–30). The lovers' own words take on an alternative value: 'She speaks. / O speak again, bright angel' (2.1.68–9); 'every tongue that speaks / But Romeo's name speaks heavenly eloquence' (3.2.32–3). In this way the drama explores and questions discursive conventions while also formulating new expressions of desire. This is what makes it momentous (both of its historical moment and enduringly significant in sexual discourse): 'The play's pivotal role in later depictions of desire stems from the way it juxtaposes historical and emergent conceptions.'[25]

Critical and cultural tendencies to 'universalize' the tragedy ignore the ideological factors that shape the drama and later human crises to which it supposedly relates. For example, Davis quotes an Australian director of the play likening its prejudices to that of the Christian–Muslim conflict in Bosnia and (multiplying the easy equivalence) to the tensions experienced by teenagers in a Brisbane Mall. Ironically, turning the play into a template for understanding various historical problems actually glosses over historical meaning. The tragic significance of the play, of genocide in the Balkans and of racism in Australia, becomes a misleadingly easy point about 'the human spirit'. Davis cites cultural materialist arguments to show that the 'sexual, class and ethnic factors' that produce such tragedy and different human experience are elided in these universalizing readings.[26] He recognizes that romantic love operates like ideology when figured as a universal truth (here Davis references Callaghan, Porter and Goldberg, all of whose work will be discussed in the next chapter). Hailing the relationship between Romeo and Juliet as a timeless ideal naturalizes one brand of heterosexuality. As is always the case, this ideological power is effective in its invisibility.

But Davis argues that as a tragedy *Romeo and Juliet* does not simply shore up this sexual ideology: it also questions it. Desire, while not a typical theme of staged tragedy at this point in literary history, is appropriate to it because of the focus it puts on selfhood (tragedy, after all, is the story of individuals). Different amatory discourses conceptualize the self differently. Ovid's *Metamorphoses* (a hugely influential classical text that was translated into English in 1567 by Arthur Golding) depicts the destructive pressure desire puts on the self: for example, Jove repeatedly transforms himself into animals when trying to fulfil his passions and Narcissus destroys himself in his impossible attempt to satisfy his desire. On the other hand, Platonism saw 'love as desire for what one lacks, either a specific quality or a lost or missing element of the self'.[27] In this view desire is a part of and a longing for the true self. *Romeo and Juliet* draws on these alternative ideas but also interrogates them:

> ■ the play proceeds by exploring the limits of the Platonic, Ovidian and Petrarchan tropes. The seriousness of narcissistic absorption is questioned (underlined by Mercutio's quips at romantic indulgence); yet the full consequence of desire is not realised in Platonic union but deferred to its aftermath. None of the conventional models can quite convey what is at stake in the lovers' story, and the discourse of desire must be revised.[28] □

Validating none of the earlier discourses of love (and related conceptions of selfhood) which it stages, *Romeo and Juliet* has its protagonists attempt to develop a new one. The lovers intensify the personalized idea of love, whereby they are bound together and separate from the world and their old selves. However, society continues to circumscribe their story, creating a tragic disjunction. This means that the ideal selves Romeo and Juliet create to experience their desire contribute to their destruction: 'Self-transcendence can be experienced but not as a kind of timeless ecstasy; instead it becomes entwined with unfulfilled desire.'[29]

But even if this desire finally proves fatal for the self, it also helps to constitute it. The illicit nature of the Capulet–Montague love sees both Romeo and Juliet striking out from their familial identities to 'selfhood'. Furthermore, the secret nature of this transgression of patriarchal authority gives the individuals an inward depth and sense of purpose. This interiority is evident when Juliet equivocates with her mother:

> ■ O, how my heart abhors
> To hear him named, and cannot come to him
> To wreak the love I bore my cousin
> Upon his body that hath slaughtered him. □
>
> (3.5.99–102)

Desire gives Juliet a private meaning and personal depth. It also develops 'intentionality': 'desire *for* someone, effected through imagination, speech and action. Desire marks the self as agent, and tragic desire portrays the onus of agency'.[30] Juliet and Romeo both realize this at key moments in their tragedy: 'My dismal scene I needs must act alone' (4.3.19); 'I come hither armed against myself' (5.3.65). Desire is therefore a way of making identity. Note that this argument differs significantly from early criticisms of the play's tragedy that regarded Romeo and Juliet as passive victims of misfortune. Davis's analysis sees the play participating in ideas of subjectivity that emerge (in his view) in the sixteenth century, whereby the self is defined by its interiority and agency. Ironically, as inheritors of this understanding of selfhood, twentieth-century critics demand three-dimensional characters whose actions shape their destiny; since this concept of selfhood is only just appearing in *Romeo and Juliet,* critics cannot find it there. (Indeed, part of the point of the tragedy is that these selves are constantly at risk of being swallowed up by the social forms that surround them.) However, if the play shows desire as fostering selfhood, it also pushes past the individual to 'an intersubjective union'.[31] In their love for one another Romeo and Juliet redefine each *other*: 'Romeo, doff thy name, / And for thy name, which is no part of thee, / Take all myself' (2.1.90–2). And their language expresses a deep sense of reciprocity. For example, they use Petrarchan discourse only to rewrite it significantly, turning the male monologue into a male–female dialogue (as in the shared sonnet of their first meeting [1.4.206–19]).

As idealistic as such desirous subjectivity may be, the play constantly qualifies its romantic vision with a more sceptical one. For one thing, the dialogue naturalizes a connection between sex and violence. Thus the Montague servant puns on rape and murder: 'I will be civil with the maids, I will cut off their heads' (1.1.21–2); Friar Laurence likens birth and death: 'The earth that's nature's mother is her tomb; / What is her burying grave, that is her womb' (2.2.9–10); and Romeo calls the Capulet tomb a 'womb of death' (5.3.45). In regarding these links as naturalized rather than natural, Davis departs from a psychoanalytical view of the death-drive as universal, and instead sees it as an ideological condition of a particular (tragic) society. The play's perspective on desire is ambivalent: both a romantic ideal and self-destructive tragedy. Both of these views inhere in the fatal ending.

Davis's stimulating article skilfully adapts psychoanalytical themes to a historicist understanding of the way the concept and representation of desire changes over time. Shakespeare does not create an entirely new or uniquely authentic expression of desire in the play, but rather writes with and against the discourses of his age. The lasting impact of the play on amatory language is 'a notion of desire as lost presence', which is found in later Shakespearean plays such as *Hamlet, Othello, Macbeth* and *Antony and Cleopatra* and continues into novels of the nineteenth and twentieth centuries, such as the work of Charles Dickens, Henry James and F. Scott Fitzgerald. Just as its protagonists are firmly emplotted in a temporal world, *Romeo and Juliet* is a timely text.

## HUGH GRADY (2009)

The final chapter of Hugh Grady's book, *Shakespeare and Impure Aesthetics*, focuses on *Romeo and Juliet*. Like Davis, Grady puts psychoanalysis in conversation with other theories. Indeed, as its title suggests, the book is more properly 'aesthetic' (concerned with art) than psychoanalytical. However, since he draws on psychoanalytical thought and explicitly addresses (and rejects) the *Liebestod* concept that is so attractive to other critics discussed in this chapter, Grady's argument is considered alongside them. Where psychoanalytical critics (especially Kristeva) see *Romeo and Juliet* as exposing death as the 'true goal' of desire, Grady claims that the larger impact of the play actually enforces the opposition between the two.[32]

The argument synthesizes various theories and critical approaches. Building on Susan Snyder's work (see Chapter 4 above), Grady identifies a movement from comedy to tragedy in the drama. But drawing on the theories of the historian Philippe Ariès, he detects in this generic pattern a larger cultural shift in attitudes to death:

> ■ We move from a 'comic', 'pre-modern' world of harmony between the social and the natural, into a 'tragic' . . . , 'modern', and dissociated one. As Ariès suggests, the meaning of sex and death changes as we move from one era to the other, and *Romeo and Juliet* displays this change as a shift in genre halfway through its plot. The harmony between sex and death described by Friar Laurence [2.2.9–10] becomes the rupture in the social fabric brought about first by Romeo and Juliet's transgressive, mutual passion, and then by the deaths Romeo becomes involved in.[33] □

After the medieval period a new and dangerous association between love and death was felt; *Romeo and Juliet* tracks this change. However, Grady maintains that this pattern is not the whole story. By emphasizing instead the aesthetic status and function of death in the play, he accounts for the way audiences tend not to view the narrative as a wrong-headed adolescent death-drive.

Nevertheless, Grady does not reject psychoanalysis outright, but instead values theories that explain aesthetic motivation psychoanalytically. He cites Hanna Segal's account of art as a productive reaction to loss: 'a desire for restoration and re-creation'.[34] Indeed, it is partly this deeper drive within the aesthetic that helps him to reject readings of *Romeo and Juliet* as a *Liebestod* myth. The play is a work of art that strives to compensate for death, rather than embrace its annihilation. While there are moments where the lovers seem to conflate erotic desire with desire for death, the larger drama militates against this connection. In the first place, the comedic content of the opening acts stress possibility rather than inevitable destruction. Furthermore, the play's emphatically social setting ('Two households', 'fair Verona' [Prologue, 1–2]) proves not only the cause of its fatal denouement, but also provides the final sense of hope. Grady agrees with feminist critics (discussed in the next chapter) who regard Verona as violently patriarchal. The mutuality and equality of the love between Romeo and Juliet is therefore 'utopian': 'socially counter-factual but fueled by desire in a relationship of negation to the real and offering an implicit critique of the real'.[35] Their love thus rebels against the values of Veronese society. However, this same passion also offers a possible cure for social ills, as Friar Laurence recognizes: 'For this alliance may so happy prove, / To turn your households' rancour to pure love' (2.2.91–2). Since Capulet and Montague are finally reconciled, the healing potential of the lovers' desire seems to outweigh hints of a 'death-drive'.

Indeed, Grady hears in some of the play's more famous lines 'one of the key components of the aesthetic, an idealizing vision of what might be, and perhaps once was: a harmonization of the natural and the social worlds, an interpenetration and mutual influence'.[36] This 'interpenetration' is witnessed when Romeo declares, 'It is the east, and Juliet is the sun' (2.1.46), and Juliet worries that their love is 'Too like the lightning which doth cease to be / Ere one can say "It lightens" ' (2.1.162–3), then later invokes Romeo as 'day in night' and fantasizes cutting him 'out in little stars' (3.2.17, 22). With this last example Grady specifically opposes Kristeva's analysis of 'love-hatred' and instead finds art (i.e. the play) positively uniting nature and humanity. He also demonstrates that death, even in the second half of the play, is not figured in the exclusively erotic terms implied by Kristeva and others: Juliet is horrified by its putrescence when she imagines being enclosed in the tomb with the 'loathsome smells' (4.3.45) and 'fest'ring' corpse of Tybalt (4.3.42). Indeed, she is brought to this pass precisely because she hyperbolically promises the Friar she is prepared to be 'O'ercovered quite with dead men's rattling bones' (4.1.82) in order to preserve her married chastity; death is the rhetorical opposite of the love she wants to protect.

Grady clarifies that the generic movement in the play is not so much comedy to tragedy, but rather comedy to *Trauerspiel*. This German term, which broadly means 'mourning play', is adapted from the philosophical work of Walter Benjamin. Like a number of the early twentieth-century genre critics such as Bradley and Charlton, Grady notes that *Romeo and Juliet* does not behave like 'an Aristotelian tragedy' since 'chance and accident' are implicated in the final catastrophes rather than a clear-cut *hamartia*, or error.[37] For Grady, far from weakening it, these divergences from 'tragedy' help make the drama aesthetically 'perfect' (and expose the inappropriateness of the *Liebestod* model, which is predicated on inevitability).[38] Nevertheless, he invokes the alternative label *Trauerspiel* only to show that *Romeo and Juliet* finally evades this designation too. Where a *Trauerspiel* proper (such as *Hamlet*) arrives at total loss, even of meaning, *Romeo and Juliet* offers comfort. Romeo's dream of revivification (5.1.6–9) and Juliet's feigned death flirt with the possibility that the play could end differently, and the fatal conclusion produces social harmony. The audience is left with two self-consciously aesthetic conceptions of the lovers: the promised golden statues and the 'story' (5.3.309) of the play itself. In this work of art the dead couple become

> ■ emblems of highly valued accomplishments: the intensity of their love survives their death for us, and that is the source of the sense of an offsetting satisfaction in the midst of the vicarious mourning we undertake for these two saints of love. If all art is a mourning, it is also a consolation within mourning, a way to carry with us the possibilities that reality has expressed but not really killed.[39] □

Grady's twenty-first-century analysis of the play thus insists on a positive final impact. Many feminist critics, to whom we turn in the next chapter, are rather less consoled.

## CHAPTER EIGHT

# Juliet and Her Romeo: Feminism, Gender Studies and Queer Theory

As one of only three women in the Shakespeare dramatic canon to be named in the title of her play, Juliet has usefully inspired a range of insightful feminist readings. Following in the footsteps of researchers such as Charlotte Lennox and proto-feminists like Anna Jameson, critics of the twentieth and twenty-first centuries pay particular attention to the innovations of Juliet's tragic status. However, earlier (relatively straightforward) attempts to proclaim the critical interest of female characters are replaced by more complex questions about the nature of sexual identities and the historical specificity of gender roles. The diversification of feminist criticism means that such questions are approached from different methodological perspectives. Related but significantly different concerns motivate Queer Theorists, who expose some of the hetero-normative assumptions of criticism that eulogize the play's supposed celebration of an ideal romantic love. By the end of the twentieth century gender studies recognize masculinity as a gendered category, so that Romeo becomes as ideologically interesting as Juliet. In the 1970s, Coppélia Kahn puts such questions in a broadly psychoanalytical framework.

### COPPÉLIA KAHN (1977–78)

Like many of the critics considered in the previous chapter, Coppélia Kahn is interested in the child–parent relationship in the play; specifically, in how Romeo and Juliet grow up and separate themselves from their parents. However, Kahn's perspective is feminist and she views the dynamic of the play as being underpinned by a patriarchal structure. It is this patriarchal 'milieu' which connects Verona with its English audience, even though the world of the play presents it on a tragic scale. Veronese patriarchy operates through the feud. The Prologue defines the conflict as 'their parents' strife' and 'their parents' rage' (Prologue 8, 10); it is an opposition, according to Kahn, fostered and perpetuated by the older generation. Placing it at the centre of her argument, Kahn treats the feud as more consistently serious and meaningful to the tragedy than many of the other critics we have encountered earlier in this Guide. For example, H. B. Charlton (see Chapter 4 above) found the feud to be a 'dead letter' – an element of the play that should have produced tragic inevitability but which failed to do so; Susan Snyder (see Chapter 4 above) regarded it as a comic obstacle that looks set to be overcome until the death of Mercutio turns it tragic. Kahn does not respond to the details which prompt these less credulous reactions to the feud. There is nothing in this analysis about the risibility of the two old men trying to join in a street fight as their wives drily remark on their unfitness for the brawl: 'A crutch, a crutch – why call you for a sword?' (1.1.72). Nor is Capulet's willingness to tolerate Romeo at his family party acknowledged.

However, while Kahn elides the tonal complexity of the feud, her analysis does provide insight into the way in which it 'constitutes socialization into patriarchal roles' for Verona's sons and daughters.[1] She points out that the feud emphasizes familial identities, even to the extent of determining the social relationships young Capulets and Montagues can enter into. Furthermore, for the sons, the feud provides an adolescent space where they can 'prove themselves men by phallic violence on behalf of their fathers, instead of by the courtship and sexual experimentation that would lead towards marriage and separation from the paternal house'.[2] The feud thus sustains an intensified version of patriarchy that keeps sons in a tightly endogamous relationship with their fathers, even as they grow up. The discourse of the feud structures the whole society of Verona, from the heads of household down to the servants (who were considered part of the 'family' network in Elizabethan England). Even Mercutio – neither a Capulet nor a Montague – participates in it. So pervasive and effective is this violent discourse that no other language signifies. Romeo deploys wordplay in an attempt to pacify Tybalt: 'And so, good Capulet, which name I tender / As dearly as mine own, be satisfied' (3.1.70–1). The words *tender, dearly* and *satisfied* invite Tybalt to see himself as valued, even cherished, and as having been paid a debt. These puns do not work, whereas Mercutio's puns on Tybalt's name ('rat-catcher' [3.1.74]) successfully stoke rage. It is the feud which produces social meaning in Verona.

Even love in this feuding society is merely another form of aggression. Mercutio instructs Romeo: 'If love be rough with you, be rough with love; / Prick love for pricking, and you beat love down' (1.4.25–6). In other words, subjugate love (and by extension, the beloved) before it (and she) subjugates you. However, in loving Juliet, Romeo rebels against this (particularly violent) patriarchal order, as he re-identifies himself through his relationship with this Capulet woman rather than his Montague father. This resistance is, Kahn argues, central to the dynamic of the play: 'the conflict between manhood as aggression on behalf of the father, and manhood as loving a woman, is at the bottom of the tragedy, and not to be overcome'.[3] Kahn's feminist reading views gender structures as constitutive of the tragedy.

Juliet's female experience is very different from Romeo's male one: 'Unlike its sons, Verona's daughters have, in effect, no adolescence, no sanctioned period of experiment with adult identities or activities.'[4] Juliet is expected to switch straight from being a child (still looked after by her nurse) to being a married woman. While Romeo roams the street with his friends and never shares the stage with his parents, Juliet is kept within Capulet spaces (apart from brief religious excursions Kahn does not note). Her primary role as a Capulet daughter is to secure a patriarchal future. Capulet reveals: 'Earth hath swallowed all my hopes but she; / She's the hopeful lady of my earth' (1.2.14–15). The polyglot pun on *fille de terre* ('heiress'; literally 'daughter of earth') indicates that Capulet looks to Juliet to provide him with future heirs. His patriarchal authority over his daughter is shown to be despotic as he capriciously changes his mind about the speed with which Juliet should be married off, and as he violently threatens his daughter with disinheritance when she proves unwilling. Kahn draws a telling parallel between Capulet and Tybalt, as both men react with sudden violence to potential threats to their sense of order; the nephew shares the standards upheld by his uncle.

Both protagonists seek escape from Verona's aggression through surrogate parents, with Romeo turning to Friar Laurence and Juliet to the Nurse. However, these relationships again adumbrate different male and female experience. Romeo finds a figure who is 'outside that system' and who will plot to free the pair from their feuding families; Juliet's surrogate mother is taken from within the Capulet household and will ultimately fail to help her in her married identity.[5] Nevertheless, like Romeo, Juliet rejects her prescribed role as Capulet daughter, not only by her exogamous love of a Montague, but also in exercising choice and expressing desire.

But these rebellions cannot survive. At the end of the play the opposition between 'Eros and Thanatos' (love and death), which 'seems to drive the plot along', collapses.[6] Kahn here separates out impulses which other critics (especially those discussed in Chapter 7) understand as working in tandem, only to recognize their ultimate integration. This is manifest even at a situational level as the sex–death connection is realized in 'The blood-spattered entrance to this tomb that has been figured as a womb [which] recalls both a defloration or initiation into sexuality and a birth'. The effect is profoundly ambivalent as 'Imagery and action combine to assert that death is a transcendent form of sexual consummation, and further, that it is rebirth into a higher stage of existence – the counterpart of an adulthood never fully achieved in life.'[7] Kahn adds to this commentary on the tragedy's paradoxical catharsis a final gender reversal and rejection on the part of the lovers of the patriarchal roles scripted for them. She points out that where tradition dictates that the female moves to the male household, Romeo takes his final rest in the Capulet rather than the Montague tomb. Furthermore, he drinks poison while Juliet uses the phallic dagger against herself. As elsewhere in the article, Kahn's analysis reveals both the structural significance of gender roles and Shakespeare's bold rejection of them. At times the argument oversimplifies some of the details of the play, but it does essential work in illuminating the tragedy's socially innovative nature.

## MARIANNE NOVY (1984)

Marianne Novy continues the feminist interpretation of *Romeo and Juliet* as a gender tragedy in her book *Love's Argument: Gender Relations in Shakespeare*. This work recognizes that the impact of gender differs according to genre, with distinctions between male and female characters operating with greater rigidity in tragedy than in comedy. However, *Romeo and Juliet*, like the other double-faced tragedies *Troilus and Cressida* and *Antony and Cleopatra*, has comic features that create a gendered structure distinct from tragedies such as *Hamlet*, *King Lear*, *Macbeth* and *Othello*. In *Romeo and Juliet* the male and female characters act as each other's audience; Romeo never once displays the distrust for Juliet that is shown towards women by his tragic counterparts in the canon; and Juliet, unlike other tragic women, remains adept at playing a role (the 'obedient daughter') in a (failed) attempt to protect Romeo. Such features suggest that gender roles are more flexible in the love tragedy; however, this adaptability is engulfed by a society where traditional distinctions are deep-rooted and damaging. *Romeo and Juliet* is decidedly uncomic in its 'blood feud that calls on men to define their masculinity by violence'.[8] Novy's argument thus sees the separation of Romeo and Juliet from the social environment of Verona as a rejection of typical gender roles. The resulting tension produces the tragedy.

In their private relationship, Romeo and Juliet refigure the terms in which love is expressed. Elsewhere in Verona sex is equated with violence: Benvolio counsels that 'A right fair mark, fair coz, is soonest hit' (1.1.203); Romeo conceives of being in love as being struck by 'Cupid's arrow' (1.1.205) and puts his failed courtship in martial terms: 'She will not stay the siege of loving terms, / Nor bide th'encounter of assailing eyes' (1.1.208–9); Mercutio describes Romeo as 'stabbed with a white wench's black eye, run through the ear with a love-song, the very pin of his heart cleft with the blind bow-boy's butt-shaft' (2.3.12–15); and in rebuffing Romeo's love, Rosaline is immune from its violence: 'From love's weak childish bow she lives unharmed' (1.1.207).[9] But Romeo and Juliet develop an alternatively reciprocal model of love. Romeo tells Friar Laurence: 'I have been feasting with mine enemy, / Where on a sudden one hath wounded me / That's by me wounded' (2.2.49–51). Earlier he describes Juliet not as a fortress to be attacked, but as a means of protection if she reciprocates his love: 'Alack, there lies more peril in thine eye / Than twenty of their swords. Look thou but sweet, / And I am proof against their enmity' (2.1.114–16). Aggression is jettisoned from amorous expression. Where Romeo does use violent imagery in his declarations of love for Juliet, it is self-directed. He offers to destroy his own name: 'Had I it written, I would tear the word' (2.1.100). If such language makes the lovers unconventionally tragic, they do not simply evince comic values in a tragic world. Shakespeare's romantic comedies are populated with lovers who frequently disguise themselves and who only gradually overcome inhibitions to declare their love frankly; Romeo and Juliet are candid from their first meeting. But even as Romeo is boldly direct, he carefully eschews the aggressive line of Verona's romantic discourse. He describes his 'unworthiest hand' (1.4.206) and assures Juliet that his potentially sinful touch is nevertheless 'gentle' (1.4.207), offering 'a tender kiss' if it is too 'rough' (1.4.209). Granted the metaphorical dominance of a saint to Romeo's pilgrim, Juliet is not trapped into silence in the usual Petrarchan mode, but free to join in the sonnet and willingly accept a kiss, even as she says 'Saints do not move' (1.4.218). This reciprocity characterizes their love; 'they share the initiative' again at their next meeting in the orchard scene, when a soliloquy is transformed into a dialogue.[10] In other plays distrust creeps into romantic relationships, but these two lovers' absolute trust in one another is accentuated by the fact that it is instead words that provoke their suspicion, and simply the reality of happiness itself: 'I am afeard, / Being in night, all this is but a dream, / Too flattering sweet to be substantial' (2.1.182–4). Novy claims that their declarations set 'the beloved outside the social framework: Romeo compares Juliet to the sun, her eyes to the stars; Juliet more consciously imagines removing him from society' when she meditates on him denying his father and refusing his name.[11] It might be objected that while Juliet's proposal is indeed an imaginative rejection of society, Romeo's poetic comparisons are rooted in a fairly conventional romantic discourse and are not therefore rebelliously antisocial. But Novy goes on to suggest that their rhetoric is indeed carefully calibrated, and can 'imply both mutuality and patriarchy'. Romeo identifies Juliet as 'my lady' (2.1.53), and Juliet says that if they marry, 'all my fortunes at thy foot I'll lay, / And follow thee, my lord, throughout the world' (2.1.190–1); 'This could reflect either reciprocity of service or a conventional shift from female power in courtship to male power in marriage.'[12] The commercial imagery that resonates throughout the play is recalculated by the lovers. Juliet figures consummation as a loss and a victory where male and female virginity are of equivalent value: 'learn me how to lose a winning match, / Played for a pair of stainless maidenhoods' (3.2.12–13). She conceives of herself as property but also as a possessor: 'O, I have bought the mansion of a love, / But not possessed it; and though I am sold, / Not yet enjoyed' (3.2.26–8). Novy argues that the lovers 'transcend' the social figuration of female subordination and the concerns for financial gain (so evident in the Capulet interest in Paris), and yet there remains an 'asymmetry' that is kept rooted in patriarchy (Juliet imagines herself possessing 'love' rather than Romeo, though she herself is an object that is 'sold').[13] In this way, even as the lovers redefine love they are unable to escape the pernicious social hierarchies of Verona.

Novy argues that pre-existing gender structures are not simply unfair or constrictive, but actually produce the tragedy. Romeo's love of Juliet isolates him from his friends, not simply because of the feud, but because of the way the male youth of Verona think about women and sex. Novy points out that neither Benvolio nor Mercutio are fanatical about the Montague cause, and might not object to Juliet for being Capulet. But the aggressively bawdy masculine conception of sexual relations prohibits Romeo from sharing news about his marriage. Dragged back into the feud with the death of Mercutio, Romeo's lament indicates how deep-seated the associations between masculinity and violence are: 'O sweet Juliet, / Thy beauty hath made me effeminate' (3.1.113–14). He is a 'man' in the fullest sense of the pun that emerges when he arrives at the scene of the argument between Tybalt and Mercutio:

TYBALT: Well, peace be with you, sir, here comes my man.
MERCUTIO: But I'll be hanged, sir, if he wear your livery.
Marry, go before to field, he'll be your follower;
Your worship in that sense may call him 'man'.

(3.1.55–8)

Romeo is the 'man' Tybalt looks for and not, as in Mercutio's wordplay, a manservant. But Romeo's masculinity or 'manliness' does in fact entrap him as fortune's 'man – its pawn': he joins in a fatal fight that will banish him from his wife.[14] The problematic nature of gender roles is thus integral to the unfolding of the tragic action. Novy also notes Friar Laurence's retrograde attitude to gender difference when he tellingly uses 'womanish' to mean weak when he talks to Romeo (3.3.109) and to Juliet (4.1.119). However, she does more to explain how this outlook impinges on the plot: the Friar's assumptions about female limitations cause him to advise Juliet to feign obedience and death rather than to help her escape to her husband (though he is also motivated by a desire to stage a reconciliation). Similarly, the Nurse counsels Juliet to conform to a passive role and simply accept the husband chosen for her, according to patriarchal norms, by her father. Juliet's performance of a 'feminine' passive part (apparent obedience and death) parallels Romeo's 'manly' return to violence: 'failure to transcend the gender polarization of their society makes disaster inevitable'.[15]

The particular tragic effect of the play is, in Novy's view, the product of this practical failure and a sense of the lovers' contrary purity and separation from society. Their purity is symbolized in their private language, most evident in the parting scene the morning after their consummation (3.5). In translating the nightingale into a lark and back again the lovers make 'a verbal transformation of the world – a creation of a private world through words – as a metaphor for a relationship'.[16] Protected by secrecy and especially innocent in its youth, this love is subject to a particularly poignant tragedy. The relationship functions as a corrective to the violent hierarchies of their society, but is ultimately subsumed by its greater force. As a close investigation of the impact of gender roles in the play, Novy's criticism is enlightening, particularly because she carefully relates patriarchal structures to action within the play. However, this early feminist work is again stymied by a rather narrow conception of gender and a relatively blunt appraisal of the complexities of the play itself.

## EDWARD SNOW (1985)

Edward Snow's elegant and richly detailed essay 'Language and Sexual Difference in *Romeo and Juliet*' is also concerned with transcendence – the distance between the lovers' imaginative experience of love and the realities of life that ensnare them. However, where other critics have focused on the separation between the lovers and their society, Snow zooms in still closer and considers the difference between Romeo's rhetoric and that of Juliet: 'the language of *Romeo and Juliet* is most intricately concerned not with the opposition between passion and the social order but with the difference between the sexes: and . . . its subtler affirmations have to do not with romantic love but female ontology.'[17] Language is important because it is not only the means by which desire is communicated; it also produces love. For example, when the couple boldly speak their feelings to each other they are sheltered by the formal boundaries of the sonnet. Later, Juliet unwittingly and magically participates in Romeo's line when she appears at the window:

ROMEO: That I might touch that cheek!
JULIET: Ay me!
ROMEO: She speaks!
(2.1.68)

Then, as she muses on the metaphysics of the name 'Romeo', she seems to produce the physical Romeo himself. Yet within this linguistically realized relationship there are crucial and, Snow argues, gendered differences.

Moving beyond the usual commentary on Romeo's rhetorical growth in the play, from a drily formal Petrarchan pose to a more sincere language of passion, Snow identifies a linguistic consistency in the part:

> ■ The imaginative universe generated by Romeo's desire is dominated by eyesight, and remains subject to greater rational control than Juliet's. His metaphors assemble reality 'out there,' and provide access to it through perspectives that tend to make him an onlooker rather than a participant. There is a kind of metonymic fascination in his language with parts and extremities, especially when viewed from a distance, against a backdrop that heightens the sensation of outline and boundary.[18] □

Romeo says Juliet 'hangs upon the cheek of night / As a rich jewel in an Ethiop's ear' (1.4.158–9); he avers 'by yonder blessèd moon I vow, / That tips with silver all these fruit-tree tops' (2.1.150–1); a rope-ladder will take him 'to the high topgallant' of his joy (2.3.177); and the view from Juliet's window shows him that 'jocund day / Stands tiptoe on the misty mountain tops' (3.5.9–10). When he creates images of Juliet, Romeo puts her at a distance and stretches to touch her; his figures are composed of enumerable and orderly parts: 'See how she leans her cheek upon her hand. / O that I were a glove upon that hand, / That I might touch that cheek!' (2.1.66–8). But his happy conceptions are frequently shadowed by a sense of the 'temporary and provisional'; he cannot conceive of an enduring blissful transformation.[19] When Romeo puts himself in the images he develops (he is more frequently a spectator than a participant in these visions), it is often as an 'unchanging object' tossed around by external forces: 'he that hath the steerage of my course / Direct my suit' (1.4.110–11); 'Thou desperate pilot, now at once run on / The dashing rocks thy sea-sick weary bark' (5.3.117–18).[20] (However, this imaginary role is quite different from his activity in the plot, where he is constantly on the move – scaling walls, duelling, making love, travelling to and from Mantua, breaking into the Capulet tomb.) Romeo cannot look present happiness in the face without moving it into the future, either as a promise of fuller joy or as a tragic threat. This trait is exemplified in Romeo's report of a dream in the final act:

■ If I may trust the flattering truth of sleep,
My dreams presage some joyful news at hand.
My bosom's lord sits lightly in his throne,
And all this day an unaccustomed spirit
Lifts me above the ground with cheerful thoughts.
I dreamt my lady came and found me dead –
Strange dream that gives a dead man leave to think! –
And breathed such life with kisses in my lips
That I revived and was an emperor.
Ah me, how sweet is love itself possessed,
When but love's shadows are so rich in joy. □

(5.1.1–11)

Snow points out that the glorious transformation Romeo thinks is 'presaged' has already happened: Romeo's experience of love with Juliet has revived him. By pushing it into the future Romeo 'transforms it from a metaphor of the consummated relationship into an ironic foreshadowing of its tragic conclusion', where Juliet attempts to suck poison from his lips so she can 'die with a restorative' (5.3.166).[21] At other times when Romeo articulates a sense of present happiness he sees it in the context of future tragedy:

■ come what sorrow can,
It cannot countervail the exchange of joy
That one short minute gives me in her sight...
Then love-devouring death do what he dare,
It is enough I may but call her mine. □

(2.5.3–8)

Snow sees in such remarks an affinity with other tragic heroes in the Shakespeare canon, who conceptualize love as 'moments of satisfaction rather than a process of growth, and hence ... experience happiness within it against a backdrop of apocalyptic loss'.[22] This astute observation puts *Romeo and Juliet* in an illuminating comparison with plays too often seen as superior to it. Romeo is by no means equivalent to the obsessively jealous Othello; in fact, the link between them only highlights Romeo's 'unthreatened responsiveness to the energies sexual desire releases in Juliet'.[23] But there is a generic link in a gendered attitude that works out fatally.

Juliet's imagery is much more extravagant than Romeo's, and unlike her lover she makes figures with wholes rather than parts. In return for his name, which is 'no part' of him, Juliet offers 'all myself' (2.1.91–2), and she hopes that 'runnaways' eyes may wink, and Romeo / Leap to these arms, untalked of and unseen' (3.2.6–7). Snow declares: 'She manages to be both subject and object in love without inner conflict or contradiction', shrewdly analyzing complex imagery that has tripped up some critics: 'O, I have bought the mansion of a love, / But not possessed it; and though I am sold, / Not yet enjoyed' (3.2.26–8). Instead of standing at a distance from her imagery, Juliet centres in it, and produces a 'depth' of interiority: 'My bounty is as boundless as the sea, / My love as deep' (2.1.176–7). Such features make Juliet's language risky and adventurous. Snow suggests: 'Juliet's sensations tend in general to be more "piercing" and ontologically dangerous than Romeo's. [In] her imagination . . . perceptual experience spontaneously invades and emanates from the self, instead of becoming the structuring activity it is for Romeo, even when he is most enraptured.'[24] Juliet generates a sense of her 'self' through her erotic experiences, even though her 'self' is the subject that produces this passion:

■ My only love sprung from my only hate,
Too early seen unknown and known too late.
Prodigious birth of love it is to me
That I must love a loathèd enemy. □

(1.4.251–4)

This imagery sees Juliet submitting herself to the forces of desire; she possesses and is possessed by love and hate ('my only love', 'my only hate'). Her 'I' (both the word and the self it represents) is associated with assent ('ay'):

NURSE: 'Yea', quoth my husband, 'fall'st upon thy face?
Thou wilt fall backward when thou comest to age,
Wilt thou not, Jule?' It stinted and said 'Ay'.
JULIET: And stint thou too, I pray thee, Nurse, say I.

(1.3.57–60)

The story of the play finds Juliet fulfilling this prophecy and assenting passionately to a sexual relationship. Snow suggests that the idea of a moral 'fall' from innocence and submission to masculine authority (alluded to here, when we first meet Juliet) is corrected by her active and self-willed assent. Sex is not contaminated by guilt for Juliet. Instead she eagerly anticipates the full 'strangeness' of the unknown erotic moment, which she conceives as 'intimate' rather than violent or an oppression to be feared: 'Come gentle night, come loving black-browed night, / Give me my Romeo' (3.2.20–1).[25] This and other metaphors bring love close to Juliet; she does not push it into the imaginative and grammatical distance like Romeo, who often frames his images in the subjunctive: 'What if her eyes were there, they in her head?' (2.1.61); 'O that I were a glove upon that hand, / That I might touch that cheek!' (2.1.67–8). While a critical commonplace holds that Romeo matures out of his tendency to poetic abstraction, Snow argues that Romeo still partly seems to enjoy figuration for its own sake, to prefer to keep it at an imaginative level rather than to realize it. By contrast, Juliet's equally imaginative poetry has a passionate reality that brings future possibility into the present: 'Come night, come Romeo, come thou day in night; / For thou wilt lie upon the wings of night / Whiter than new snow upon a raven's back' (3.2.17–19). Romeo's images maintain a kind of rational order, so that Juliet substitutes poetically but logically for the 'sun' which rises in the 'east' (2.1.46); but Juliet herself forms more outlandish images that

> ■ loosen the boundaries that fix the rational universe in place, and draw it into a state of continual flux: Romeo is both night and day in night, she both waits for him in the night as he wings his way toward her and is herself the winged night on whose back he lies like new snow – all in the space of two lines.[26] □

This subtle close textual analysis brings fantastic vigour to the question of gender difference in the play; Snow rigorously shows how desire is linguistically produced but also maintains its thrill even under the academic microscope. This work adds to the accounts of Juliet's unconventional behaviour a detailed sense of how her passion is presented.

Snow regards the different images used by the lovers as demonstrating their linguistic compatibility and phenomenological dissimilarity. Romeo's 'lack' is counterbalanced by 'an overflowing in Juliet'.[27] Romeo's more passive figures are met by the activity of Juliet's images. Intriguingly, this inverts the behavioural difference found by Novy, who saw the tragedy as emanating from the pair's residual adherence to gender norms: Romeo leapt to fatal action in killing Tybalt and Juliet acquiesced to the passive part of pretended obedience and death. Snow's language analysis shows a deeper refiguration of gendered expectations. He maintains that this is finally borne out in the death scene where Romeo 'rests' himself with Juliet, and Juliet actualizes Romeo's desire to rest on her breast: 'O happy dagger, / This is thy sheath. There [rest], and let me die' (5.3.169–70).[28] Throughout the play Juliet experiences desire not as a subjugation of the self, but as a means of realizing it. However, the society of the play-world plots a different story for her: the Capulets arrange a marriage for Juliet in disregard of her will, and puns in the very first scene figure female experience of sex as punishment ('I will be civil with the maids, I will cut off their heads' [1.1.21–2]). However, in Snow's view the male characters who are positioned hierarchically above women are also losers 'in the realm of primary experience'.[29] Thus, according to Snow, Juliet enjoys an 'instinctual wisdom' about erotic matters, whereas Romeo kisses 'by th' book' (1.4.223). This point takes a rather essentialist line on male/female difference which not all readers will feel comfortable with, and it is certainly worth keeping the practical restrictions faced by Juliet and other female characters in mind when celebrating the heroine's emotional liberation.

At the conclusion of the play 'sexual difference' again has the two protagonists approaching death in distinct ways. Romeo enters the tomb and death as an imaginary space, where time is not operational and Juliet is held against her will: 'death's pale flag is not advancèd there . . . Shall I believe . . . that the lean abhorrèd monster keeps / Thee here' (5.3.96–105). Juliet, on the other hand, confronts the real immediacy of the tomb. She wakens into perfect clarity: 'I do remember well where I should be' (5.3.149). Before drinking the sleeping potion she acknowledges the reality of the passage of time in the tomb, where her cousin lies 'fest'ring' (4.3.42). Snow also finds a contrast in the toast both lovers drink to one another. Juliet imagines that Tybalt's ghost seeks out his murderer, and she wilfully drinks in an effort to 'cross over' to the place of death: 'Stay, Tybalt, stay! / Romeo, Romeo, Romeo! Here's drink – I drink to thee' (4.3.56–7). Whereas Romeo 'fixes himself in the scene of his own death' rather than trying to cross over; when he says 'Here's to my love' (5.3.119); the gesture is 'nostalgic, not directional'.[30] The subtle difference between the two lovers may be a little overplayed here, but there is a striking difference in the posthumous record left behind: Romeo leaves his father a letter to clear up any misunderstandings and explain the situation; Juliet (whose suicide is 'brief' [5.3.169]) is indifferent to any judgements made of her.

Snow's article is a highly engaging response to the play that sheds linguistic light on the tragedy's gender structures. In dwelling on the minutiae of the play's poetry Snow goes beyond the more obvious commentary on the different social positions of the protagonists. However, his focus is narrowly reserved for the lovers themselves, and so the larger points about gender difference are less convincing, located as they are in a couple also thought to exceed 'a common bound'.[31] Just three years later Joseph Porter devotes a full book to redressing the critical balance, making his subject the enigmatic and energetic Mercutio.

## JOSEPH PORTER (1988)

*Shakespeare's Mercutio: His History and Drama* puts Mercutio at the centre of the play's meaning. Porter's book is divided into three parts: Part 1 establishes Mercutio's connection with Mercury and details representations of the god in classical, medieval and Renaissance times (highlighting his associations with homosexuality, travel, theft, boundaries, and other themes); Part 2 concentrates on Mercutio as he appears in the Shakespearean text; and Part 3 tracks Mercutio's changing appearances in 'adaptations, promptbooks, stage performances, and films', uncovering 'the history of his transformations' as 'one of manifold strategies of pre-emption, containment, and accommodation'.[32]

Such attention to Mercutio might seem surprising given that this character, as Porter observes, has no influence on the plot until he dies. However, the cultural significance of Mercury endows Mercutio with a rich thematic resonance. Furthermore, as a linguistic phenomenon, Mercutio represents a key stage in Shakespeare's development as a writer of characters with 'distinctive speech'.[33] Accordingly, in Part 2, Porter scrutinizes Mercutio's language very closely and recommends that his readers should have a copy of the text with them as they work through his argument.

Mercutio inhabits the 'dominant space' in Verona, that is, the masculine, public realm where decisions are made. This sphere is in 'dialectical opposition' to the private domestic space of the Capulet household and the secrecy of the marriage of Romeo and Juliet.[34] More specifically, Mercutio also functions as a principle of opposition to the love that Romeo champions. Even so, as his ribald wordplay makes clear, Mercutio is certainly not anti-sex. Indeed, his insistence on sex aligns him with the serving-men who open the play and with the Nurse, who all embrace an earthy frankness about sexual matters; in sharp contrast, Benvolio and Romeo manage to discuss love without mentioning sex. Of course, Mercutio is frequently found mocking Romeo (though the two are never given a scene alone together), as he tries to rescue his friend from romance, wanting him instead for the 'world of male comradeship'.[35] In their dialogues Mercutio is the active figure, who initiates conversation and directs the banter; Romeo, on the back foot, can only react (this reading complements Snow's analysis of Romeo as a passive onlooker in his own images).

However, Porter finds more to Mercutio than a bawdy counterpoint to Romeo's romance. Mercutio's allusive connection with the god Mercury is found in both his name and characterization. In attempting to snap Romeo out of his infatuation, Mercutio behaves like his classical namesake who had the same lesson for Odysseus and the Trojan Aeneas. Given that in Virgil's narrative Mercury drew the latter away from

Queen Dido to found 'Rome', Aeneas having been dispossessed by a war caused by the sexual misdeeds of another 'Paris', the story gains 'Trojan–Roman' overtones (perhaps also hinted at in 'Juliet'/Julius). The god, who also escorted souls of the dead to the afterlife (a 'psycho-pomp'), is thought by Porter to lurk in Mercutio's most famous speech:

> ■ Inasmuch as the Queen Mab speech is prompted by Romeo's mention of his dream and is itself both about dreams and dream-like, it may be that behind the fairies' midwife stands the classical deliverer of dreams [Mercury]. Inasmuch as this uncanny speech seems to catch everyone including the speaker unaware, it may be that what we have is a kind of possession by Mercutio by the god. Or, to put the matter differently, it may be that here the god looms through the man. If so, the face he presents is more disturbing than in the first part of the scene. And in the chill forebodings that darken the end of the scene there may be traces of Mercury's role as psycho-pomp. Indeed parts of the speech itself may come from beyond the grave inasmuch as Shakespeare seems possibly to have added to it after writing Mercutio's death.[36] □

This quotation exemplifies Porter's ludic methodology, which works by poetic associations (in the same vein as Mercutio, who spins out dialogue by snatching at and developing particular connotations). Porter identifies himself as a poststructuralist, and therefore draws on a variety of different ideas and sources without privileging any one particular narrative. The notion of the slippery god appearing through Mercutio puts the tragedy on a supernatural scale. Indeed Mercury's weird presence brings a dark threat to the play. Mercutio wraps up his speech by dismissing 'fantasy' as

> ■ more inconstant than the wind who woos
> Even now the frozen bosom of the north;
> And being angered puffs away from thence,
> Turning his side to the dew-dropping south. □
>
> (1.4.98–101)

As a figure of the wind as well as dreams, Mercury is doubly present in this image of inconstancy and, still more presciently, anger. In the words 'puffs away from thence' Porter is reminded of Mercury disappearing after his first meeting with Aeneas. The god's link with Mercutio gives that character an association with an 'inhuman vindictiveness' that makes Romeo's misgivings about the future apt.[37] So Mercutio is not to be oversimplified as a benign joker who has only a distantly symbolic role in the play (the death of the comic figure inaugurating the more tragic movement of the second part of the play). He is strikingly aggressive, even in comparison to the famously fiery Tybalt: it is Mercutio who prods Tybalt into violence in 3.1. Given the sexual nature of Mercutio's language, his aggression also has a 'phallic component' that Porter relates 'distantly' to 'Mercury's phallicism'.[38] These characteristics are translated into a tragic force levelled against Romeo, because of Romeo's responsibility for Mercutio's death (this is stressed three times: in a descriptive stage direction [3.1.88.0], in Mercutio's accusation [3.1.102–3] and in Benvolio's report of the killings [3.1.164–9]). Mercutio dies cursing Romeo and marking his distance from his friend by addressing him with the formal 'you' instead of the intimate 'thou' (the pronoun he continues to use for Benvolio).

Although Mercutio ostensibly leaves the action when he dies, Porter draws on the concept of liminality (developed by the anthropologists Gennep and Turner) to explain the character's continued role in the play. Liminal stages are the moments 'in between' major events such as life and death. Mercutio has what Porter calls an extended 'exit limin, or threshold' in between his death and the last reference to him at 5.3.75. Thus Mercutio lingers as a pervasive presence in the play until its final scene. Though this is the first time Shakespeare produces such an 'exit limin' in one play (Richard II exerts an ongoing hold across the series of history plays), the effect is reprised by the eponymous protagonist of *Julius Caesar* and miraculously by Hermione in *The Winter's Tale*. In *Romeo and Juliet* Mercutio remains after death in explicit references to him that indicate both a continued influence and a sense of loss. For example, just before entering the tomb, Romeo recognizes the man he has just killed as 'Mercutio's kinsman' before naming him 'noble County Paris!' (5.3.75). As an audience, we miss Mercutio in a way that we do not miss Lady Montague (whose non-attendance at the conclusion is explained), or Benvolio and the Nurse (whose absence is not). Porter here clarifies the impact of Mercutio's ongoing 'role', though at times the associative analysis can seem strained, with proposals that Mercutio inheres in tonal references to wind, aspiration, scorn, and so on, or that he is found in Capulet's tragic decision to bring Juliet's wedding day forward from Thursday to 'Wednesday – *mercredi*, Mercury's day'.[39] Nevertheless, his speculation that the actor playing Mercutio may have doubled the part with the Prince is intriguing, and more plausibly suggests that Mercutio's influence may lie beneath even the last lines of the play.

Mercutio not only has a lengthy 'exit limin' but also, Porter contends, functions as a principle of liminality even before he dies:

■ he embodies the liminality of the Mercury who presides over the wild border regions, the herm who stands by the roadside to guide a wayfarer or a *romeo*. Boundaries – that of the ancient feud, those of gender and generation, those between night and day and life and death – crisscross

> Mercutio's play, and much of its action transpires at such Mercurially liminal times and sites as dawn, the city walls, the garden and balcony, the interurban road, and the entrance to the tomb. Above all others Mercutio before his death manifests this liminality in his behaviour, as when he turns aside from his companions as if rapt in his talk of dreams, fantasy, and the wind that, in Benvolio's words, 'blows us from ourselves' [1.4.102].[40] □

This commentary smartly elucidates Mercutio's relationship to the many oppositions countless critics have recognized in the play. His marginality becomes thematically and even actively functional. Mercutio curses 'A plague a both your houses! (3.1.99–100, 106). In this malediction Porter sees the god Mercury left angry without 'any *romei* to direct'; he curses the houses themselves. Identifying a triad that later Queer Theorists will continue to explore (the loving enemies Romeo and Juliet, and Mercutio), Porter contends that the cursing Mercutio here swaps places with Romeo, taking on the part of enemy. Mercutio stands between the two houses that have destroyed him, and therefore also between the two lovers, who are likewise subject to his curse. Therefore 'in Mercutio's final tragic configuration the liminal has become central, the god of the wild border region has become god of the agora [market place]'.[41] It is through his marginality that Mercutio helps to unleash the tragic disaster of the play. This interpretation successfully shows the much more profound significance of a character who had often been seen as a mechanical trigger for more tragic events.

Thus Porter's creative analysis usefully shifts attention from the central couple to an enigmatic character whose meaning had been underresearched. In doing so, Porter also squares up to feminist accounts of the play that locate Mercutio firmly in the camp of a violent masculinity out of which Romeo must mature. He accuses Kahn and Novy (among others) of 'psychosexual prescriptivism' – that is, of imposing a narrative that insists that heterosexual love should replace and correct earlier homosexual bonding.[42] For Porter, Mercutio functions as evidence that *Romeo and Juliet* does not straightforwardly conform to such a pattern, partly because he does not fit into the binary model of masculinity identified by feminists: men who seek to dominate women/men who desire a mutually loving relationship with women. Porter is right to argue that Mercutio's fluid complexity is not effectively labelled by such a crude distinction; but he fails to confront this attractive character's unattractive misogyny. The claim that Mercutio's 'light intermittent misogyny does not in the least entail antifeminism' is somewhat unconvincing, especially since offhand misogyny is all the more invidious because it is casual.[43] Nevertheless, the reading paves the way for more ideologically charged accounts of the play's interrogation not just of the romance of Romeo and Juliet, but of the heteronormative standards they supposedly embody. It is this very paradigm that the feminist critic Dympna Callagan insists is an inescapable ideological effect of the play. We turn now to her article of 1994.

## DYMPNA CALLAGHAN (1994)

Feminism is given a Marxist structure in Dympna Callaghan's article 'The Ideology of Romantic Love: The Case of *Romeo and Juliet*'. Callaghan argues that the play was produced at a time when 'institutions' we now think of as natural – 'romantic love and the family' – were in the process of being 'naturalized'; *Romeo and Juliet* participates in that enduring change of understanding.[44] The tragedy holds feminist interest for Callaghan because the formulation of 'transhistorical romantic love' is 'one of the most efficient and irresistible interpellations of the female subject, securing her complicity in apparently unchangeable structures of oppression, particularly compulsory heterosexuality and bourgeois marriage'.[45] In other words, the fantasy of romantic love is the means by which women are kept within a hierarchal structure that privileges men, their desires strictly regulated into a narrowly heterosexual mould. Callaghan thus challenges not only non-feminist readings that fail to recognize the significance of gender, but also (implicitly) readings that celebrate Juliet's frank expression of sexual desire as a liberation. As one of the most iconic texts about 'romantic love', *Romeo and Juliet* does ideological work: it makes us think that its story about desire is timeless instead of historically specific. However, this supposed timelessness is merely an effect produced through the story's endless repetition, not only the play's repeated performances and adaptations down the centuries, but also within the text itself, where the lovers' tragedy is repeatedly re-narrated: the Prologue outlines the story before the play proper dramatizes it again, the Friar (needlessly) recounts it in the final scene and the Prince closes the play saying that there will be 'more talk of these sad things' (5.3.307) and affirming 'never was a story of more woe / Than this of Juliet and her Romeo' (5.3.309–10). Furthermore, the promised statues of the lovers reify their love in perpetuity. Callaghan exposes the fallacy of 'timelessness', which she regards as having been engineered by the text itself. She also explicitly rejects the 'universalizing' readings of psychoanalytical accounts (including Kristeva's – see Chapter 7 above). In doing so she builds on the work of the New Historicist Stephen Greenblatt, who claims that the model of 'selfhood' that psychoanalysis takes as fundamental to the human condition across time was developed during the early modern period, and is therefore historically specific rather than timeless. (Critics working on medieval literature challenge this aetiology of selfhood.)

While Callaghan approves Greenblatt's contestation of psychoanalysis she rejects his understanding of history – or rather histories – as endlessly multiple, made up of innumerable stories. Instead, she lays out a materialist agenda that is informed by Marxist methodology and which sees history as 'structured material conflict'.[46] She is concerned to show not how *Romeo and Juliet* neutrally exemplifies aspects of its historical context, but how it actively participates 'in the ideological/historical conditions of its own making'.[47]

The narrative situation of *Romeo and Juliet* is aligned with its historical context: there is a movement from a feudal society (organized according to family loyalty) to a centralized state. This shift makes the Prince a major figure in the play as he wrests authority from the Montague and Capulet patriarchs. However, this political process is not separate from the play's love story since the reconceptualization of sexual desire is integral to the Prince's project. The plot sees the love of Romeo and Juliet ambivalently pinioned between two different meanings: it is both transgressive and orthodox. This is because the play works as a hinge between an old and new social order; the meaning of the young love is accordingly split between these two paradigms. There are hints within the play of desire's curious status as a psychic drive that is nevertheless socialized. Callaghan quotes from the Queen Mab speech:

■ And in this state she gallops night by night
Through lovers' brains, and then they dream of love;
On courtiers' knees, that dream on curtsies straight;
O'er lawyers' fingers, who straight dream on fees;
O'er ladies' lips, who straight on kisses dream,
Which oft the angry Mab with blisters plagues,
Because their breath with sweetmeats tainted are . . .
Sometime she driveth o'er a soldier's neck,
And then dreams he of cutting foreign throats,
Of breaches, ambuscados, Spanish blades . . .
This is the hag, when maids lie on their backs,
That presses them and learns them first to bear,
Making them women of good carriage. □

(1.4.68–92)

The scenario of the dream claims desire for the unconscious, but the details reveal its socially structured nature: only soldiers not maids get to dream of slitting throats. Bearing this socialized condition of love in mind, it is perhaps less surprising that Callaghan should view Prince Escalus as 'the play's pivotal figure rather than the tragic couple'.[48] While this may seem like a counter-intuitive suggestion, Callaghan's reading is focused on the ideological structures of the play that go unnoticed *because* they are ideological. Building up a case for the Prince's centrality, she argues that he helps to organize the dramatic structure of the play by issuing commands at the beginning, middle and end (in having him do so Shakespeare chooses to alter his immediate source, Brooke). The Prince is empowered to condemn subjects to death, and in trying to end the feud he also attempts to supplant an older feudal order. Callaghan detects a further symbolic resonance: 'Escalus strives to control the flow of blood, a metonym of lineage, class, and succession – the very essence of the patriarchal imperative.'[49] Political order is intertwined with the sexual relationships that generate it. The movement from feudal society to an absolutist state is also a movement from endogamous 'fatal loins' (Prologue 5) to exogamy. Juliet's equivocation with her mother marks this shift as she transfers apparent love for her cousin to the non-Capulet Romeo; she wants to: 'wreak the love I bore my cousin / Upon his body that hath slaughtered him' (3.5.101–2). Her desire is transgressive in terms of the endogamous values of the feuding families, but orthodox in the Prince's new exogamous state.

The patriarchs to whom the Prince is opposed appear as diminished. Capulet blusters into the opening street fight calling for his 'long sword' (1.1.71) only for his wife to caution him that he would better call for 'A crutch, a crutch' (1.1.72). The women here 'deflate the exaggerated phallic proportions of their husbands' and Capulet is again undermined later in the same act when he is unable to contain the young Tybalt.[50] Thus where early genre critics saw dramaturgical weakness in the feuding fathers' comical impotence (see Chapter 4 above), Callaghan finds an ideological transition that is part of a real-life historical change. The Prince secures his power over the feudal/feuding patriarchs in the final resolution of the conflict, which Callaghan terms 'a belated public solemnization of the marriage contract'.[51] Agreeing to peace means submitting to the Prince, who busily asserts his authority by commandeering the letter Balthazar brings from Romeo to his father. Callaghan's interpretation exposes the power-play that can be overlooked in considerations of the play's emotional content.

But it is the consequences the sociopolitical realignment has for women (rather than the displaced patriarchs) that most interests Callaghan. The refiguration of 'love' that accompanies and assists the change in social structure has its root, Callaghan determines, in the Protestant Church. Earlier religious writings condemned women for rampant desire (virginity was prized as the most sanctified sexual state by the Catholic Church), but Protestant (and especially Puritan) writers instead idealized companionate marriage where women were afforded a 'desiring subjectivity' that was also 'pliant' to male authority.[52] Women thus escape the financial exchanges of parentally organized marriages, but their free romantic choice is put in the service of a social order that keeps the husband as the head of the wife – the difference is she is now expected to submit to an oppressive hierarchy with willing love. Callaghan thinks that earlier models of romantic love that eroticized illegitimate passions such as adultery may have been less constraining for women.

However, *Romeo and Juliet* stages the emergence of the newer sexual attitudes. The lovers' dialogue translates Catholic imagery into the language of sexual desire: Romeo's 'pilgrim' 'purges' his 'sin' by kissing a 'saint'. And where other critics accept the love as ideal, Callaghan exposes the way it has been 'idealized'. The play is 'about the power relation between the amorous couple and the outside world';[53] defying a violent authority, their love is depicted as freeing. One aspect of this is the couple's freedom from the financial considerations that determine feudal marriage arrangements. Romeo asserts his economic independence when he insists the Nurse takes a payment from him (2.3.170–2) and the lovers' metaphors reclaim the monetary consequences of their relationship as their own rather than as belonging to their parents: 'O dear account! My life is my foe's debt' (1.4.231); 'As that vast shore washed with the farthest sea, / I should adventure for such merchandise' (2.1.126–7); 'They are but beggars that can count their worth; / But my true love is grown to such excess, / I cannot sum up sum of half my wealth' (2.5.32–4). In this last quotation Juliet redefines 'wealth' as love that she rather than her father possesses. Callaghan stipulates that both the message and lyricism of such formulations contribute to the idealizing drive of the play, which work to cover over a more fraught financial situation in the early modern marriage, where 'companionate' wives struggled to have a say in the property controlled by the husbands to whom they were also subject.

Callaghan coolly appraises the 'female desire' represented in the play as: 'benign and unthreatening, easily recruited to emergent absolutism and nascent capitalism'.[54] This somewhat bleak assessment marks Callaghan's considerable distance from critics such as Snow, who celebrate Juliet's sexual liberation and regard her as experiencing a truer ontology of desire than Romeo. But for Callaghan this supposed authenticity is itself a product of the play's idealization of desire and is governed by its deeper, enslaving ideological structure. The only hints of an alternative female eroticism are glimpsed in the Nurse's bawdiness, where nursing ('giving suck') retains a sexual dimension. Callaghan objects to straightforwardly comic readings of this character that ignore her 'indelible maternal memory': 'I never shall forget' (1.3.26); 'I do bear a brain' (1.3.31).[55] Nevertheless, the scene of the Nurse's sexualized reminiscence is locked within a private female space in an emphatically patriarchal house. And Callaghan insists that the play quashes the alternatives to the ideology of heterosexual romantic love. Drawing on the work of Bruce Smith, she points out that Mercutio's different erotic mode is killed off halfway through the play and believes no happy ending can be imagined for what Romeo's friend represents. By contrast, the comedic aspects of the play mean that a positive outcome for Romeo and Juliet is well within grasp. We might note here that Callaghan can conceive of the lovers' survival because she sees their relationship as embodying (albeit in idealistic form) what would become a standard familial unit of the state: a companionate marriage. Other critics, such as Kristeva, who interpret the love as an intense and real ideal, cannot imagine any outcome in which it might endure.

Callaghan's essay is much more theoretically rigorous than earlier feminist accounts of the play. She moves far beyond the relatively straightforward declarations of Juliet's interpretative merits and simple assessments of the play as either sexist or pro-women, to identify the way the play does 'the work of culture, instigating and perpetuating the production of socially necessary formations of desire'.[56] However, her insistence on the play's complicity in a heteronormative paradigm is controversial, not least to Queer Theorists, who argue that critics have been blind to the range of sexual possibilities manifest in the play. Jonathan Goldberg levels this criticism against earlier feminist critics, and it is to his article on *Romeo and Juliet* that we now turn.

## JONATHAN GOLDBERG (1994)

Jonathan Goldberg's article, '*Romeo and Juliet*'s Open Rs', was first published in a collection of essays entitled *Queering the Renaissance*. This anthology aimed to challenge the 'heterosexist assumptions' of formalist, historicist and even feminist criticism.[57] Goldberg's piece makes this point by arguing that *Romeo and Juliet* has been misconstrued by generations of commentators who celebrate the protagonists' love as simultaneously 'withdrawn' from society's problems and also a social 'aspiration'.[58] Like Callaghan, he sees the play as bound up in a restrictive ideology that idealizes married heterosexuality to fix social order; but unlike Callaghan, Goldberg regards editors, critics and schoolteachers, rather than the play itself, as the proponents of this ideology. Thus he directly rejects the terms of Kahn's feminist reading, which he thinks prescriptively associates 'growing up' with 'a single heterosexual trajectory'.[59] Instead, Goldberg elucidates a more complex set of social and sexual interactions.

Goldberg opens his analysis by redefining the heterosexual marriage between Romeo and Juliet (finally blessed by Capulet and Montague in the last scene) as part of a 'homosocial order' – that is, a social structure determined by relations between men. The old patriarchs shake hands over their children's corpses, so that the marriage serves to secure a social bond. Goldberg identifies a

> ■ configuration that continually triangulates the relation of Romeo and Juliet, adding in every instance a third term that gives the lie to the shelter of their love. Romeo and Paris as possible husbands, still fighting over the body of Juliet in the final scene of the play; Capulet and Paris as the patriarchal couple trading Juliet between them; Romeo and Tybalt as enemies and yet as lovers, joined and divided by Juliet.[60] □

This analysis resists the familiar critical notion that Romeo and Juliet's love is blissfully separate from Veronese society: 'Indeed, what makes their love so valuable is that it serves as a nexus for the social and can be mystified as outside the social.'[61] Goldberg's 'queer' reading locates 'sodomitical' transgressions alongside these patriarchal appropriations of the lovers' romance. 'Sodomy' refers here not simply to sexual intercourse between two men, but to any relationship that disrupts the 'patriarchal organization' said to inhere in married heterosexuality and the homosocial order it supports.[62]

This argument rejects the supposedly unique and transcendental quality of Romeo and Juliet's love. Goldberg points out that Romeo is initially in love with Rosaline; the alienated lover follows the advice of both Benvolio and the Friar in switching his affections to a more appreciative figure. Juliet replaces Rosaline in a substitution accentuated by their shared Capulet identity and the floral connection in the 'rose' present in both Rosaline's name and Juliet's famous speech (2.1.86–7). Extending the chain of associations, Goldberg also sees Romeo standing in for Rosaline when Juliet exchanges him for the rose (2.1.88–90). Thus substitutions that at one level work to shore up a patriarchal society (one woman can easily be replaced by another, leaving men free to go about their business) also unleash transgressive energy. Goldberg contends: 'the coupling of Romeo and Juliet is not a unique moment of heterosexual perfection and privacy but part of a series whose substitutions do not respect either the uniqueness of individuals or the boundaries of gender difference'.[63] In the midst of these sequential replacements desire refigures gender identity. Famously, Romeo claims that he has been effeminized by his love for Juliet (3.1.113–14); but Goldberg also speculates that Juliet is masculinized when Romeo exclaims that she is the 'sun' defeating the 'envious moon' (2.1.46–7), so that the mythological sun god Apollo replaces the moon goddess Diana. Furthermore, he connects Rosaline to her cross-dressing namesake in *As You Like It*, and to both the young man of the *Sonnets* (who like Rosaline squanders his beauty by failing to procreate) *and* the 'dark lady' (who represents the threat of unmarried sexuality).

The 'move across gender ... allows a subject position for women that is not confined within patriarchal boundaries'.[64] For Goldberg, 'queering' an understanding of the play's sexual and social structures liberates female characters and viewers far more effectively than feminist readings that insist on strictly heterosexual roles (whereby men and women must conform to particular gender types).

Juliet is here figured as a queer, and not just a heterosexual, object (and subject) of desire. As a Capulet, she is forbidden to the Montague Romeo; but she is also repeatedly described as Death's lover, as when Capulet laments to Paris: Death has 'lain with thy wife. There she lies, / Flower as she was, deflow'red by him' (4.4.62–3). Goldberg elaborates:

> ■ Such imaginings of the sexual act as taking place in the wrong place ('the place death' [2.1.107]) and with the wrong partner only further the sense that the sexual field in which desire operates in the play is the forbidden desire named sodomy. The ungenerative locus of death allies the sexual act to the supposedly sterile and unreproductive practice of usury associated with the young man and with Rosaline's self-hoarding and waste, themselves as suggestive of sodomy as they are of masturbatory activities as well.[65] □

An illegitimate lover and a legitimate wife, a living woman and an apparently dead body, Juliet hovers between licit and illicit desires. It is precisely such ambiguity that signifies the play's queer impulses. Thus Goldberg is critical of modern editors who remove the prevarication of a textual crux in the play when Mercutio teases the lovelorn Romeo with lewd talk about his mistress: 'ah that she were, / An open *Et cætera*' (Q1); 'o that she were / An open, or' (Q2). Modern editors often supply the elided bawdy term: 'An open-arse' (2.1.39). However, Goldberg suggests this 'open place', which is tellingly not named in the early editions, both 'hits and deflects' desire.[66] More importantly, this space is open to desire in its full variety. Mercutio speaks his desire for Romeo by speaking of and as Rosaline: 'I conjure thee by Rosaline's bright eyes' (2.1.18); Goldberg recognizes 'Mercutio's rivalry for a place that anyone might occupy'.[67] The analysis thus reveals the energetic circulation of desire in the play.

However, not all feminists would accept Goldberg's erasure of gender distinctions as politically enabling for women. Goldberg pays little heed to the different social roles available for men and women, and thus obscures the historical conditions which are a necessary starting point for many feminist theorists (not least Callaghan). Instead he regards gender-typing as inextricably and causally linked with heterosexual social structures. Goldberg thus criticizes readings that 'enforce a compulsory heterosexuality' as 'complicit with the domestication of women and with the scapegoating of men'.[68] Such an argument is dependent on a rather narrow definition of heterosexuality: one which is tightly tethered to a patriarchal imperative. Any desire that flouts this order, even when between man and woman (Romeo and Juliet), is redefined as sodomy in its most largely metaphorical sense. This argument brilliantly exposes the full spectrum of sexual desires in this play, not just between Romeo and Juliet, but between Rosaline, Romeo, Juliet, Paris, Tybalt, Mercutio, and so on. Goldberg also astutely demonstrates the interplay between sexual and social relationships, and insists that we recognize differences between early modern and modern sexual identities. However, in reducing the meaning of 'heterosexuality' to patriarchal oppression, and enlarging the scope of 'sodomy' to include all other desires, he also risks flattening the variegated sexual impulses he seeks to identify.

## ROBERT N. WATSON AND STEPHEN DICKEY (2005)

The continuing capacity of gender criticism to reconceptualize literature and expose ideological blind spots is demonstrated by Robert N. Watson and Stephen Dickey's article, 'Wherefore Art Thou Tereu? Juliet and the Legacy of Rape'. It opens by antagonistically implying previous editors and critics have deliberately misread the play: 'the seemingly exhaustive commentary on Shakespeare's *Romeo and Juliet* has contrived to ignore a cluster of allusions linking the hero to the most notorious rapists of classical culture: Tereus, Hades, Tarquin, and Paris'. Seeking to 'break free' from the 'high-romantic reputation' of the 'balcony' scene, they argue that a threat of sexual violation permeates the adolescent courtship. They thereby posit a complex understanding of sexual aggression as part of a 'spectrum' of desire that replaces 'an absolute binary of rape and consent'.[69] Thus this article not only reinterprets the play's romance, but also makes an intervention into discourse about sexuality.

Focusing first on the scene at Juliet's window, Watson and Dickey reread Romeo's traditionally understood romantic enthusiasm as potentially menacing. In the first instance, Romeo's breaking-and-entering and secretive gazing at Juliet for a full 49 lines before he reveals his presence have voyeuristic associations. Comments in the dialogue serve to strengthen these implications. Romeo explains that he discovered the garden 'By love, that first did prompt me to inquire: / He lent me counsel, and I lent him eyes' (2.1.123–4), and Juliet describes him as 'bescreened in night' (2.1.95). A little earlier, Mercutio's dirty jokes imply that Romeo looks for a 'straight leg, and quivering thigh, / And the demesnes that there adjacent lie' (2.1.20–1). And in the first scene Romeo complains that Rosaline refused to 'bide th'encounter of assailing eyes' (1.1.209). Watson and Dickey also point out that the second-act Chorus calls Romeo 'bewitchèd by the charm of looks' (2.0.6); although they miss out the line's first word which details that Romeo *and* Juliet are 'Alike' in this visual enchantment. Their point is not that Romeo needs to be recategorized as a peeping Tom, but rather that the possibility that he is and that sexual desire might be uncomfortably close to sexual perversion, is a tension that Shakespeare explores.

Much of the threat Watson and Dickey detect is found in the allusive and figurative language of the scene. For example, in Romeo's offer to swear 'by yonder blessèd moon' (2.1.150) they perceive a reference to the classical story of Actaeon, a hunter who was turned into a stag for seeing the moon goddess Diana naked, and then torn apart by his own hounds. This somewhat distant allusion might have been more apparent to classically literate Renaissance audiences, especially since Juliet 'warns [Romeo] that he may be hunted down and torn apart by a pack if he is noticed there'. However, this commentary makes its case by introducing a metaphor not found in the text (Juliet speaks more straightforwardly of 'murder' at the hands of 'any' of her 'kinsmen' who find him [2.1.108–13]). Watson and Dickey also associate one of Romeo's most famous conceits – 'that I were a glove upon that hand, / That I might touch that cheek!' (2.1.67–8) – with 'degrading analogues' where poets fantasize about transformation into a beloved's garters.[70] The caution sounded by other characters strengthens this unusual and somewhat associative argument. Juliet knows that she should be wary of 'lovers' perjuries' at which 'They say Jove laughs' (2.1.135–6) and sharply questions him: 'What satisfaction canst thou have tonight?' (2.1.169). Having proposed marriage to Romeo, she still wonders if he 'meanest not well' (2.1.193), and the Nurse is likewise worried he leads Juliet in 'a fool's paradise' (2.3.154–5). Similarly, the Friar assumes that the stop-out Romeo needs 'pardon' for 'sin' (2.2.44). Such comments articulate the dangers inherent in the wooing scenes that are obscured by the play's now iconic status.

Romeo is here presented as a potential predator, and not the harmless sonneteer of most criticism. It would be easy to misread this argument as a crude attack on Romeo that rests on dubious intertextual associations. But the point is not that Romeo *is* a fully-fledged sexual miscreant, but that Shakespeare fosters a sense of uncertainty about his actions through allusive hints and a charged situation. Juliet is necessarily alert to the possibility that this young Montague is attempting a 'Disingenuous seduction' to score sexual points against an enemy (following a similar logic to that voiced by the sexually aggressive servants in the first scene [1.1.21–30]). Refusing to acknowledge this tension,

Watson and Dickey claim, 'does no justice to the dangers Juliet must accept in pursuing' the love story.[71] Rather than distinguish, like other critics, Romeo's participation in Verona's masculine aggression and his love for Juliet, they suggest that Romeo's phallic violence in stabbing Tybalt 'looks very much like a displacement of the confrontation in the newlyweds' bedroom'.[72] Romeo himself realizes: 'Now I have stained the childhood of our joy / With blood removed but little from her own' (3.3.94–5). The commentary opens out an interpretative space between rape and consent that reveals the physical and social risks faced by Juliet.

The second 'balcony' scene – where Romeo leaves Juliet after consummating their marriage – replays in a different form the uncomfortable associations of the first: earlier in the play Romeo broke into Juliet's private space, now (after taking her virginity) he runs away. Classical allusions strengthen the sense of possible violation. Watson and Dickey spot references in Juliet's dialogue to tales of rape from Ovid's *Metamorphoses* (a well-known Latin narrative poem written in the first century AD). Thus when she tries to prevent Romeo from leaving she claims to hear the song of the 'nightingale' rather than the 'lark' (3.5.2). Since Ovid's Philomel is transformed into a nightingale after being raped by her brother-in-law Tereus, Elizabethan writers often used the bird to emblematize sexual violence. This association is deepened by Juliet's locating the nightingale on a 'pom'granate tree' (3.5.4), which hints at another Ovidian tale. Persephone was raped by Hades (the god of the Underworld): having eaten seeds from an Underworld pomegranate tree Persephone was forced to spend part of the year as Hades' bride. Watson and Dickey think this connection is confirmed by references echoing throughout the play that metaphorically marry Juliet to 'death and the Underworld' (1.4.247–8; 3.2.136–7; 3.5.139; 4.4.54–5; 4.4.61–6; 5.3.102–5), as well as Capulet's remark that 'Earth hath swallowed all my hopes but she' (1.2.14). The classical frame of reference raises anxiety about sexual violence, and complicates its definition. Similarly, the name 'Paris' connotes the classical figure who was notorious for starting the Trojan war by carrying Helen away from her legitimate husband; he 'occupies a middle category: not exactly a rapist in the most obvious criminal sense . . . but someone using force to take a woman to his bed, with destructive consequences'.[73] *Romeo and Juliet* continues to verge on the edge of violation through to its final moments, as Paris suspects Romeo of planning 'villainous shame / To the dead bodies' (5.3.52–3) in the Capulet tomb. Juliet's suicide looks like the reaction of a raped woman such as Lucrece – the Roman matron raped by Tarquin, whose plight is told by Shakespeare in the narrative poem *The Rape of Lucrece*.

Watson and Dickey conclude their article by addressing the controversial nature of their position that 'Rape is . . . the threat encompassing and permeating the physical actions, the psychological tensions, and the classical allusions of what is widely deemed the ultimate love story.'[74] They quote the comments made when the article had been rejected for publication by another journal. It was objected that they should have distinguished between 'seduction, courtship, and rape' since 'culture works to elide' those categories. Watson and Dickey counter that their point is 'exactly the opposite: that the culture, as is morally imperative, works to distinguish these things, which in experience can often be murky and shifting'.[75] It is easy to see why their argument met with disapproval: it makes a conceptually (and emotionally) difficult point about sexual behaviour, and locates this idea in a play we have spent centuries celebrating (to varying degrees) as idealistically romantic. Their scholarship performs essential critical work in forcing us to reassess established 'truths' and modes of thinking. However, while their suggestion that violence haunts lovemaking usefully pinpoints moments of slippage in the play, other methodological elisions weaken the case. Throughout the article they frequently refer to Shakespeare's source, Arthur Brooke's *The Tragicall Historye of Romeus and Juliet* (1562), in tandem with the tragedy itself. Brooke's Romeus emerges as more clearly threatening than Shakespeare's Romeo; but the earlier text is cited to shore up the argument about the Shakespearean play, when it might just as easily be claimed that Shakespeare toned down the ambiguities of the narrative account. Nevertheless, the central thesis of the article cleverly refocuses the sexual themes of the play and detects tensions and allusions that are otherwise concealed by the play's iconic reputation.

Negotiating the play's (overly) familiar qualities is also crucial to the 'interpreters' we encounter in the next chapter, where we move from written responses to the medium of film.

# CHAPTER NINE

# From fair Verona to Verona Beach: Shakespeare on Film

The majority of people experience *Romeo and Juliet* extra-textually, that is, they recognize those names as symbolic of tragic love without ever having read Shakespeare's play. But then, as Chapter 1's discussion of Quarto 1 and Quarto 2 shows, 'Shakespeare's play' is a deceptively straightforward term for a slippery concept. The innumerable and varied adaptations of *Romeo and Juliet* in different forms of media (ballet, opera, puppet show, manga, and so on) are evidence both for and against the universality of the Shakespearean text: it is a story that keeps being retold across time and cultures, but it needs to be reshaped to fit new contexts. This chapter considers two of the most famous adaptations of the play in our time: the films of Franco Zeffirelli and Baz Luhrmann. These adaptations offer valuable interpretations of Shakespeare's drama (much like the plays of Otway and Garrick discussed in Chapter 2), and function as works of art in their own right (just as Shakespeare's text is itself an adaptation of a famous story).

## FRANCO ZEFFIRELLI, *ROMEO AND JULIET* (1968)

Franco Zeffirelli's *Romeo and Juliet* was the most commercially successful Shakespeare film of its day. Contemporary reviews were mixed but the film was a hit with the newly emergent youth market of the 1960s. Eight years earlier, Zeffirelli had staged a production of the play at the Old Vic in London; however, he altered the text to make a film in its own right, rather than a screening of a theatrical production.[1] Influenced by Italian neo-realist directors such as Roberto Rossellini and Luchino Visconti, Zeffirelli avoided any sense of 'staginess' in his film. The camera (at times shaky, as if handheld) appeared to capture events as they happened. Thus even though the film was set in Renaissance Italy, audiences were invited to connect to 'real' and 'natural' action. Indeed the historical distance from both Renaissance Italy and the early modern Shakespearean text is elided in Zeffirelli's universalizing vision. He sees

Shakespeare's plays as applying 'to every human being on earth, no matter what [their] cultural background'.[2] But in order to sustain this idea Zeffirelli necessarily makes cuts.

Like Otway and Garrick before him (see Chapter 2 above), Zeffirelli removes passages of Shakespeare's dialogue so that only one-third remains.[3] As we have seen, for many critics language is not merely a vehicle for dialogue in *Romeo and Juliet*, but is the play's central theme: the lovers interrogate the signifying system by questioning 'what's in a name' (see Chapter 5 above). Zeffirelli edits out anything that seems unfamiliarly Elizabethan to modern ears and reclaims the story as exclusively emotional. Where the play's lovers communicate through stylised Petrarchan dialogue, Zeffirelli uses close-ups of the lovers' faces to reveal the formation of a less wordy attachment. Body language becomes part of the film's meaning, as the young couple's physical demonstrativeness conveys an immature enthusiasm. Zeffirelli carefully selected actors who naturally conveyed naiveté: at 15 and 16, respectively, Olivia Hussey and Leonard Whiting were not 'performing' youthful innocence. As unknowns, they did not remind the audience of other roles, so that they could simply 'be' Romeo and Juliet. The actors' relative inexperience in performance suited Zeffirelli's preference for dialogue spoken naturalistically rather than with poetic regard for metre. Indeed, in place of complex conceits, classical references and rhetorical figures, the actors make various non-verbal sounds: Mercutio *mmm*s and *ahh*s his way through the Queen Mab speech, Romeo grunts and yelps when he fights, and the lovers' kisses are remarkably noisy.

At only one moment does the film break off from an apparently realist mode: the emotional high point of the lovers' first meeting. The difference is registered not in the delivery of the lines, but in the way the film frames them. Russell Jackson explains 'the diegetic music for the song' – that is, music that fits the narrative and fictional situation – 'at first appropriate for the resources of the musicians seen in the hall, is replaced by the fuller symphonic orchestration of nondiegetic music'.[4] The folk singer interrupts the Renaissance dance to deliver a song and is encircled by an audience. Robert Shaughnessy usefully likens this moment to the 'conventions of the musical and, more particularly, the emergent codes of pop music television and film'. Rota's 'Love Theme' frames the lovers' shared sonnet so that their words occupy 'the slot which, in a pop song, would be filled by a guitar solo'.[5] The lovers are briefly lifted out of their Renaissance world, and their love is communicated not in the Elizabethan attire of a Petrarchan sonnet, but through the more familiar form of 1960s popular music.

While the emotional content of the love story is accentuated, the younger generation's culpability for the feudal violence is tempered. The fight between Tybalt and Mercutio registers real competitiveness and social aggression as the pair taunt one another in front of an appreciative crowd of youths. But there is also a note of humour that demonstrates that the real antagonism is not meant to be fatal. At one point Tybalt manages to get a sword to Mercutio's throat; Mercutio looks nervous for an instant then leans back, feigning exaggerated relaxation and making both characters laugh. Romeo parts them out of an anxiety that an accident might happen, ironically causing that accident. Misfortune rather than serious misbehaviour precipitates the tragedy. And at Mercutio's death Zeffirelli brilliantly captures the generic hybridity of Shakespeare's text. Only Tybalt realizes that he has seriously wounded Mercutio; his horror at the sight of blood clarifies that the killing is unintentional. Mercutio continues to jest, making the most of his comic role until the very end. But as death approaches and his curses become real, comedy and tragedy are put in horrifying proximity. The dying boy staggers up a set of steps (as to a raised stage) and the unwitting crowd provide jeering applause at every step, assuming this is part of his performance. Zeffirelli shows us Mercutio's perspective through a blurred focus. The crowd roar with laughter at Mercutio's death; tragedy bleeds through comedy.

Zeffirelli is thus careful to absolve the younger generation of responsibility for the tragedy's violence. When he races after Tybalt, Romeo's rage has a distinctly immature quality that sees him flailing wildly. Like Garrick, Zeffirelli eventually decided to cut the scene of Romeo's killing of Paris, remarking that it turned the young lover into an 'Ugly boy, ugly boy!'[6] This film presents the lovers as innocent victims of misfortune rather than complex moral agents. The removal of Romeo's scene with the Apothecary – when he exploits the druggist's poverty to buy poison – likewise simplifies the hero's character. Similarly, Juliet is a passionate child. When seeking the Friar's help to escape bigamy with Paris she does not threaten suicide, so that her offers to be covered with 'dead men's rattling bones' sound like childish hyperbole rather than a true determination to confront danger. She flings herself sobbing at the Friar's feet just as she had earlier clung to her Nurse's skirts when her father shouted. Zeffirelli's portrayal concentrates on her love and innocence, rather than on the Shakespearean Juliet's flouting of gender roles as she organizes her own wedding and funeral.

Jack Jorgens claims that Zeffirelli's *Romeo and Juliet* is 'a "youth movie" of the 1960s which glorifies the young and caricatures the old, a Renaissance *Graduate*'.[7] Despite its historical setting, the film's aesthetics connect it to contemporary culture. Robert Shaughnessy details the 'cod-medieval graphics' of the title 'that also invoke the Tolkienesque album-cover artwork of acid rock'; the 'psychedelic red and yellow doublet and hose' of the Capulet servants that recalls 'the characteristics of the Haight-Ashbury and Carnaby Street' in contrast to the 'Montagues whose dark-hued sartorial conservatism identifies them more closely with the world of the straights'; the appearance of Romeo as 'a gentler kind of hippie (carrying not a sword but a flower, signifying his desire to make love rather than war) and a remnant from an earlier era, with an aura of innocence reminiscent of the young Cliff Richard'; and the use of hair as 'a crucial signifier throughout the film' whereby Romeo's 'neat Beatles-style moptop' gets gradually messier and Juliet 'literally lets her hair down ... at the moment of soft-core sexual abandon in the balcony scene'.[8]

Yet if the film consciously connects to the popular signifiers of 1960s youth culture, it also avoids engaging with its political substance. The year of the film's release, 1968, was a year of 'revolution'. Eastern European students and workers demonstrated against repressive Communist regimes. In the United States students led protests against the Vietnam War and nuclear armament; the civil rights movement grew (despite the assassination of Martin Luther King in that year); and feminism found new force through demonstrations at the Miss America contest. But Zeffirelli's young characters are too innocent for their love to function as a conscious protest against the world shaped by adults. Russell Jackson argues:

> ■ Neither of them expresses or indicates dislike of their parents and when she tries to defy her father Juliet shows no signs of sharing a modern audience's understanding of her situation as a consequence of living in patriarchy ... they have no insight into what is going on beyond anger and frustration at the impediments to their love. In this respect Romeo and Juliet are far removed from the more activist members of the generation of 1968. What is 'contemporary' in Zeffirelli's version resides in the couple's frank expression of sexual desire and their haircuts, and in a fundamental ordinariness.[9] □

Zeffirelli purges the text not only of the rhetoric that allows Romeo and Juliet to meditate on the problems they face, but also of any sense that their society has condemned them to tragedy. This couple are simply victims of misfortune. Twenty-eight years later, in another film consciously geared to the youth market, Baz Luhrmann presents a more complex view of adolescent culpability in the tragedy.

## BAZ LUHRMANN, *WILLIAM SHAKESPEARE'S ROMEO + JULIET* (1996)

In its very title Luhrmann's film signals a playful relationship with its textual origins. On the one hand the apparently gratuitous inclusion of Shakespeare's full name reverently devolves authority to 'the bard';

but on the other, the twentieth-century Australian director implicitly claims this same authority: Luhrmann's vision of *Romeo and Juliet* is authentically Shakespearean. Furthermore, while the presence of the name implies tradition, the substitution of the graffiti-like symbol '+' for the word 'and' marks a new appropriation of the old tale. Even before the film starts, Luhrmann's postmodern aesthetic exposes the illusion of a neat relationship between author, text and adaptor.

The film itself constantly 'foregrounds its own status as a mediated representation'.[10] The DVD menu is organized around a decaying proscenium arch (the framework of an old-fashioned theatre) which also appears in the action as the site of Mercutio's death. The film opens with an old-fashioned television zooming into view to engulf the whole screen; at the end, this television shrinks down again and disappears. Luhrmann repeatedly draws our attention to the various 'frames' we habitually look past, insisting that we recognize our position as viewers of a represented fiction. James N. Loehlin notes that (in complete contrast to Zeffirelli's naturalistic use of the camera) Luhrmann's film 'reels with dizzying hand-held shots, slam zooms and swish pans, as well as . . . changing film speeds, jump cuts and lush, unnatural saturation of colour'.[11] Similarly, rather than settling into one cinematic mode, the film quotes multiple genres such as Westerns, news reports, music videos and soap operas, to name but a few. As José Arroyo puts it, the film is 'set in a "constructed" world, one that is different enough from a "real" one to allow for different ways of being and knowing, but with enough similarities to permit understanding'. We are never allowed to forget that we are watching an unreal fiction, and are instead invited to think about 'what this constructed world stands for and how it comments on our own'.[12] As we consume Luhrmann's entertaining tragedy we are also forced to notice how the media cues particular emotional responses.

Part of the film's strange unreality lies in its impossible combination of temporalities: Elizabethan language is spoken by teenagers with 1990s haircuts; these teenagers drive brand-new 1970s cars in an oddly futuristic world where neon lights sit alongside crumbling ruins. Michael Anderegg describes this amalgamation as

> ■ a future that is really a past; a 'there' that is really 'here;' a story that is freshly being told yet again – the effect intensified by the way Luhrmann ratchets up the sense of fate and foreknowledge already present in the play: this is a story already over before it begins. What is most 'postmodern' about the film is its ransacking of the past both for its subject matter and for its style.[13] □

Luhrmann's postmodern aesthetic thus helps to communicate the text's sense of fate (the sense of the lovers' future being always already determined) and explores what it means for a text to function as a 'timeless' myth.

The original quality of the Shakespearean language is also put in question. On one level, Luhrmann's film straightforwardly explicates Elizabethan language. Shakespearean metaphors are literalized to unlock their meaning for modern audiences. For example, Shakespeare's Romeo calls Juliet a 'bright angel' (2.1.69), and so Luhrmann's Juliet attends the Capulet costume party dressed as an angel. (Compare the way Zeffirelli removes Elizabethan oxymora from the dialogue but makes a similar point visually, as when Romeo throws a flower on the wreckage of the latest fray instead of lamenting 'O brawling love, O loving hate' [1.1.172]).[14] However, Luhrmann's film, like Shakespeare's play, interrogates the function of language, but by different means. Luhrmann cuts significant portions of dialogue but he also translates it into various forms of media. Snatches of Shakespearean language appear in newspaper headlines, on billboard advertisements, on the barrel of a gun, on a petrol-station sign, as the brand name of a courier company, and tattooed onto an actor's skin. Words are supposed to have 'depth' through meaning, but here Shakespearean language is literally superficial, emblazoned as it is on various surfaces. Barbara Hodgdon argues that 'the film restyles textual culture as fashion or fetish'.[15] In reducing language to a mere brand, the film makes a postmodern point about the impossibility of originality in the present and of accessing the real origins of the past (Shakespearean language is fractured into scraps of speeches and clichés). Yet this postmodern awareness of the worn-out quality of language is not dissimilar from Shakespeare's early modern concern for the artificiality of Petrarchan rhetoric (see Chapter 6 above). In freeing himself from a 'faithful' adaptation of the full Shakespearean text, Luhrmann engages with some of its more complex questions.

Nevertheless, many commentators see Luhrmann's Romeo and Juliet as simplified versions of Shakespeare's characters. Juliet, for example, does not rail against Romeo on learning of his murder of her cousin, nor does she equivocate with her mother about her love for Romeo/hate for Tybalt's murderer, and she feels no suspicion of the Friar. Anderegg complains this 'Juliet, robbed of these enriching traits, emotions, motives, and inconsistencies of character, is an ideal Victorian Juliet, perhaps, but she is far from the Juliet Shakespeare created.'[16] (Similar reductions were also visited upon both Garrick's and Zeffirelli's Juliets.) However, while Luhrmann might have stripped his protagonists of some of their textual richness, his portrayal explores alternative complexities. Where Zeffirelli deliberately chose actors with no screen history to colour their portrayal of Romeo and Juliet, Luhrmann cast Claire Danes and Leonardo DiCaprio as performers already known for roles as 'misunderstood adolescents' in *My So-Called Life, This Boy's Life* and *The Basketball Diaries*.[17] In this way Luhrmann hints at the role-playing *within* the Shakespearean parts. For example, Luhrmann's Romeo is found smoking a cigarette and writing in a journal, semi-consciously performing the anti-hero role (in the DVD commentary Luhrmann lists James Dean, Byron and Kurt Cobain as relevant types). This representation translates Shakespeare's Petrarchan wannabe into a modern idiom. Furthermore, the film plays with different cultural identities. Barbara Hodgdon comments: 'Just as *Romeo + Juliet* is not precisely a chick flick – one where more tears than blood are shed – but, given its coterie of boys who crash cars and carry big guns, can be "re-branded" within a masculine discursive space, DiCaprio's Romeo straddles several cultural masculinities.'[18] The film's setting in the fictionalized 'Verona Beach' also enables play with racial identities: 'it takes place, not in a Eurocentric culture, but in a multicultural borderland – a mythic geographical space open to variant readings (Miami, California, Mexico) – the film not only accentuates the performative possibilities for "othering" but ties its representation of gender to somewhat slippery markers of ethnicity and class.'[19] Characterological interiority may not be as fully developed in the film as in Shakespeare's drama, but Luhrmann's adaptation provides another perspective on the identities shaped externally by culture.

Luhrmann also captures the protagonists' yearning for authentic experience. In the play this longing is seen in Romeo's endeavours to throw himself into Petrarchan passion and Juliet's attempts to reach beyond language. The film figures this desire visually as nostalgia for an imaginary past. Loehlin notes that where Dave Paris attends the Capulet masked ball as a modern man, costumed as an astronaut, Romeo and Juliet 'are dressed as a knight in shining armour and a Botticelli angel'.[20] Just as Shakespeare's Romeo and Juliet remain locked in their names and in language more generally (see Chapter 5 above), Luhrmann's lovers are limited to mere clichés when attempting to reach back to a past that never really existed. Indeed the postmodern mode of the film as a whole makes the inaccessibility of authenticity a condition of its form. Nevertheless the lovers are granted fleeting moments of separation that mark their difference from the worn-out world they occupy. Water is a recurrent symbol throughout the film that links the couple together: Juliet is first seen with her face submerged in the water of a washbowl; Romeo plunges his face into water to rinse off an acid trip; they catch sight of one another through a fish tank; and the 'balcony' scene is relocated to a swimming pool. Water silences and slows down the frenetic activity of the film, perhaps even hinting at a spiritual dimension to their love.[21] Other shots frame the lovers in separate spaces, as when they kiss in a lift or are hidden beneath bed sheets.

In a significant alteration to the play, the couple's isolation is maintained in their suicide scene. Shakespeare's lovers are deprived of privacy in their last moments: Romeo has to fend off Paris to get to Juliet, and then drags his corpse into the already well-populated Capulet tomb; Juliet's last conversation is with the Friar rather than her husband. Like Garrick and Zeffirelli, Luhrmann does not allow his Romeo to kill Paris. And neither does the Friar intrude on the couple's final moment of intimacy. Luhrmann shifts the action from the tomb to a church, which becomes a fantasy space occupied only by the lovers. As in Garrick's adaptation, Juliet wakes in time for Romeo to see her before he dies. The pair may not have a conversation like their eighteenth-century counterparts, but the shared look gives them a last moment of togetherness and allows each to die solely focused on the other.

The vast proportions of the church (which wishfully enlarge the tiny spaces of earlier snatched intimacies) are gloriously bedecked with traditional candles and modern neon crosses. Luhrmann has literalized the 'feasting presence full of light' (5.3.86) and encourages his audience to consume a gorgeous tragedy. Juliet's gunshot wound to the head produces only an artful trickle of blood. The beautiful corpses lie together as the camera hovers above them and zooms out to the operatic score of the '*Liebestod*' from Wagner's *Tristan und Isolde*. Even before the film has ended it produces nostalgia for itself, as we are shown a montage of the lovers' 'best' moments. And yet Luhrmann does not permit his audience only to swoon at the lovely pathos of it all. Barbara Hodgdon argues:

> ■ Although the thousand-candle tableau may suggest that love is all there is, its garish MTV excess also clearly marks it as an imported fantasy, something cooked up when an old play confronts a new medium. And that is precisely the point: highlighting the tension between the two, Luhrmann's film juxtaposes medium and message, has it both ways. As the candle-flames dissolve into bubbles to freeze frame the lovers' underwater kiss, a long fade to white, accompanied by the *liebestod*'s final strains, dissolves in turn to the 'social real' – a white-sheeted body on a hospital trolley.[22] □

Even as viewers revel in the sentimentality and fabulous aesthetics, they are also forced to critique that response and recognize the tragedy's function as consumer entertainment. The jarring juxtaposition between the hyper-romantic death scene and the newsreel version of reality exposes the constructed nature of both. There is no 'real' space left for the lovers.

Luhrmann's film ends bleakly, without the Capulet–Montague reconciliation scripted by Shakespeare. Instead the two fathers stand dumbly by ambulances. (Only earlier in the film was reconciliation glimpsed in the Friar's fantasy of peace.) Yet if the adults fail to make amends, it is significant that Luhrmann does not represent the story's youth as blameless victims either of fate (like Zeffirelli) or adult society (like Otway). Luhrmann's gun-toting teenagers share real responsibility for the tragedy's violence. Where Zeffirelli's Tybalt looked horrified at his accidental killing of Mercutio, Luhrmann's Tybalt shows no regret. *William Shakespeare's Romeo + Juliet* not only speaks to a youth market, it also speaks about them. It remains a popular and perspicacious adaptation of the play in the twenty-first century.

# Conclusion

In the very last words of the play, the Prince asserts the superlative status of *Romeo and Juliet*: 'For never was a story of more woe / Than this of Juliet and her Romeo' (5.3.309–10). Popular opinion seems to concur: *Romeo and Juliet* remains one of Western culture's most iconic love stories. It continues to be adapted in wildly various forms: in 2004 the Icelandic company Verstuport performed the play on trapeze; Sonia Leong illustrated a manga version in 2007; Tom Morris directed octogenarian lovers in *Juliet and her Romeo* for the Bristol Old Vic in 2010; the same year saw a collaboration between Mudlark and the Royal Shakespeare Company that performed the play (*Such Tweet Sorrow*) across five weeks on Twitter and other online social platforms; and garden gnomes replaced teenagers and found a happy ending in the 2011 animation, *Gnomeo and Juliet* (perhaps proving Garrick's point about the dangers of puns). The cultural appetite for this tale seems to be insatiable. However, we have seen that over the last four centuries some critics have been rather less confident than the Prince in the play's tragic value (or, at least, find weakness rather than wonder in its 'woe'). Even so, the range and depth of critical insights into *Romeo and Juliet* are testament to its intellectual (as well as its emotional) profundity. Scholarship has repeatedly recorded Shakespeare's formal, poetic and social innovations in this work. In her appropriation of the sonnet, epithalamium and tragedy, one of literature's most famous heroines is generically experimental; organizing her own wedding and funeral, she is also socially bold. *Romeo and Juliet*'s linguistic, Petrarchan, psychoanalytical, gendered and sexual aspects continue to provoke new debate. As is shown by Grady's methodological fusions between aesthetic theory and psychoanalysis, and Watson and Dickey's contentious exposure of sinister threats in seductive poetry, criticism keeps moving. The relatively new willingness to engage with the tragedy in its multiple texts (Quarto 1 and Quarto 2) also means that returning to the play itself demands flexibility.

One of the most exciting critical developments in Shakespeare studies in recent years has taken place in theatre history. With their paradigm-shifting book, *Shakespeare in Parts*, Simon Palfrey and Tiffany Stern reveal the practical and interpretative centrality of the actor's 'part' in early modern theatre. Rather than rehearsing from full scripts containing all of the play's dialogue, actors were given 'roles' that included only their lines and the two or three words that cued each speech. By scrutinizing 'parts', Palfrey and Stern show how Shakespeare shaped character in directly dramatic ways. For example, they determine that the cues for an actor's dialogue help the performer understand the world he inhabits: in the case of the Romeo-actor the first-act cues concentrate the (un)romantic advice to shift affections and thus 'express the prevailing sexual ethos of Verona's young men'.[1] Similarly, the structure of parts actively conditions the way an actor inhabits character. On the occasions when the Juliet-actor cues another actor's speech with half-lines (as opposed to the more usual full-lines), the words are ambiguous, so that player is left uncertain as to whether the speech forms a soliloquy (cuing the end of a scene) or dialogue. In this way 'The actor is often forced to commit absolutely to the emotion, and to the passion and physicality of its expression ... without quite knowing whether satisfaction will come immediately, soon, or not at all.'[2] Such an insight consolidates Edward Snow's analysis of Juliet's language as conceptually daring, and Watson and Dickey's point about Juliet's risky trust in Romeo. *Shakespeare in Parts* looks set to have a large and long-lasting impact on the way critics approach and conceptualize early modern drama.

The turn of the twenty-first century has also seen a 'turn to religion' in both Shakespearean criticism and Renaissance research more broadly. Scholars have attended to the religious saturation of post-Reformation culture, and in particular the tensions experienced in Protestant England – a nation that had a Catholic heritage and which was surrounded by Catholic European neighbours. Beatrice Groves demonstrates the dual influence on Shakespeare of both Protestant 'texts' and Catholic 'traditions' in her book, *Texts and Traditions: Religion in Shakespeare 1592–1603*. She detects in *Romeo and Juliet* allusions to Easter or what she terms a 'paschal motif', especially in the tomb scene and the hopes for revivification.[3] In connecting this Christian theme of salvation with the tragedy's paradoxically comedic impulses, Groves clears the ground for readings that are alert to the interactions between religious ideas and literary form. *Romeo and Juliet*'s Catholic setting and content holds interpretative potential for those interested in the sectarian fissures of the age. Given the play's theologically charged vocabulary (for example, the lovers' shared sonnet centres on metaphors of palmers, saints, icons, sin, prayer and repentance), we should expect more explorations of these topics in the future.

Related to the developments in religious criticism is the historicist interest in Shakespeare that has prevailed since the 1980s. *Romeo and Juliet* has proved to be a less obvious starting point for such research than other plays in the Shakespeare canon, but a recent article by Glenn Clark indicates the historical applications of the tragedy. In 'The Civil Mutinies of *Romeo and Juliet*' Clark interrogates the early modern permutations of the idea of 'civility', ranging from aristocratic violence to 'cultivated refinement and productive sociability'.[4] Dramatizing various forms of civil defiance, *Romeo and Juliet* is said to rethink distinctions of rank, so that Clark usefully opens the play out to politicized interpretation. The emotional valence of the play's love story has sometimes overshadowed its social structures (though feminist critics have exposed the links between the two); there is space and opportunity for scholars to redress the balance.

This Guide has shown that claims for the play's 'timelessness' are problematic: *Romeo and Juliet* is shaped by a specifically Elizabethan literary and cultural context and is adapted to meet the demands of successive ages thereafter. Nevertheless, the drama's enduring appeal is incontestable. A continuing critical challenge of the play remains that of distinguishing between what it says about love, sex, death, family and friendship, and what we want it to say. *Romeo and Juliet* promises to hold our academic and emotional interest for a long time to come.

# Notes

## INTRODUCTION

1. Brian Vickers (ed.), *Shakespeare: The Critical Heritage, Volume 2: 1693–1733* (London and Boston: Routledge & Kegan Paul 1995), p. 189.
2. A. C. Bradley, *Shakespearean Tragedy* (1904; R/P London: Penguin, 1991), p. 19.

## CHAPTER ONE

1. Jill Levenson (ed.), *Romeo and Juliet* (Oxford: Oxford University Press, 2000), p. 103.
2. Levenson (2000), p. 111.
3. Lukas Erne (ed.), *The First Quarto of Romeo and Juliet* (Cambridge: Cambridge University Press, 2007), p. 26.
4. Erne (2007), p. 26.
5. Erne (2007), pp. 30–1.
6. Erne (2007), p. 31.
7. Erne (2007), p. 32.
8. Erne (2007), p. 32.
9. Erne (2007), pp. 27–8.
10. Erne (2007), pp. 34–5, 29–30.
11. Amy J. Riess and George Walton Williams, '"Tragical Mirth": From *Romeo* to *Dream*', *Shakespeare Quarterly* 43:2 (Summer 1992), p. 215.
12. Riess and Williams (1992), p. 217.
13. John Marston, *The Scourge of Villanie* (London, 1598), sig. [H4r].
14. Marston (1598), sig. [H4r].
15. Anonymous, *The Three Parnassus Plays*, ed. J. B. Leishman (London: Nicholson & Watson, 1949), p. 183.
16. Henry Porter, *The Two Angry Women of Abingdon* (London, 1599), sig. Gr.
17. Porter (1599), sig. Gv.
18. Mary Bly, 'Bawdy Puns and Lustful Virgins: The Legacy of Juliet's Desire in Comedies of the Early 1600s', *Shakespeare Survey* 49 (1996), p. 97.
19. Porter (1599), sig. D2r.
20. Porter (1599), sig. Gr.
21. Porter (1599), sig. G2r.
22. Porter (1599), sig. G2v.
23. John Ford, *'Tis Pity She's a Whore*, ed. Martin Wiggins (London: A&C Black, 2003).
24. Robert Burton, *The Anatomy of Melancholy*, ed. Holbrook Jackson (New York: New York Review of Books, 2001), Pt. 3, Sec. 2, Mem. 4, p. 187.
25. Burton (2001), Pt. 3, Sec. 2, Mem. 4, p. 188.
26. Burton (2001), Pt. 3, Sec. 2, Mem. 4, p. 189.
27. Burton (2001), Pt. 3, Sec. 2, Mem. 4, p. 186.

## CHAPTER TWO

1. Samuel Pepys, *Diary*, ed. Robert Latham and William Matthews, 10 vols (London: G. Bell, 1970), Vol. 3, p. 39.
2. Susan J. Owen, *Restoration Theatre and Crisis* (Oxford: Clarendon Press, 1996), p. 131.
3. Michael Dobson, *The Making of the National Poet* (Oxford: Clarendon Press, 1992), pp. 77–8.
4. Thomas Otway, *The History and Fall of Caius Marius* (London, 1692), p. 62.
5. Otway (1692), p. 63.
6. Jessica Munns, '"The Dark Disorders of a Divided State": Otway and Shakespeare's *Romeo and Juliet*', *Comparative Drama* 19:4 (Winter 1985–86), pp. 347–62.
7. Otway (1692), p. 18.
8. Otway (1692), p. 64.
9. Otway (1692), p. 64.
10. Otway (1692), pp. 64–5.
11. Otway (1692), p. 65.
12. Nicholas Rowe, *Works of Mr. William Shakespear* (London, 1709), p. xxvi.
13. Rowe, p. xxxi.
14. David Garrick, *Romeo and Juliet* (London: J. & R. Tonson & S. Draper, 1753), sig. A3r.
15. George C. Branam, 'The Genesis of David Garrick's *Romeo and Juliet*', *Shakespeare Quarterly* 35:2 (Summer 1984), p. 178.
16. Garrick (1753), pp. 65–6.
17. Garrick (1753), p. 69.
18. Charlotte Lennox, *Shakespear Illustrated: or the Novels and Histories, on which the Plays of Shakespear are Founded, Collected and Translated from the Original*, Vol. I (London, 1753), p. 89.
19. Lennox (1753), p. 99.
20. Levenson (2000), p. 4.
21. Lennox (1753), p. 94.
22. Lennox (1753), p. 95.
23. Lennox (1753), p. 97.
24. Lennox (1753), p. 98.
25. Samuel Johnson (ed.), *The Plays of William Shakespeare*, Vol. I (London, 1765), pp. viii–ix.
26. Samuel Johnson (1765) in Brian Vickers (ed.), *Shakespeare: The Critical Heritage, Volume V: 1765–1774* (London and Boston: Routledge & Kegan Paul, 1995), p. 155.
27. Vickers 5, p. 155.
28. Johnson (1765), p. xxiv.
29. Vickers 5, pp. 152–3.
30. Vickers 5, p. 154.
31. Vickers 5, p. 154.

## CHAPTER THREE

1. Schlegel, in, Jonathan Bate (ed.), *The Romantics on Shakespeare* (London: Penguin, 1992), p. 511.

2. Schlegel (1992), p. 511.
3. Schlegel (1992), pp. 511–12.
4. Schlegel (1992), p. 512.
5. Schlegel (1992), p. 513.
6. Samuel Taylor Coleridge, *Coleridge on Shakespeare: A Selection of the Essays, Notes and Lectures of Samuel Taylor Coleridge on the Poems and Plays of Shakespeare*, ed. Terence Hawkes (London: Penguin, 1969), p. 155.
7. Coleridge (1969), p. 136.
8. Coleridge (1969), p. 139.
9. Coleridge (1969), p. 140.
10. Coleridge (1969), pp. 147–8.
11. Coleridge (1969), p. 134.
12. Coleridge (1969), p. 149.
13. Coleridge (1969), p. 150.
14. Coleridge (1969), p. 151.
15. Coleridge (1969), p. 137.
16. Coleridge (1969), p. 138.
17. Coleridge (1969), pp. 134–5.
18. Coleridge (1969), p. 144.
19. Coleridge (1969), p. 145.
20. Hazlitt, in Bate, *Romantics on Shakespeare*, p. 520.
21. Hazlitt (1992), p. 521.
22. Philip Davis, 'Nineteenth-Century Juliet', *Shakespeare Survey* 49 (1996), 139.
23. Hazlitt (1992), pp. 521–2.
24. Cheri L. Larsen Hoeckley (ed.), 'Introduction', in Anna Jameson, *Shakespeare's Heroines* (Peterborough, ONT: Broadview, 2005), p. 9.
25. Jameson (2005), p. 125.
26. Jameson (2005), p. 142.
27. Jameson (2005), p. 136.
28. Jameson (2005), p. 133.
29. Jameson (2005), p. 127.
30. Jameson (2005), p. 127.
31. Jameson (2005), p. 137.
32. Davis (1996), pp. 134–5.
33. Jameson (2005), p. 126.
34. Hoeckley (2005), p. 21.
35. Jameson (2005), p. 141.
36. Jameson (2005), p. 144.
37. Davis (1996), p. 132.
38. Jameson (2005), pp. 147–8.
39. Edward Dowden, *Shakspere: A Critical Study of His Mind and Art* (London: Routledge, 1948), p. 95.
40. Dowden (1948), p. 96.
41. Dowden (1948), p. 101.
42. Dowden (1948), p. 107.
43. Dowden (1948), pp. 107–8.
44. Dowden (1948), p. 108.
45. Dowden (1948), p. 110.
46. Dowden (1948), pp. 117–18.
47. Dowden (1948), p. 122.
48. Dowden (1948), pp. 123–4.

49. As quoted in Ann Thompson and Sasha Roberts (eds), *Women Reading Shakespeare 1660–1900: An Anthology of Criticism* (Manchester: Manchester University Press, 1997), p. 185.
50. Helena Faucit, *On Some of Shakespeare's Characters* (1885; R/P Edinburgh and London: William Blackwood & Sons, 1887), p. 115.
51. Faucit (1887), p. 117.
52. Faucit (1887), p. 90.
53. Faucit (1887), p. 85.
54. Faucit (1887), p. 113.
55. Faucit (1887), p. 89.
56. Faucit (1887), pp. 107–8.
57. Faucit (1887), p. 109.
58. Faucit (1887), pp. 118–19.
59. Faucit (1887), pp. 139–40.
60. Faucit (1887), p. 154.

## CHAPTER FOUR

1. A. C. Bradley, *Shakespearean Tragedy* (1904; R/P London: Penguin, 1991), p. 21.
2. Bradley (1904), p. 33.
3. Bradley (1904), p. 47.
4. Bradley (1904), p. 38.
5. Bradley (1904), p. 29.
6. Bradley (1904), pp. 24–5.
7. Bradley (1904), p. 34.
8. H. B. Charlton, *Shakespearian Tragedy* (Cambridge: Cambridge University Press, 1948), p. 49.
9. Charlton (1948), p. 49.
10. Charlton (1948), p. 50.
11. Charlton (1948), p. 51.
12. Charlton (1948), p. 51.
13. Charlton (1948), pp. 52, 60.
14. Charlton (1948), pp. 56–8.
15. Charlton (1948), p. 58.
16. Charlton (1948), p. 61.
17. Charlton (1948), p. 61.
18. Charlton (1948), p. 62.
19. Franklin M. Dickey, *Not Wisely But Too Well: Shakespeare's Love Tragedies* (San Marino, CA: Huntington Library, 1957), p. 102.
20. Dickey (1957), p. 116.
21. Dickey (1957), p. 103.
22. Dickey (1957), pp. 104–6.
23. Dickey (1957), p. 106.
24. Dickey (1957), p. 111.
25. Dickey (1957), p. 113.
26. Dickey (1957), p. 116.
27. Dickey (1957), p. 116.
28. Dickey (1957), p. 116.
29. Dickey (1957), p. 104.
30. Dickey (1957), p. 115.

31. John Lawlor, '*Romeo and Juliet*', in John Russell Brown and Bernard Harris (eds), *Early Shakespeare* (London: Edward Arnold, 1961), p. 123.
32. Lawlor (1961), pp. 130, 124.
33. Lawlor (1961), p. 125.
34. Lawlor (1961), pp. 125–6.
35. Lawlor (1961), p. 127.
36. Lawlor (1961), p. 127.
37. Lawlor (1961), pp. 130–1.
38. Lawlor (1961), p. 132.
39. Lawlor (1961), pp. 133, 135.
40. Lawlor (1961), p. 139.
41. Lawlor (1961), p. 138.
42. Lawlor (1961), p. 142.
43. Nicholas Brooke, *Shakespeare's Early Tragedies* (London: Methuen, 1968), p. 88.
44. Brooke (1968), p. 90.
45. Brooke (1968), p. 81.
46. Brooke (1968), p. 94.
47. Brooke (1968), p. 87.
48. Brooke (1968), p. 96.
49. Brooke (1968), p. 82.
50. Brooke (1968), p. 83.
51. Brooke (1968), p. 83.
52. Brooke (1968), p. 100.
53. Brooke (1968), p. 99.
54. Brooke (1968), p. 101.
55. Brooke (1968), p. 105.
56. Susan Snyder, '*Romeo and Juliet*: Comedy into Tragedy', *Essays in Criticism* 20:4 (October 1970), p. 391.
57. Snyder (1970), p. 391.
58. Snyder (1970), p. 394.
59. Snyder (1970), p. 394.
60. Snyder (1970), p. 400.
61. Gary M. McCown, '"Runnawayes Eyes" and Juliet's Epithalamium', *Shakespeare Quarterly* 27:2 (Spring 1976), p. 150.
62. McCown (1976), p. 153.
63. McCown (1976), p. 162.
64. McCown (1976), p. 166.
65. McCown (1976), p. 168.
66. McCown (1976), pp. 170, 169.
67. Martha Tuck Rozett, 'The Comic Structures of Tragic Endings: The Suicide Scenes of *Romeo and Juliet* and *Antony and Cleopatra*', *Shakespeare Quarterly* 36:2 (Summer 1985), p. 152.
68. Rozett (1985), p. 154.
69. Rozett (1985), p. 157.
70. Rozett (1985), p. 164.

## CHAPTER FIVE

1. Caroline F. E. Spurgeon, *Shakespeare's Imagery and What It Tells Us* (Cambridge: Cambridge University Press, 1935), p. 307.

2. Spurgeon (1935), p. 310.
3. Spurgeon (1935), p. 310.
4. Spurgeon (1935), p. 312.
5. Spurgeon (1935), p. 310.
6. M. M. Mahood, *Shakespeare's Wordplay* (London: Methuen, 1957), p. 56.
7. Mahood, p. 57.
8. Mahood, pp. 62–3.
9. Mahood, p. 72.
10. Harry Levin, 'Form and Formality in *Romeo and Juliet*', *Shakespeare Quarterly* 11:1 (Winter 1960), p. 4.
11. Levin (1960), p. 4.
12. Levin (1960), p. 5.
13. Levin (1960), p. 9.
14. Levin (1960), p. 6.
15. Levin (1960), p. 9.
16. James L. Calderwood, '*Romeo and Juliet*: A Formal Dwelling', in John F. Andrews (ed.), *Romeo and Juliet: Critical Essays* (New York and London: Garland Publishing, 1993), p. 87.
17. Calderwood (1993), p. 90.
18. Calderwood (1993), pp. 90–1.
19. Calderwood (1993), p. 92.
20. Calderwood (1993), p. 100.
21. Calderwood (1993), p. 101.
22. Calderwood (1993), p. 112.
23. Calderwood (1993), p. 114.
24. Michael Goldman, *Shakespeare and the Energies of Drama* (Princeton, NJ: Princeton University Press, 1972), p. 33.
25. Goldman (1972), p. 35.
26. Goldman (1972), p. 36.
27. Goldman (1972), p. 37.
28. Goldman (1972), p. 38.
29. Goldman (1972), p. 33.
30. Goldman (1972), p. 43.
31. Jacques Derrida, 'Aphorism Countertime', trans. Nicholas Royle, in Derek Attridge (ed.), *Acts of Literature* (New York and London: Routledge, 1992), p. 416.
32. Attridge (1992), p. 414.
33. Derrida (1992), p. 417.
34. Derrida (1992), p. 432.
35. Derrida (1992), p. 427.
36. Derrida (1992), p. 423.
37. Derrida (1992), p. 420.
38. Derrida (1992), p. 422.
39. Derrida (1992), p. 423.
40. Derrida (1992), p. 425.
41. Derrida (1992), p. 426.
42. Derrida (1992), pp. 426–7.
43. Derrida (1992), p. 433.
44. Catherine Belsey, 'The Name of the Rose in *Romeo and Juliet*', *Yearbook of English Studies* 23 (1993), p. 126.
45. Belsey (1993), p. 126.

46. Belsey (1993), p. 127.
47. Belsey (1993), p. 131.
48. Belsey (1993), p. 132.
49. Belsey (1993), p. 132.
50. Belsey (1993), p. 138.
51. Belsey (1993), p. 141.
52. Belsey (1993), p. 140.
53. Belsey (1993), p. 141.
54. Belsey (1993), p. 142.
55. Kiernan Ryan, *Shakespeare*, 3rd edn (Basingstoke: Palgrave Macmillan, 2002), p. 71.
56. Ryan (2002), p. 74.
57. Ryan (2002), p. 74.
58. Ryan (2002), pp. 78–9.
59. Ryan (2002), p. 80.
60. Ryan (2002), p. 81.
61. Ryan (2002), p. 83.
62. Laurie Maguire, *Shakespeare's Names* (Oxford: Oxford University Press, 2007), p. 59.
63. Maguire (2007), p. 54.
64. Maguire (2007), p. 54.
65. Maguire (2007), p. 59.
66. Maguire (2007), p. 67.
67. Maguire (2007), p. 63.
68. Maguire (2007), p. 71.

## CHAPTER SIX

1. Leonard Forster, *The Icy Fire* (Cambridge: Cambridge University Press, 1969), p. 51.
2. Rosalie L. Colie, *Shakespeare's Living Art* (Princeton, NJ: Princeton University Press, 1974), pp. 136, 138, 137.
3. Colie quotes a textual variant: 'when he shall die'.
4. Colie (1974), p. 142.
5. Colie (1974), p. 143.
6. Colie (1974), p. 145.
7. Colie (1974), p. 145.
8. Ralph Berry, *The Shakespearean Metaphor: Studies in Language and Form* (London and Basingstoke: Macmillan, 1978), p. 37.
9. Berry (1978), p. 38.
10. Berry (1978), p. 39.
11. Berry (1978), p. 40.
12. Berry (1978), p. 41.
13. Berry (1978), p. 42.
14. Berry (1978), p. 44.
15. Berry (1978), p. 46.
16. Ann Pasternak Slater, 'Petrarchanism Come True in *Romeo and Juliet*', in Werner Habicht, D. J. Palmer and Roger Pringle (eds), *Images of Shakespeare* (Newark: University of Delaware Press, 1988), p. 133.

17. Slater (1988), p. 138.
18. Gayle Whittier, 'The Sonnet's Body and the Body Sonnetized in *Romeo and Juliet*', *Shakespeare Quarterly* 40:1 (Spring 1989), p. 27.
19. Whittier (1989), p. 28.
20. Whittier (1989), p. 30.
21. Whittier (1989), p. 32.
22. Whittier (1989), p. 37.
23. Whittier (1989), p. 32.
24. Whittier (1989), p. 33.
25. Whittier (1989), p. 35.
26. Whittier (1989), p. 36.
27. Whittier (1989), p. 40.
28. Diana E. Henderson, *Passion Made Public: Elizabethan Lyric, Gender, and Performance* (Urbana and Chicago: University of Illinois Press, 1995), p. 4.
29. Henderson (1995), p. 5.
30. Henderson (1995), p. 6.
31. Henderson (1995), p. 218.
32. Henderson (1995), p. 219.

## CHAPTER SEVEN

1. Norman Rabkin, *Shakespeare and the Common Understanding* (New York: Free Press; London: Collier-Macmillan, 1967), p. 151.
2. Rabkin (1967), p. 163.
3. Rabkin (1967), p. 164.
4. Rabkin (1967), pp. 179–80.
5. Rabkin (1967), p. 180.
6. Rabkin (1967), p. 181.
7. Rabkin (1967), p. 181.
8. Rabkin (1967), p. 183.
9. Julia Kristeva, '*Romeo and Juliet*: Love-Hatred in the Couple', in R. S. White (ed.), *Romeo and Juliet: Critical Essays* (Basingstoke: Palgrave Macmillan, 2001), p. 68.
10. Kristeva (2001), p. 69.
11. Kristeva (2001), p. 70.
12. Kristeva (2001), p. 71.
13. Kristeva (2001), p. 70.
14. Kristeva (2001), p. 69.
15. Kristeva (2001), p. 72. Kristeva quotes the textual variant 'when he shall die'.
16. Kristeva (2001), p. 73.
17. Kristeva (2001), pp. 74–5.
18. Kristeva (2001), p. 75.
19. Kristeva (2001), P. 77.
20. Kristeva (2001), p. 79.
21. Kristeva (2001), p. 80.
22. Lloyd Davis, '"Death-Marked Love": Desire and Presence in *Romeo and Juliet*', *Shakespeare Survey* 49 (1996), p. 57.
23. Davis (1996), p. 58.
24. Davis (1996), p. 59.
25. Davis (1996), p. 59.

26. Davis (1996), p. 61.
27. Davis (1996), p. 61.
28. Davis (1996), p. 63.
29. Davis (1996), p. 64.
30. Davis (1996), p. 65.
31. Davis (1996), p. 65.
32. Hugh Grady, *Shakespeare and Impure Aesthetics* (Cambridge: Cambridge University Press, 2009), p. 194.
33. Grady (2009), p. 214.
34. Grady (2009), p. 197.
35. Grady (2009), pp. 210–11.
36. Grady (2009), pp. 214–15.
37. Grady (2009), p. 223.
38. Grady (2009), p. 222.
39. Grady (2009), pp. 223–4.

## CHAPTER EIGHT

1. Coppélia Kahn, 'Coming of Age in Verona', in Ruth Swift Lenz, Gayle Greene and Carol Thomas Neely (eds), *The Woman's Part: Feminist Criticism of Shakespeare* (Urbana: University of Illinois Press, 1980), p. 172.
2. Kahn (1980), p. 173.
3. Kahn (1980), p. 179.
4. Kahn (1980), p. 180.
5. Kahn (1980), p. 182.
6. Kahn (1980), p. 185.
7. Kahn (1980), p. 188.
8. Marianne Novy, *Love's Argument: Gender Relations in Shakespeare* (Chapel Hill: University of North Carolina Press, 1984), p. 100.
9. Novy here quotes the Quarto 1 reading; Levenson's Quarto 2 edition reads: 'From love's weak childish bow she lives uncharmed' (1.1.207).
10. Novy (1984), p. 102.
11. Novy (1984), p. 103.
12. Novy (1984), p. 104.
13. Novy (1984), p. 105.
14. Novy (1984), p. 107.
15. Novy (1984), p. 108.
16. Novy (1984), pp. 108–9.
17. Edward Snow, 'Language and Sexual Difference in *Romeo and Juliet*', in Peter Erickson and Coppélia Kahn (eds), *Shakespeare's 'Rough Magic': Renaissance Essays in Honor of C. L. Barber* (Newark: University of Delaware Press, 1985), p. 170.
18. Snow (1985), p. 170.
19. Snow (1985), p. 171.
20. Snow (1985), p. 171.
21. Snow (1985), p. 172.
22. Snow (1985), p. 172.
23. Snow (1985), p. 173.
24. Snow (1985), p. 174.
25. Snow (1985), p. 176.

26. Snow (1985), p. 177.
27. Snow (1985), p. 178.
28. Snow's reading itself rests on the Quarto 1 variant 'rest'; Levenson's Quarto 2 edition has 'There rust'.
29. Snow (1985), p. 185.
30. Snow (1985), p. 188.
31. Snow (1985), p. 168.
32. Joseph Porter, *Shakespeare's Mercutio: His History and Drama* (Chapel Hill and London: University of North Carolina Press, 1988), p. 167.
33. Porter (1988), p. 99.
34. Porter (1988), p. 101.
35. Porter (1988), p. 107.
36. Porter (1988), p. 104.
37. Porter (1988), p. 106.
38. Porter (1988), p. 111.
39. Porter (1988), p. 117.
40. Porter (1988), p. 118.
41. Porter (1988), p. 119.
42. Porter (1988), p. 149.
43. Porter (1988), p. 198.
44. Dympna Callaghan, 'The Ideology of Romantic Love: The Case of Romeo and Juliet', in Dympna Callaghan, Lorraine Helms and Jyotsna Singh, *The Weyward Sisters: Shakespeare and Feminist Politics* (Oxford: Blackwell, 1994), p. 59.
45. Callaghan (1994), pp. 59–60.
46. Callaghan (1994), p. 71.
47. Callaghan (1994), p. 72.
48. Callaghan (1994), p. 74.
49. Callaghan (1994), p. 75.
50. Callaghan (1994), p. 76.
51. Callaghan (1994), p. 78.
52. Callaghan (1994), p.79.
53. Callaghan (1994), p. 81.
54. Callaghan (1994), p. 84.
55. Callaghan (1994), p. 85.
56. Callaghan (1994), p. 88.
57. Jonathan Goldberg, 'Introduction', in Jonathan Goldberg (ed.), *Queering the Renaissance* (Durham, NC: Duke University Press, 1994), p. 3.
58. Jonathan Goldberg, '*Romeo and Juliet*'s Open Rs', in Goldberg (ed.), *Queering the Renaissance*, p. 218.
59. Goldberg (1994), p. 220.
60. Goldberg (1994), pp. 219–20.
61. Goldberg (1994), p. 220.
62. Goldberg (1994), p. 225.
63. Goldberg (1994), p. 222.
64. Goldberg (1994), p. 227.
65. Goldberg (1994), p. 228.
66. Goldberg (1994), p.230.
67. Goldberg (1994), p. 231.
68. Goldberg (1994), p. 227.

69. Robert N. Watson and Stephen Dickey, 'Wherefore Art Thou Tereu? Juliet and the Legacy of Rape', *Renaissance Quarterly* 58:1 (2005), p. 127.
70. Watson and Dickey (2005), p.130.
71. Watson and Dickey (2005), pp. 133–4.
72. Watson and Dickey (2005), p. 132.
73. Watson and Dickey (2005), p. 144.
74. Watson and Dickey (2005), p. 148.
75. Watson and Dickey (2005), pp. 151–2.

## CHAPTER NINE

1. Jill L. Levenson, *Shakespeare in Performance: Romeo and Juliet* (Manchester: Manchester University Press, 1987), p. 108.
2. As quoted in Robert Hapgood, 'Popularizing Shakespeare: The Artistry of Franco Zeffirelli', in Lynda E. Boose and Richard Burt (eds), *Shakespeare, the Movie* (London and New York: Routledge, 1997), p. 81.
3. Levenson (1987), p. 110.
4. Russell Jackson, *Shakespeare Films in the Making: Vision, Production and Reception* (Cambridge: Cambridge University Press, 2007), p. 205.
5. Robert Shaughnessy, '*Romeo and Juliet*: The Rock and Roll Years', in Pascale Aebischer, Edward J. Esche and Nigel Wheale (eds), *Remaking Shakespeare: Performance Across Media, Genres and Cultures* (Basingstoke: Palgrave Macmillan, 2003), pp. 184–5.
6. As quoted in Shaughnessy (2003), p. 182.
7. Jack Jorgens, 'Franco Zeffirelli's *Romeo and Juliet*', in John F. Andrews (ed.), *Romeo and Juliet: Critical Essays* (New York: Garland, 1993), p. 170.
8. Shaughnessy (2003), pp. 182–3.
9. Jackson (2007), p. 208.
10. James N. Loehlin, ' "These Violent Delights Have Violent Ends": Baz Luhrmann's Millennial Shakespeare', in Mark Thornton Burnett and Ramona Wray (eds), *Shakespeare, Film, Fin de Siècle* (London: Macmillan, 2000), p. 123.
11. Loehlin (2000), p. 123.
12. José Arroyo, 'Kiss Kiss, Bang Bang', in José Arroyo (ed.), *Action/Spectacle Cinema: A Sight and Sound Reader* (London: BFI, 2000), pp. 206–7.
13. Michael Anderegg, 'James Dean Meets the Pirate's Daughter: Passion and Parody in *William Shakespeare's Romeo + Juliet* and *Shakespeare in Love*', in Richard Burt and Lynda E. Boose (eds), *Shakespeare, The Movie II* (London and New York: Routledge, 2003), p. 59.
14. Jorgens (1993), p. 172.
15. Barbara Hodgdon, '*William Shakespeare's Romeo + Juliet*: Everything's Nice in America?', *Shakespeare Survey* 52 (1999), p. 89.
16. Anderegg (2003), p. 62.
17. Loehlin (2000), p. 122.
18. Hodgdon (1999), p. 93.
19. Hodgdon (1999), p. 95.
20. Loehlin (2000), p. 129.
21. Loehlin (2000), p. 128.
22. Hodgdon (1999), p. 98.

## CONCLUSION

1. Simon Palfrey and Tiffany Stern, *Shakespeare in Parts* (Oxford: Oxford University Press, 2007), p. 102.
2. Palfrey and Stern (2007), p. 149.
3. Beatrice Groves, *Texts and Traditions: Religion in Shakespeare 1592–1603* (Oxford: Clarendon Press, 2007), pp. 60–88.
4. Glenn Clark, 'The Civil Mutinies of *Romeo and Juliet*', *English Literary Renaissance* 41:2 (Spring 2011), p. 288.

# Select Bibliography


## EDITIONS OF *ROMEO AND JULIET*

Blakemore Evans, G. and J. J. M. Tobin (eds), *The Riverside Shakespeare: Second Edition* (Boston and New York: Houghton Mifflin, 1997).
Erne, Lukas (ed.), *The First Quarto of Romeo and Juliet* (Cambridge: Cambridge University Press, 2007).
Johnson, Samuel (ed.), *The Plays of William Shakespeare*: Volume 1 (London, 1765).
Levenson, Jill (ed.), *Romeo and Juliet* (Oxford: Oxford University Press, 2000).
Rowe, Nicholas (ed.), *Works of Mr. William Shakespear* (London, 1709).

## EARLY REFERENCES

Anonymous, *The Three Parnassus Plays*, ed. J. B. Leishman (London: Nicholson & Watson, 1949).
Burton, Robert, *The Anatomy of Melancholy*, ed. Holbrook Jackson (New York: New York Review of Books, 2001).
Ford, John, *'Tis Pity She's a Whore*, ed. Martin Wiggins (London: A&C Black, 2003).
Marston, John, *Jack Drum's Entertainment* (London, 1601).
——, *The Scourge of Villanie* (London, 1598).
Pepys, Samuel, *Diary*, ed. Robert Latham and William Matthews, 10 vols (London: G. Bell, 1970).
Porter, Henry, *The Two Angry Women of Abingdon* (London, 1599).

## ADAPTATIONS

Garrick, David, *Romeo and Juliet* (London: J. & R. Tonson & S. Draper, 1753).
Otway, Thomas, *The History and Fall of Caius Marius* (London, 1692).

## CRITICISM

### Seventeenth- and Eighteenth-Century Responses

Johnson, Samuel (ed.), *The Plays of William Shakespeare*: Volume 1 (London, 1765).
Lennox, Charlotte, *Shakespear Illustrated: or the Novels and Histories, on which the Plays of Shakespear are Founded, Collected and Translated from the Original*: Volume 1 (London, 1753).
Rowe, Nicholas (ed.), *Works of Mr. William Shakespear* (London, 1709).
Vickers, Brian (ed.), *Shakespeare: The Critical Heritage: Volume 2: 1693–1733* (London and Boston: Routledge & Kegan Paul 1995).

## Romantic and Victorian Criticism

Bate, Jonathan (ed.), *The Romantics on Shakespeare* (London: Penguin, 1992).

Dowden, Edward, *Shakspere: A Critical Study of His Mind and Art* (London: Routledge, 1948).

Faucit, Helena, *On Some of Shakespeare's Characters* (Edinburgh and London: William Blackwood & Sons, 1887).

Hawkes, Terence (ed.), *Coleridge on Shakespeare: A Selection of the Essays, Notes and Lectures of Samuel Taylor Coleridge on the Poems and Plays of Shakespeare* (London: Penguin, 1969).

Jameson, Anna, *Shakespeare's Heroines*, ed. Cheri L. Larsen Hoeckley (Peterborough, ONT: Broadview, 2005).

Vickers, Brian (ed.), *Shakespeare: The Critical Heritage: Volume 5: 1765–1774* (London and Boston: Routledge & Kegan Paul, 1995).

## Genre Criticism

Bradley, A. C., *Shakespearean Tragedy* (1904; R/P London: Penguin, 1991).

Brooke, Nicholas, *Shakespeare's Early Tragedies* (London: Methuen, 1968).

Charlton, H. B., *Shakespearian Tragedy* (Cambridge: Cambridge University Press, 1948).

Dickey, Franklin M., *Not Wisely But Too Well: Shakespeare's Love Tragedies* (San Marino, CA: Huntington Library, 1957).

Lawlor, John, '*Romeo and Juliet*', in John Russell Brown and Bernard Harris (eds), *Early Shakespeare* (London: Edward Arnold, 1961).

McCown, Gary M., '"Runnawayes Eyes" and Juliet's Epithalamium', *Shakespeare Quarterly* 27:2 (Spring 1976), pp. 150–70.

Rozett, Martha Tuck, 'The Comic Structures of Tragic Endings: The Suicide Scenes in *Romeo and Juliet* and *Antony and Cleopatra*', *Shakespeare Quarterly* 36:2 (Summer 1985), pp. 152–64.

Snyder, Susan, '*Romeo and Juliet*: Comedy into Tragedy', *Essays in Criticism* 20:4 (October 1970), pp. 391–402.

## Language and Deconstruction

Belsey, Catherine, 'The Name of the Rose in *Romeo and Juliet*', *Yearbook of English Studies* 23 (1993), pp. 126–42.

Calderwood, James L., '*Romeo and Juliet*: A Formal Dwelling', in John F. Andrews (ed.), *Romeo and Juliet: Critical Essays* (New York and London: Garland, 1993).

Derrida, Jacques, 'Aphorism Countertime', trans. Nicholas Royle, in Derek Attridge (ed.), *Acts of Literature* (New York and London: Routledge, 1992).

Goldman, Michael, *Shakespeare and the Energies of Drama* (Princeton, NJ: Princeton University Press, 1972).

Levin, Harry, 'Form and Formality in *Romeo and Juliet*', *Shakespeare Quarterly* 11:1 (Winter 1960), pp. 3–11.

Maguire, Laurie, *Shakespeare's Names* (Oxford: Oxford University Press, 2007).

Mahood, M. M., *Shakespeare's Wordplay* (London: Methuen, 1957).

Ryan, Kiernan, *Shakespeare*, 3rd edn (Basingstoke: Palgrave Macmillan, 2002).

Spurgeon, Caroline F. E., *Shakespeare's Imagery and What It Tells Us* (Cambridge: Cambridge University Press, 1935).

## Reading Petrarchism

Berry, Ralph, *The Shakespearean Metaphor: Studies in Language and Form* (London and Basingstoke: Macmillan, 1978).

Colie, Rosalie L., *Shakespeare's Living Art* (Princeton, NJ: Princeton University Press, 1974).

Henderson, Diana E., *Passion Made Public: Elizabethan Lyric, Gender, and Performance* (Urbana and Chicago: University of Illinois Press, 1995).

Slater, Ann Pasternak, 'Petrarchanism Come True in *Romeo and Juliet*', in Werner Habicht, D. J. Palmer and Roger Pringle (eds), *Images of Shakespeare* (Newark: University of Delaware Press, 1988).

Whittier, Gayle, 'The Sonnet's Body and the Body Sonnetized in *Romeo and Juliet*', *Shakespeare Quarterly* 40:1 (Spring 1989), pp. 27–41.

## Psychoanalytical Criticism

Davis, Lloyd, '"Death-Marked Love": Desire and Presence in *Romeo and Juliet*', *Shakespeare Survey* 49 (1996), pp. 57–67.

Grady, Hugh, *Shakespeare and Impure Aesthetics* (Cambridge: Cambridge University Press, 2009).

Kristeva, Julia, '*Romeo and Juliet*: Love-Hatred in the Couple', in R. S. White (ed.), *Romeo and Juliet: Critical Essays* (Basingstoke: Palgrave Macmillan, 2001).

Rabkin, Norman, *Shakespeare and the Common Understanding* (New York: Free Press; London: Collier-Macmillan, 1967).

## Feminism, Gender Studies and Queer Theory

Callaghan, Dympna, 'The Ideology of Romantic Love: The Case of Romeo and Juliet', in Dympna Callaghan, Lorraine Helms, and Jyotsna Singh, *The Weyward Sisters: Shakespeare and Feminist Politics* (Oxford: Blackwell, 1994).

Goldberg, Jonathan, '*Romeo and Juliet*'s Open Rs', in Jonathan Goldberg (ed.), *Queering the Renaissance* (Durham, NC: Duke University Press, 1994).

Kahn, Coppélia, 'Coming of Age in Verona', in Ruth Swift Lenz, Gayle Greene and Carol Thomas Neely (eds), *The Woman's Part: Feminist Criticism of Shakespeare* (Urbana: University of Illinois Press, 1980).

Novy, Marianne, *Love's Argument: Gender Relations in Shakespeare* (Chapel Hill: University of North Carolina Press, 1984).

Porter, Joseph, *Shakespeare's Mercutio: His History and Drama* (Chapel Hill and London: University of North Carolina Press, 1988).

Snow, Edward, 'Language and Sexual Difference in *Romeo and Juliet*', in Peter Erickson and Coppélia Kahn (eds), *Shakespeare's 'Rough Magic': Renaissance Essays in Honor of C. L. Barber* (Newark: University of Delaware Press, 1985).

Watson Robert N., and Stephen Dickey, 'Wherefore Art Thou Tereu? Juliet and the Legacy of Rape', *Renaissance Quarterly* 58:1 (2005), pp. 127–56.

## Shakespeare on Film

Anderegg, Michael, 'James Dean Meets the Pirate's Daughter: Passion and Parody in *William Shakespeare's Romeo + Juliet* and *Shakespeare in Love*', in Richard Burt and

Lynda E. Boose (eds), *Shakespeare, The Movie II* (London and New York: Routledge, 2003).

Arroyo, José, 'Kiss Kiss, Bang Bang', in José Arroyo (ed.), *Action/Spectacle Cinema: A Sight and Sound Reader* (London: BFI, 2000).

Hapgood, Robert, 'Popularizing Shakespeare: The Artistry of Franco Zeffirelli', in Lynda E. Boose and Richard Burt (eds), *Shakespeare, the Movie* (London and New York: Routledge, 1997).

Hodgdon, Barbara, '*William Shakespeare's Romeo + Juliet*: Everything's Nice in America?', *Shakespeare Survey* 52 (1999), pp. 88–98.

Jackson, Russell, *Shakespeare Films in the Making: Vision, Production and Reception* (Cambridge: Cambridge University Press, 2007).

Jorgens, Jack, 'Franco Zeffirell's *Romeo and Juliet*', in John F. Andrews (ed.), *Romeo and Juliet: Critical Essays* (New York: Garland, 1993).

Levenson, Jill L., *Shakespeare in Performance: Romeo and Juliet* (Manchester: Manchester University Press, 1987).

Loehlin, James N., ' "These Violent Delights Have Violent Ends": Baz Luhrmann's Millennial Shakespeare', in Mark Thornton Burnett and Ramona Wray (eds), *Shakespeare, Film, Fin de Siècle* (London: Macmillan, 2000).

Shaughnessy, Robert, '*Romeo and Juliet*: The Rock and Roll Years', in Pascale Aebischer, Edward J. Esche and Nigel Wheale (eds), *Remaking Shakespeare: Performance Across Media, Genres and Cultures* (Basingstoke: Palgrave Macmillan, 2003).

## New Directions

Clark, Glenn, 'The Civil Mutinies of *Romeo and Juliet*', *English Literary Renaissance* 41:2 (Spring 2011), pp. 280–300.

Groves, Beatrice, *Texts and Traditions: Religion in Shakespeare 1592–1603* (Oxford: Clarendon Press, 2007).

Palfrey, Simon, and Tiffany Stern, *Shakespeare in Parts* (Oxford: Oxford University Press, 2007).

# Index